Coláiste n

3 903

CH00870963

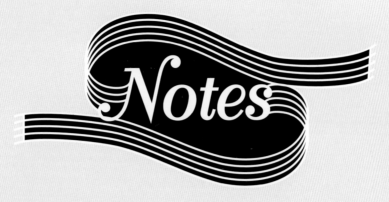

Notes

for Leaving Certificate Music

(Textbook with workbooks and CDs)

Anna-Marie Higgins & Majella Higgins

Edited by Cliona Ardiff

Published by Higgins & Higgins, "Somerton", Emmet Street, Birr, Co Offaly.

Website: http://www.leavingcertmusic.com
E-mail: info@leavingcertmusic.com

2nd Edition 2010 - Reprint 2014
© Anna-Marie Higgins and Majella Higgins

ISBN: 978-0-9560487-0-7

The authors thank Mary McFadden for her advice on the educational content of the book and workbooks and John Cooney for his contribution to the Irish music section. They appreciate the encouragement given by Ethel Glancy, Mary Melody and members of the Post-Primary Music Teachers Association, as well as Maureen Donnelly and colleagues in Manor House School, Dublin. They gratefully acknowledge the help given by Harry Ardiff, Gillian Cahill, Rena Condrot, Jonathan Grimes, Helena Lennon, Sarah Macken, Irina Nicolescu and Ainle O'Shea. Thanks also to Raymond Deane for clarifying some musical points. Further information at www.cmc.ie. A special mention goes to senior students in Somerton Music School, Birr, namely Aoife C, Aoife G, Claire, Edel, Ella, Eve, Louise, Olivia, Paddy, Pádraig, Paula, Rona, Séamus and Siobhán. They tested the material and gave invaluable feedback as the book took shape. Finally, their profound gratitude goes to Cliona Ardiff for her expertise, hard work and patience throughout the entire project.

The publishers would like to thank the following for permission to reproduce copyright material:

Seachanges by Raymond Deane © Contemporary Music Centre, Ireland. Reproduced by kind permission. Recording reproduced by permission of Universal Music. *Piano Quartet No 1* by Gerald Barry © Oxford University Press 1997. Excerpts reprinted by permission of Oxford University Press. All rights reserved. Recording reproduced by kind permission of NMC Recodings. *Symphonie Fantastique* by Berlioz, *Piano Concerto K488* by Mozart, *Romeo and Juliet Fantasy Overture* by Tchaikovsky and *Dies Irae*, all reproduced by permission of Naxos, Select Music & Video Distribution Ltd. Cantata BWV78 by Bach reproduced by permission of Haensler-Verlag. Extract from *Violin Suite No 1* included by permission of Eimear Heeney. Extracts from *Planet Express* reproduced by permission of Scott Newman and Yann O'Brien. Photograph of the uilleann pipes reproduced by permission of Terry Moylan at Na Píobairí Uilleann.

If the publishers have inadvertently overlooked any copyright holders, they will be happy to make appropriate arrangements. All rights reserved. No part of this publication may be reproduced or transmitted in any form or by any means electronic, mechanical, photocopying, recording or otherwise without prior written permission from the publishers.

Design, Layout, Typesetting and Covers: Cliona Ardiff
Music setting: Anna-Marie Higgins and Majella Higgins
Sound Recording, Editing and Mastering: Scott Newman
Recording Musicians: Aoife Corrigan, Eimear Heeney, Scott Newman, Yann O'Brien
CD duplication and packaging: Trend Digital Media, Park West, Dublin 12
Printed by Ardiff-Mahon Printers, Yarnhall Street, Dublin 1

The authors dedicate this book to Tom and Kathleen Higgins.

'I feel like taking off my shoes and running fast away.'

Coláiste na hInse Book Rental
3 9037 00019716 7

Contents

CD Track Listing

Aural Skills	1 – 54		**Bach**	1 – 26		**Mozart**	1 – 46
Irish Music	55 – 70		**Tchaikovsky**	27 – 53		**Berlioz**	47 – 67
Practical	71 – 87		**Barry**	54 – 71		**Deane**	68 – 76

Chapter 1 – Melody

Contents

Note: The accompanying Composing Workbook contains exercises based on Sections 1-13.

DESCRIPTORS FOR HIGHER LEVEL MELODY-WRITING (FROM STATE EXAMS COMMISSION [S.E.C.] MARKING SCHEME)

Q1 Continuation of a given opening

Task: Continue the opening to make a 16-bar melody. A modulation to the dominant at an appropriate point is requested in major key melodies. Performing directions must be added and a suitable instrument must be chosen for the melody.

Aim: To compose a melody that has *'excellent style and imagination, excellent awareness of shape and structure, excellent development of opening ideas and excellent point(s) of climax'*.

Q2 Setting Music to a given text

Task: Study the opening line of a verse already set to music and set the remaining words to make a melody of 16 bars (or longer). A modulation may be included. Performing directions must be added.

Aim: To set words to an original melody that shows *'excellent style and imagination, with an excellent marriage of words and music and an excellent sense of climax'*.

Q3 Composing to a given dance rhythm or Metre or form

Task: Continue the given opening of a dance tune to make a 16-bar melody, using a given form. Major tunes must modulate to the dominant at an appropriate point. Performing directions must be added and a suitable instrument must be chosen from a list.

Aim: To write a dance tune that has *'excellent style and imagination, an excellent awareness of shape and structure, an excellent development of opening ideas, excellent point(s) of climax, where the rhythmic integrity and style of the dance is maintained with flair and an excellent adherence to the given structure'*.

INTRODUCTION: TOOLS OF MELODY-WRITING

Melody-writing tools include notes and how they relate to each other, keys, time signatures, structural phrasing, articulation, dynamics and instrumental range.

Degrees of the scale

The position of a note in a scale determines its behaviour. The most important notes in any scale are the tonic and the dominant.

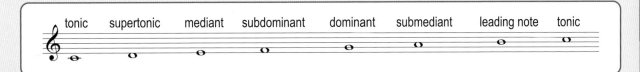

Key signatures: Major

The nine major keys on the Leaving Cert course are:

Major scales with Tonic Solfa

EXERCISE

The scale of C is written below with the tonic solfa names added. The tonic is 'd' (*doh*) and the dominant is 's' (*soh*). **Write the scale of G on the blank stave. Add tonic solfa.**

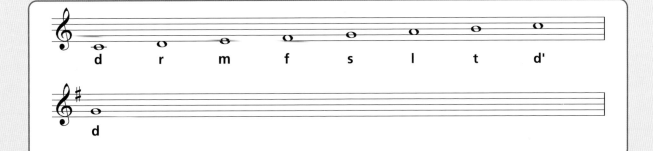

Key signatures: Minor

Major keys have the same key signatures as their relative minors. The raised 7th found in minor keys is not part of the key signature but appears as an accidental.

©Higgins & Higgins

Minor scales with Tonic Solfa

EXERCISE

The scale of A minor is written below with the tonic solfa names added. The tonic note is '*l*' (*lah*) and the dominant is '*m*' (*me*). The raised 7th changes the note '*s*' into '*se*'. **Write out the scale of E minor. Add tonic solfa.**

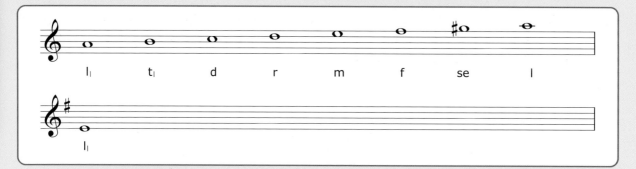

Phrasing

Structural phrasing can be indicated in one of two ways:

*   A long phrase mark begins precisely on the first note in the phrase and ends precisely on the final note in the phrase.
*   A comma (or apostrophe) is placed just after the final note in the phrase and before the first note of the next phrase. This is neat, takes up less space and tends to show the phrasing more accurately.

All subsequent phrases are usually treated in a similar way.

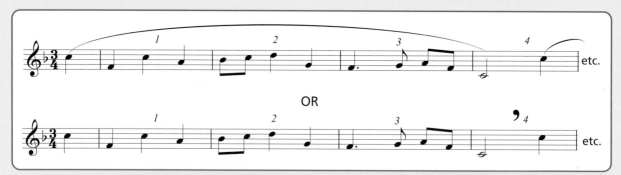

Articulation

Articulation indicates where a string player may bow or where a wind player may breathe. It helps the performer to shape the tune. Slurs and staccatos tell a musician that the notes are to be played smoothly or in a detached manner. If you have no experience of playing string or wind instruments, you may be unaware of bowing or breathing difficulties.

Possible ways of articulating the following phrase have been suggested by a violinist and by a flautist:

©Higgins & Higgins

Dynamics

It is a good idea to place an *f*, *mf*, *p* or *mp* under the first note of a phrase (not necessarily the first note of a system). Gradations in volume can be indicated by means of a crescendo or a decrescendo. Dynamics are placed below the stave and should make sense (eg. the music cannot crescendo from *ff* to *pp*). If a melody is ending with an ascending scale passage leading to the upper tonic, it would probably make more sense to use a crescendo, while downward-moving sequences might be more effective when a decrescendo is used. The melody lasts only 16 bars altogether, so the dynamics should not be too extreme.

Lower range of treble instruments

Do not write for piano, cello, bassoon or any bass instrument listed in the melody question. Your tune has to be playable on the instrument you choose eg. it cannot dip below the lowest note of that instrument. Your tune will probably not be in the style of the given phrase if it goes into the highest register of the instrument. Know the following lowest notes:

Locate these notes on the keyboard below:

EXERCISE

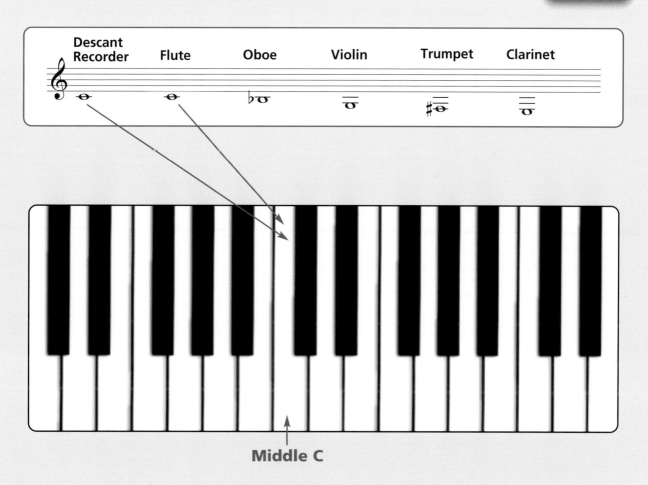

©Higgins & Higgins

Modulating to the Dominant (*Major keys only)

In order to modulate to the dominant, the fourth note of the original scale 'f' *(fah)* is raised (to become *fe*) and becomes the leading note 't' *(te)* in the dominant scale. The new key is established by placing its leading note and tonic at a cadence point.

Look at the examples below and complete the modulations in order to produce a reference section for your future exercises:

EXERCISE

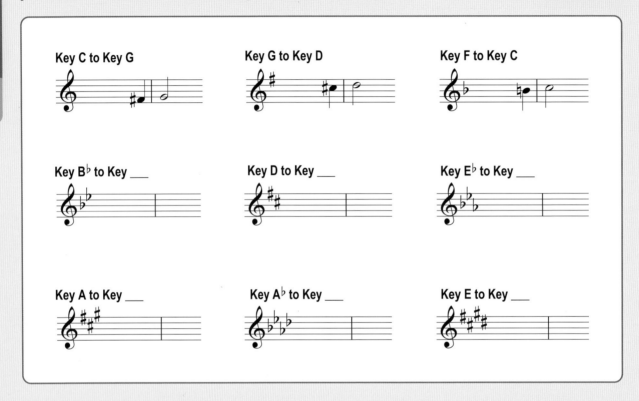

Note: Modulation is not requested in the exam when the melody is in a minor key. Minor tunes may modulate to the relative major by establishing the new key at a cadence point. The 7th is not raised in the vicinity of the modulation.

Note: **COMPOSING WORKBOOK** contains exercises based on the following sections.

©Higgins & Higgins

SECTION 1: DEVELOPING THE GIVEN MATERIAL

Before you start to work on the melody at all, write out the scale of the tune on a stave. Fill in the tonic solfa names under the scale. Put the tonic solfa names under the notes of the given phrase. Sing the phrase. At this stage your rough work looks like this:

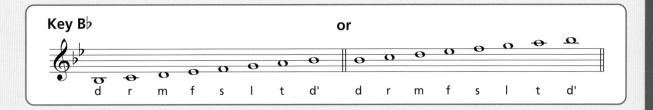

A motif, a bar or an idea could be developed rhythmically, melodically, or through inversion. **Examine the following and say how each idea is developed:**

EXERCISE

©Higgins & Higgins

SECTION 2: THE FINAL PHRASE (A²)

Bars 13-16

A 16-bar melody should have *excellent development of opening ideas* (S.E.C.). The form **AA¹BA²** allows the given material to be explored. We will look at the final phrase, **A²**.

Suggestions for composing the A² phrase:

- Retain the most striking features of the given **A** phrase
- Try to have a range of an 8ve (or more)
- Do not highlight the same tonic note in bars 15 and 16
- Make the ending strong by using a Perfect cadence: use *te* or *soh* or *ray* before the tonic
- Make the final note sound important

Examine this opening phrase:

Three possible final phrases are shown. Select the one that sounds most musical and that complies with the suggestions made above. You could start by writing in the tonic solfa names below.

To find the best solution, answer these questions:

1. How are bars 1 and 2 developed in bars 13 and 14?
2. Does this final phrase use a wide range of notes?
3. Is there a good melodic line with a mixture of leaps and steps?
4. Are there any weak leaps?
5. Do the final two chords produce an appropriate cadence?

Solution 1

Solution 2

Solution 3

©Higgins & Higgins

SECTION 3: THE ANSWERING PHRASE (A¹)

Bars 5-8

The phrase after the given phrase is called the answering phrase, **A¹**. It is a good idea:

*   to develop some of the given material
*   to modulate to the dominant key

Write out the scale in the correct key on a stave. Fill in the tonic solfa names under the scale. Work out the modulating notes and write them on the stave. At this stage your rough work should look like this:

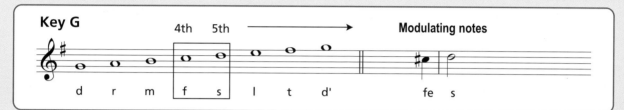

Composing the A¹ phrase

*   Bars 5-6 should resemble bars 1-2
*   In bar 6 extend the melodic range upwards (or downwards)
*   Try not to use the fourth note of the tonic key (*fah*) in bar 7 as it weakens the modulation
*   Do not sound the original tonic (*doh*) too close to the modulation
*   Having ended the phrase on the note *soh* (*doh* in the new key) do not move away from it too soon as it needs to be established

Finding and handling the modulating notes.

*   The fourth note (*fah*) of the tonic key is raised a semitone and becomes *fe*
*   Place *fe* on a weak beat in the second last bar of the phrase (usually bar 7)
*   Place the fifth note of the scale (*soh*) at the start of the final bar in the phrase (bar 8)
*   Remain on the *soh* for long enough to establish the new key
*   The notes *fe* to *soh* in the original key have become *te* to *doh* in the dominant key
*   A Perfect cadence has now been created in the new key

Examine this opening phrase:

EXERCISE

Choose the best answering phrase from three possible solutions and say why it works better than the others.

To find the best solution, answer these questions:

1. How are bars 1 and 2 developed in bars 5 and 6?
2. Does this answering phrase use a wide range of notes?
3. Is there a good melodic line with a mixture of leaps and steps?
4. Are there any weak leaps such as a leap from a non-chord note?
5. Is the modulation effective?

©Higgins & Higgins

Solution 1

Solution 2

Solution 3

SECTION 4: SEQUENCES

A sequence is a useful compositional device for the **B** phrase. In its most basic form, it lasts two bars with the second bar identical to the first, but a step lower or higher. Do not allow your sequence to repeat more than once as it risks becoming tedious.

Example

EXERCISE

Make a descending sequence by beginning the second bar a note *lower*.

Make an ascending sequence by beginning the second bar a note *higher*.

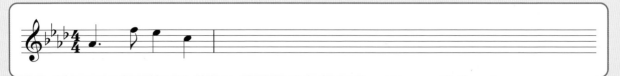

Note: *Sequences sound best when they begin on a strong melodic note such as* me.

©Higgins & Higgins

SECTION 5: THE B PHRASE

Bars 9-12

The **A** phrases show how the given material can be developed while retaining an **A** phrase outline. It is a good idea to explore a given rhythmic or melodic feature in a bit more depth in the **B** phrase. Before working on the **B** phrase, find a sequence motif.

At this stage your rough work should look like this:

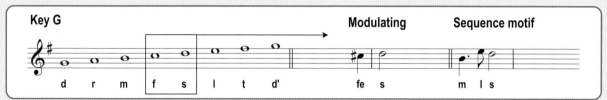

Composing the B phrase

EXERCISE

* Use a sequence in bars 9-10. Base bar 9 on a motif from the given phrase
* Make bar 10 the same as bar 9, but bring each note either down or up a step
* To guarantee a musical cadence at bars 11-12, end the phrase on any note from chord **V** (*soh*, *ray* or *te*). This produces an Imperfect cadence (ie. any chord going to chord **V**)

Opening phrases

Three possible **B** phrases are offered here. Which one of the proposed solutions produces the most musical **B** phrase? What are the good and bad points of all three versions?

To find the best solution, answer these questions:

1. What makes this phrase different from the opening **A** phrase?
2. Has any element of the **A** phrase been explored? How?
3. Is there a two-bar sequence beginning on a strong note (eg. *doh* or *me* or *soh*)?
4. Is the sequence itself a good one? Are there any unmusical leaps?
5. Does the phrase end on an Imperfect (or other) cadence?

Solution 1

Solution 2

Solution 3

©Higgins & Higgins

SECTION 6: ANACRUSIS

If a piece of music begins on the beat before a bar line, it produces an anacrusis. This 'upbeat' start occurs in the other three phrases of the melody.

Example of a phrase beginning on an upbeat:

Handling a tune that starts with an anacrusis.

* Place the phrase mark immediately after the given phrase
* Begin each subsequent phrase on the final beat of bars 4, 8 and 12
* This also ensures that bars 4, 8 and 12 are complete
* Bar 16 balances the start and has one beat less

Here is a completed tune:

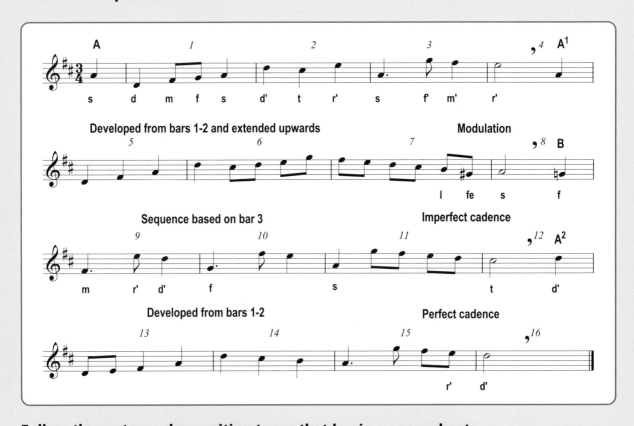

Follow these steps when writing tunes that begin on an upbeat:

* Write in the bar numbers. Indicate the structural phrasing by placing an apostrophe or comma after the third beat in bars 4, 8 and 12
* Write the tonic solfa names (in abbreviated form, eg. *d, r, m* etc.) below the given notes. Complete bar 4
* Work out the modulation in your rough work. Compose an answering phrase with that modulation. Complete bar 8
* Choose a motif from the given phrase as a basis for a sequence. Compose a **B** phrase beginning with the sequence and ending on an Imperfect cadence. Complete bar 12
* Compose a final phrase and end on a Perfect cadence. Bar 16 has fewer beats

©Higgins & Higgins

Look at the following opening phrase:

- In bar 4 indicate the end of phrase **A**
- Then begin phrase **A¹** with the same rhythm used at the start of phrase **A**
- As it is based on the **A** phrase, it is a good idea to use the same notes

EXERCISE

Complete bar 4 below.

s m f   r   d t₁ s₁   d   d' t l   s m l   f m   m r

EXERCISE

Complete bar 4 of these opening phrases.

In the 2002 and 2003 Leaving Cert exams, the opening phrase extended onto the second system. Here is a similar example:

This looks difficult, but the same composing processes used elsewhere can be applied.

- Write in the bar numbers, remembering that the upbeat at the start is not bar 1
- Write the tonic solfa names below the notes
- Indicate the end of the **A** phrase (by placing an apostrophe after the third beat in bar 4 or by ending a long phrase mark on the note before the rest)
- Complete bar 4 with a crotchet (probably the note used at the start of the **A** phrase)
- You have now successfully started the **A¹** phrase.
- Compose the remaining bars by adhering to the structure you used in other melodies

©Higgins & Higgins

SECTION 7: RHYTHM AT THE MODULATING CADENCE

There are several possible rhythms that would fit the modulating cadence (bars 7-8) of this opening phrase.

Melody

14

Modulating Cadence 1	Modulating Cadence 2	Modulating Cadence 3
Old key: fe s New key: t d'	Old key: fe s s, New key: t d' d	Old key: fe fe s New key: t t d'
This establishes the new key with a strong emphasis on the new tonic.	This retains the rhythm of bar 4 and establishes the new key.	This retains the rhythm of bar 4 and the repeated note. It also ends on the new tonic.

It is *essential* to remain in the new key right to the end of the phrase.

• In the first two examples below, the modulation has not been established as the chord outlined at the end of the phrase is the tonic of the old key instead of the tonic chord in the new key

• In the third example, an upper auxiliary does not intrude on the harmony

We saw earlier that the most straightforward modulating cadence involves just one long note at the start of bar 8. Here is a reminder:

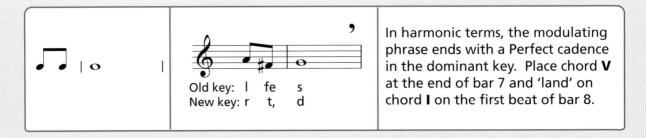

In harmonic terms, the modulating phrase ends with a Perfect cadence in the dominant key. Place chord **V** at the end of bar 7 and 'land' on chord **I** on the first beat of bar 8.

©Higgins & Higgins

Examine the following modulations to see how the new key can be established when the rhythm pattern of the phrase demands more than just one long note.

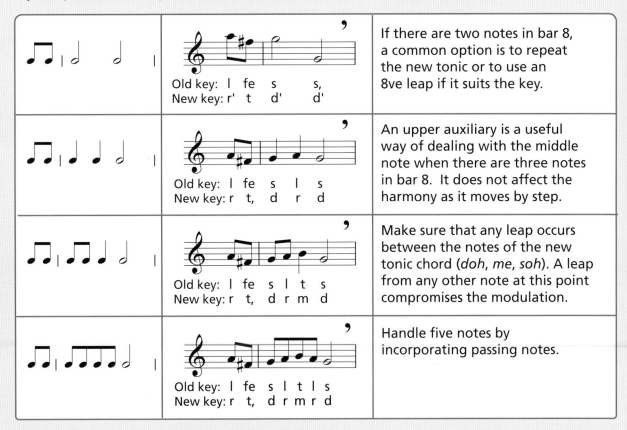

Rhythm	Notation	Description
♫ ♩ | ♩ ♩ |	Old key: l fe s s, New key: r' t d' d'	If there are two notes in bar 8, a common option is to repeat the new tonic or to use an 8ve leap if it suits the key.
♫ ♩ | ♩ ♩ ♩ |	Old key: l fe s l s New key: r t, d r d	An upper auxiliary is a useful way of dealing with the middle note when there are three notes in bar 8. It does not affect the harmony as it moves by step.
♫ ♫ | ♫ ♩ ♩ |	Old key: l fe s l t s New key: r t, d r m d	Make sure that any leap occurs between the notes of the new tonic chord (doh, me, soh). A leap from any other note at this point compromises the modulation.
♫ | ♫♫♫ ♩ |	Old key: l fe s l t l s New key: r t, d r m r d	Handle five notes by incorporating passing notes.

Note:

There are other possibilities apart from those illustrated above. These include implied modulations. However, for the purposes of the Leaving Cert exam, it is a good idea to first become familiar with these basic models.

TEMPLATE FOR A MAJOR MELODY

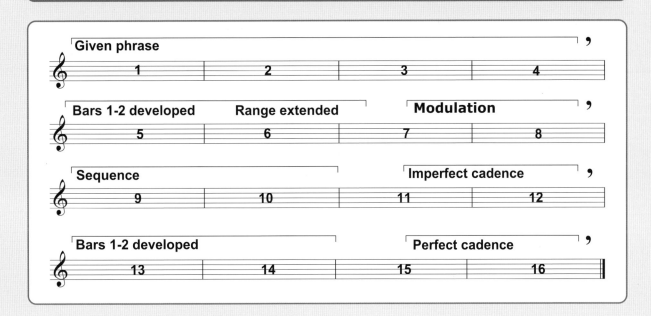

SECTION 8: COMPOUND DUPLE TIME

Compound Duple time has a time signature of $\frac{6}{8}$. Although they have the same number of quavers per bar, Compound Duple Time and Simple Triple Time are musically different.

In Simple Triple time, each bar is divided into three crotchets (or three groups of quavers) and is beaten in three.	$\frac{3}{4}$ ♩♩♩ ♫♫
In Compound Duple Time, each bar is divided into two groups of quavers and is beaten in two.	$\frac{6}{8}$ ♫♫♫

You should approach tunes in Compound Duple time as you would any other tune, making sure to use the rhythm patterns associated with this time signature. Here are some examples you could try:

Now continue the following opening to make a 16-bar melody with modulation.

EXERCISE

©Higgins & Higgins

SECTION 9: WRITING IN A MINOR KEY

Every major key is related to a minor key. They have the same key signature.

- A major scale begins and ends on its tonic, *doh*
- A minor scale begins and ends on its tonic, *lah*
- In a minor key the 7th note (*soh*) is raised a semitone (to become *se*). This raised 7th does not appear in the key signature but occurs as an accidental during the piece

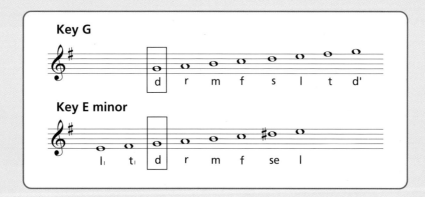

EXERCISE

The following phrase is in the key of E minor. The raised 7th is D♯. It appears three times during the phrase. Look at the intervals created between the note approaching and quitting the raised 7th. Play the phrase. **Identify all six intervals numbered here.**

To ensure that the raised 7th does not create an unmusical interval, approach and quit it with:

- tonic note a semitone higher (*lah*)
- another note from the chord of **V** (*me* and *te*)
- raised 6th but only when ascending (*fe*) and preferably not too often

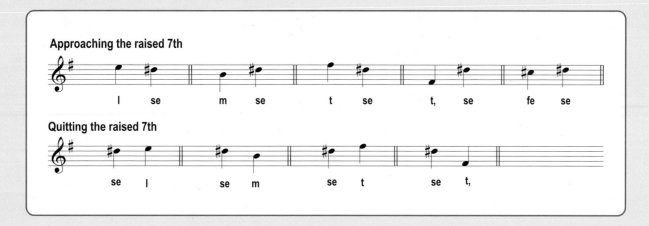

©Higgins & Higgins

SECTION 10: COMPOSING A MINOR MELODY

How do you know that the opening phrase (the A phrase) is in a minor key?

- Sing it. There will probably be an emphasis on the tonic and dominant notes (*lah* and *me*)
- There may be an accidental (the raised 7th, *se*)

The answering phrase, A¹

The answering phrase could go to the relative major and end on a Perfect cadence in the relative major key. However, when the melody is minor the question does not ask for a modulation.

- Bars 5 and 6 are a development of bars 1 and 2
- In bar 6 the range of the melody extends upwards
- Bars 7 and 8 remain in the minor key, ending the phrase on the tonic, *lah*

The B phrase

- In the **B** phrase, use a sequence in bars 9-10. Base this on a motif from phrase **A**
- End the phrase on an Imperfect cadence. Use a note from chord **V** in bars 12
- The notes of chord **V** in minor keys are *me*, *se* and *te*

The final phrase

It is important to have a strong ending. Meandering around the same few notes during the final four bars makes the overall melody sound insipid.

- Bars 13 and 14 are a development of bars 1 and 2
- Use a Perfect cadence at bars 15 and 16, ending on the tonic, *lah*

©Higgins & Higgins

SECTION 11: COMPOSING TO A DANCE METRE IN A GIVEN FORM

There are two important points to remember when tackling this task:

- The melody must retain the rhythmic characteristics and style of the dance in question
- The melody must adhere to the requested form

The dances that have already appeared on the Leaving Certificate exam papers included gigues, gavottes and minuets. The requested forms were **AA¹BB¹**, **ABB¹A¹** and **AA¹BA²**.

Composing a Gigue in AA¹BB¹ form

EXERCISE

Using this given phrase as an opening, compose a 16-bar Gigue. Write in the bar numbers and tonic solfa. Indicate the phrasing before attempting to compose the answering phrase.

- Complete bar 4
- The answering (**A¹**) phrase begins like the **A** phrase and ends in the dominant key
- Retain the main feature(s) of the **A** phrase in the answering phrase

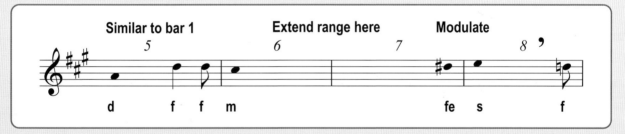

The **B** phrase begins with a sequence based on bars 2 or 3 and ends on a note from chord **V**.

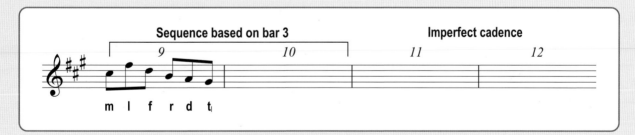

The **B¹** phrase begins like the **B** phrase but does not have a sequence.

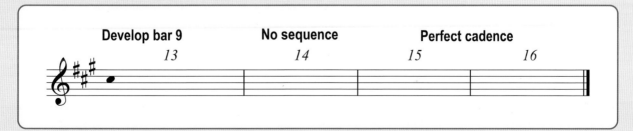

©Higgins & Higgins

SECTION 12: WORD SETTING

EXERCISE

The first line of the following verse by Bessie Shenwar has been set to music. **Set the remaining words to make a melody of 16 bars (or more, if necessary).** It is not compulsory to modulate in this melody. Although this is an exercise in free composition, it is a good idea to have a plan.

My Nana prays so hard for me
She helps with all I do
She fills me up with pies and tea
And makes a lovely stew.

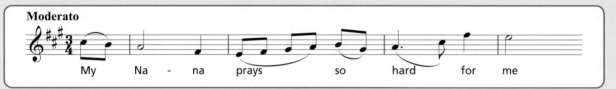

Process

- Work out the key and sing the given phrase several times
- The accents in this phrase occur on the syllables **Na**, **prays**, **hard**, **me**
- Scan the remaining lines. The accents fall on these syllables:
    Phrase 2: *helps*, *all*, *do* (only 3 strong syllables in this phrase)
    Phrase 3: *fills*, *up*, *pies*, *tea* (4 syllables)
    Phrase 4: *makes*, *love*, *stew* (3 syllables)
- In this melody, these syllables fit on the first beat of each bar. In phrases two and four, one of the strong syllables extends over two bars
- Position these words on the stave under the appropriate blank bars
- Sketch a basic rhythm that would suit the words

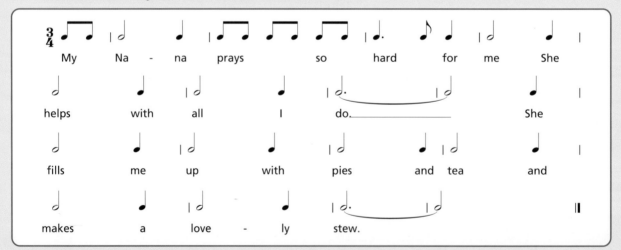

- Compare the crotchet-minim pattern with the rhythm of the given phrase. It is too repetitive and needs to be varied with quavers or dotted crotchets on important words
- It is a good idea to have a recognisable form (eg. **AA¹BA²**) when composing your tune
- The **A** phrases could have similar rhythm; the **B** phrase could introduce different rhythm, such as crotchet rests to illustrate the exclamatory nature of certain words.
- Word painting is important in order to demonstrate an affinity for the text. The climax of the verse (for example, **tea**) could be indicated by singing it with the highest note
- Compositional devices such as sequences and inversion are useful because they give the tune a sound musical foundation and prevent it from rambling

©Higgins & Higgins

SECTION 13:   ORDINARY LEVEL:
CONTINUATION OF A GIVEN OPENING

Two separate 8-bar melodies must be completed. They are usually in $\frac{4}{4}$ and $\frac{3}{4}$ time and in different keys. The first two bars of each melody are given.

Choose a suitable instrument from this list:

❏ flute   ❏ clarinet   ❏ cello   ❏ descant recorder   ❏ piano

Composing Process

*   Write in the bar numbers, the tonic solfa names and the phrase mark
*   In bar 4, use the fifth note of the scale (*soh*) to end the phrase
*   If you wish to compose an **A¹** phrase, make bar 5 and 6 *similar* to bars 1 and 2
*   If you wish to compose a **B** phrase, make bars 5 and 6 *different* from bars 1 and 2, for example you could use a sequence
*   Compose a rhythm pattern for the empty bars and write it above the stave
*   Make sure you have the correct number of beats in each bar
*   The final note could last the full bar. It is the tonic note (*doh*)
*   The best leaps are between the notes of the tonic chord (*doh, me* and *soh*)
*   Make sure that you do not leap a 7th from the leading note to the tonic (for example when you are going from *te* to *doh*, you should move up a step.)
*   Add appropriate dynamic markings (louds and softs) in bars 1 and 5
*   Which is the most suitable instrument for your finished melody on the given list? Why?

Now complete the following melody: **EXERCISE**

Apply the same process to Question 1(b):

©Higgins & Higgins

Ten Higher Level Melody Exercises

In your manuscript copy, use each of the following phrases as the opening of a 16-bar melody. Modulate at an appropriate point in the major melodies, insert expression marks and state the instrument for which you have composed each tune. Before you begin, pick out a rhythmic and a melodic feature that you will retain elsewhere in the tune.

©Higgins & Higgins

Chapter 2 – Harmony

Contents

Note: The accompanying Composing Workbook contains exercises based on all of these sections.

DESCRIPTORS FOR HIGHER LEVEL HARMONY
(FROM S.E.C. MARKING SCHEME)

Q4 Composing Melody and bass notes from a set of chords

Task 1: Compose a melody that has *'excellent style and imagination with an excellent awareness of the underlying harmonic structure and development of opening ideas and excellent point(s) of climax'*.

Task 2: Add a correct bass note that matches a correct melody note under each chord symbol as part of a good quality bass line, which shows *'a sense of musicality'* and *'an awareness of style and technical knowledge'* and is in the style of the given opening.

Q5 Composing bass notes and chord indications to a given tune

Task 1: Harmonise a tune by choosing appropriate chords that are part of a good progression and that contribute to good *'quality musical progressions and cadences overall'*.

Task 2: Add a correct bass note under a correct chord symbol, then compose a good quality bass line that has a *'sense of musicality'* and *'technical knowledge'* (including careful note placement) in the style of the given opening.

Q6 Adding a countermelody or descant to a given tune with chordal support

Task 1: Add chords that fit the melodic and descant lines and that are part of a good musical progression, with an awareness of cadences. (Bass notes, eg. an alternate bass, need not be indicated.).

Task 2: Continue the descant part *'within the harmonic framework'*, while *'adhering to the two-part style of the given opening'*. There is excellent shape and balance between phrases.

©Higgins & Higgins

INTRODUCTION: TOOLS FOR HARMONY

Intervals

An interval is the musical distance between two notes. Find out the name of this interval by counting the number of steps between the two notes, always calling the first note '1'.

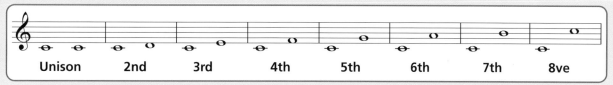

| Unison | 2nd | 3rd | 4th | 5th | 6th | 7th | 8ve |

A more detailed description is achieved by measuring the interval in semitones. Here are some more examples:

Semitones	Interval		Semitones	Interval
0	Perfect Unison		7	Perfect 5th
2	Major 2nd		9	Major 6th
4	Major 3rd		11	Major 7th
5	Perfect 4th		12	Perfect 8ve

The intervals between the notes of a major scale can now be given in more detail as follows:

| Perfect Unison | Major 2nd | Major 3rd | Perfect 4th | Perfect 5th | Major 6th | Major 7th | Perfect 8ve |

This keyboard will help you to calculate intervals visually:

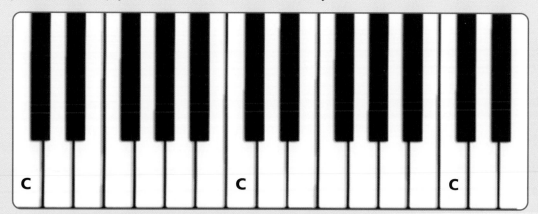

These are the semitones between middle C and the G above the treble stave:

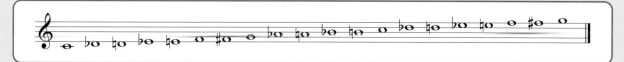

In order to work out more complicated intervals, identify the distance between the two notes eg. 2nd, 3rd, 4th. Then count the semitones. The first interval shown on the right is a 2nd. There are three semitones. It is an augmented 2nd. The next interval is a 3rd. It, too, has three semitones. It is a minor 3rd.

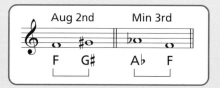

©Higgins & Higgins

Augmented and Diminished intervals

- Augmented and diminished intervals are best avoided in melodic and harmonic writing.
- The augmented 2nd occurs between the 6th and raised 7th of the minor scale.
- The augmented 4th or tritone occurs between the 4th and 7th notes of the major scale. In medieval times it was called the *diabolus in musica* ('devil in music').

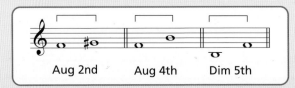

Aug 2nd   Aug 4th   Dim 5th

Semitones	Interval	Semitones	Interval
1	Minor 2nd	6	Diminished 5th
3	Minor 3rd	8	Minor 6th
6	Augmented 4th	10	Minor 7th

Naming Intervals

Work out these intervals as fully as you can:

EXERCISE

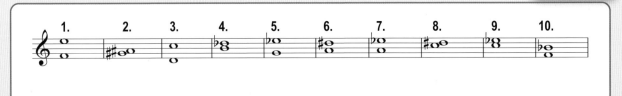

Triads and Chords

Chords are based on triads. A triad is made up of the root, the 3rd above the root and the 5th above the root eg. CEG.

- When the lowest note is the root, the chord is in root position
- When the 3rd is the lowest note, the chord is in first inversion
- When the 5th is the lowest note, the chord is in second inversion
- Roman numerals indicate the position of the chord in the scale eg. **I** and **vi**
- Inversions are shown by placing b or c beside the Roman numeral eg. **iib** and **Ic**
- Chord symbols indicate the root of the chord eg. C (root = C; bass note = C)
- Inversions are shown by giving an alternate bass eg. C/E (root = C; bass note = E)

Chord Positions

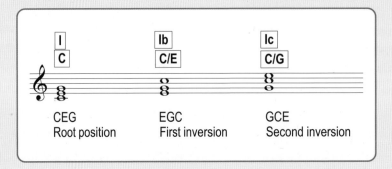

CEG   EGC   GCE
Root position First inversion Second inversion

©Higgins & Higgins

Chord Types

There are 4 semitones in a major 3rd and 3 semitones in a minor 3rd.

- Major chords have a major 3rd on the bottom and a minor 3rd on top
- Minor chords have a minor 3rd on the bottom and a major 3rd on top
- Diminished chords have a minor 3rd on the bottom and a minor 3rd on top
- Augmented chords have a major 3rd on the bottom and a major 3rd on top

Chord position	Major	Minor	Diminshed	Augmented
Chord notes ➡	G E C	G E♭ C	G♭ E♭ C	G♯ E C
Roman numerals ➡	I	i	i°	I⁺
Chord symbols ➡	C	Cm	Cdim	Caug

Dominant 7th

The position of notes in a scale often determines how those notes behave, eg. the leading note rises a step to the tonic.

- The dominant 7th chord (**V⁷**) has four notes. Above the root of chord **V**, notes are added at the interval of a 3rd, a 5th and a 7th
- The 7th causes a dissonance, so the dominant 7th is followed by chord **I** or chord **vi** to allow the 7th to 'resolve'

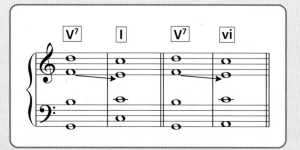

Cadential 6/4

- The tonic chord (**I**) is the only chord whose 2nd inversion is on the Leaving Cert course
- It is called 6/4 because the distance between the bass note and the other two notes in the chord are at the interval of a 6th and a 4th
- **Ic** must be used on a strong beat and has to go to **V**. The figured bass on the right demonstrates what happens

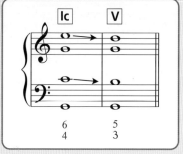

- **Ic** is 'cadential' because it works best at cadences eg. **Ic – V** and **Ic – V – I**
- ***Note:*** *Although chord **ii** should never go to **I**, it is perfectly acceptable for **ii** (or **iib**) to go to **Ic** and then to **V**. This is because chord **Ic** is like a delayed chord **V***

©Higgins & Higgins

SECTION 1: AVAILABLE CHORDS IN MAJOR KEYS FOR THE EXAM

Chord I may be used in root position, first inversion and second inversion.
Chord ii may be used in root position and first inversion.
Chord iii is not on the course.
Chord IV may be used in root position and first inversion.
Chord V may be used in root position and first inversion.
Chord V⁷ can be a useful alternative to **V** and may be used in root position and first inversion.
Chord vi may be used in root position. Its first inversion may be used but rarely sounds good.
Chord vii° is not on the course.

This gives us **13** possible chords in a major key as follows:

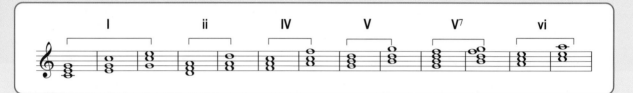

Labelling chords in a major key

EXERCISE

Look at the chords that are available for an exam question in the key of C major. Then, on the stave below, write out the chords (and inversions) that are available in the key of G major. Use chord symbols and Roman numerals.

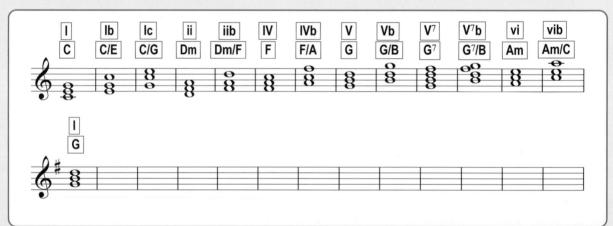

Identifying chords in different positions in the key of C major

EXERCISE

The first chord below contains the notes DFA, so it is the chord of D minor. The F is the lowest note so the chord is D minor, 1st inversion. This is written Dm/F. In the key of C major, it is chord **iib**. **Now work out the others.**

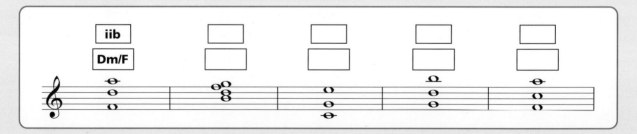

©Higgins & Higgins

Chord Bank: Major Key

This type of chord bank appears on the Leaving Cert exam paper. Learn how to fill it in. If you write the chord symbols incorrectly here, you risk entering them incorrectly in your answer, so watch out for sharps, flats, minor chords (m) and diminished chords (dim).

Key: C							
Notes of chord	G E C	A F D	B G E	C A F	D B G	E C A	F D B
Chord symbol	C	Dm	Em	F	G	Am	Bdim
Roman numeral	I	ii	iii	IV	V	vi	vii°

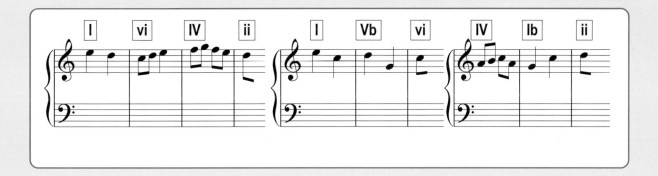

SECTION 2: CHORD POSITIONS AND PROGRESSIONS

In a harmony exercise we must match suitable chords with a melody. Moving from one chord to the next is called a chord progression. There are good and bad chord progressions.

- Moving between **I**, **IV** and **V** is usually strong eg; **IV–V; V–I**
- Cadential progressions are very strong eg. **V–vi; IV–I**
- Progressions that result in a rising 4th in the bass are strong eg. **I–IV; ii–V**
- Progressions that produce a falling 3rd in the bass are strong eg. **I–vi; IV–ii**
- On the other hand, progressions that cause a rising 3rd in the bass across a barline are weak, unless they are part of the same chord. Choose a stronger progression than **ii–IV** and **IV–vi** when going from one bar to the next
- A bass line that ascends by step is good eg. **I–ii; IV–V**
- A bass line that descends by step is good eg. **I–Vb–vi; IV–Ib–ii**

Supply the bass line for these extracts. Use minims.

EXERCISE

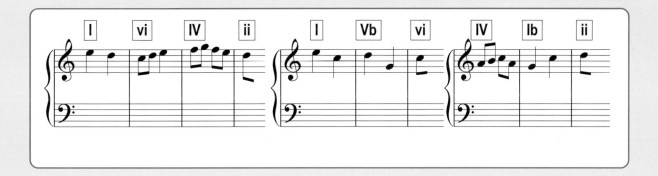

Chord	Strong progressions	General Comment
I	I-ii I-IV I-V I-vi	Generally, **I** can go to any chord, eg. many pop songs begin with **I-vi**. **Ic** occurs on a strong beat and goes to **V**. **Ic** is like a suspended **V**. **Ib** cannot be used if the 3rd note is in the treble part, as it would result in a doubled major 3rd.
ii	ii-V	Do not use **ii-I** because it is very weak. However, **iib-Ic-V** is fine. **ii** can go to **vi** if there is no other available progression. If the bass rises a 3rd over a barline, avoid **ii-IV**.
IV	IV-I IV-ii IV-V	Avoid **IV-vi** when it causes a rising 3rd in the bass, especially if this occurs over a barline. **IVb** cannot be used if the 3rd note is in the treble part, as it would result in a doubled major 3rd.
V	V-I V-vi V-IV	The leading note (in **V**) must rise a step. **V-ii** is very weak. Do not use it, unless the **V** is at the end of one phrase and **ii** is at the start of the next phrase. **Vb** cannot be used if the leading note is in the treble part, as it would result in a doubled major 3rd.
V⁷	V⁷-I V⁷-vi	The 7th note in **V** must resolve down a step.
vi	vi-IV vi-ii	Do not use **vi-I** if it causes a rising 3rd in the bass, especially if this happens over a barline. **vib** often sounds weak.

SECTION 3: CADENCES

The two chords used at the end of a phrase form a cadence. The four cadences are:

Perfect cadence	**V-I** or **V⁷-1**
Plagal cadence	**IV-I**
Interrupted cadence	**V-vi** or **V⁷-vi**
Imperfect cadence	**I-V** or **ii-V** or **IV-V** **V⁷** is not used in Imperfect cadences as the 7th must resolve.

Identify these cadences:

EXERCISE

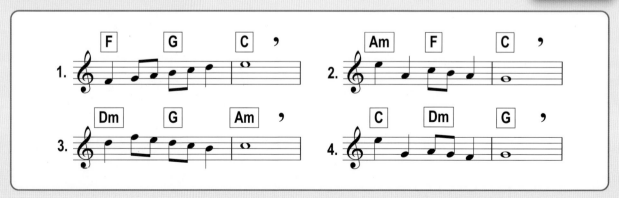

©Higgins & Higgins

Cadences in the key of C

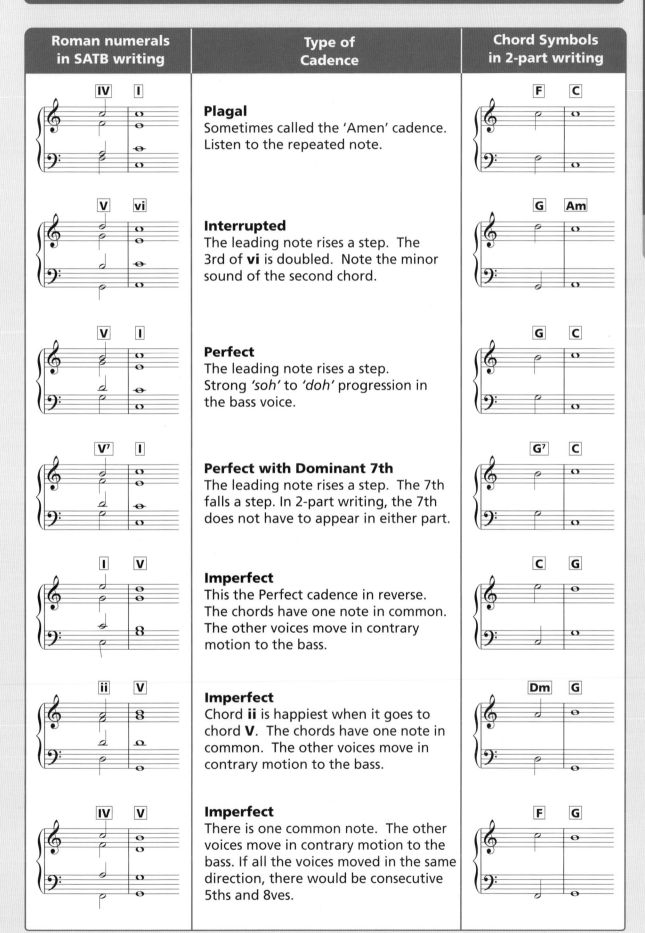

Roman numerals in SATB writing	Type of Cadence	Chord Symbols in 2-part writing
IV I	**Plagal** Sometimes called the 'Amen' cadence. Listen to the repeated note.	F C
V vi	**Interrupted** The leading note rises a step. The 3rd of **vi** is doubled. Note the minor sound of the second chord.	G Am
V I	**Perfect** The leading note rises a step. Strong 'soh' to 'doh' progression in the bass voice.	G C
V⁷ I	**Perfect with Dominant 7th** The leading note rises a step. The 7th falls a step. In 2-part writing, the 7th does not have to appear in either part.	G⁷ C
I V	**Imperfect** This the Perfect cadence in reverse. The chords have one note in common. The other voices move in contrary motion to the bass.	C G
ii V	**Imperfect** Chord **ii** is happiest when it goes to chord **V**. The chords have one note in common. The other voices move in contrary motion to the bass.	Dm G
IV V	**Imperfect** There is one common note. The other voices move in contrary motion to the bass. If all the voices moved in the same direction, there would be consecutive 5ths and 8ves.	F G

©Higgins & Higgins

SECTION 4: AVAILABLE CHORDS IN MINOR KEYS FOR THE EXAM

- **Chord i** may be used in root position, first inversion and second inversion
- **Chord ii°** may be used only in first inversion. Root position is not accepted
- **Chord III⁺** is not on the course
- **Chord iv** may be used in root position and first inversion
- **Chord V** may be used in root position and first inversion. The leading note has an accidental
- **Chord V⁷** may be used in root position and first inversion. The leading note has an accidental
- **Chord VI** may be used in root position. Avoid its first inversion
- **Chord vii°** is not on the course
- This gives us **12** possible chords in a minor key as follows:

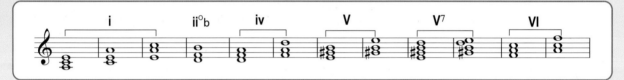

Labelling chords in minor keys

Look at the chords that are available for an exam question in the key of A minor. Then write out the chords (and inversions) that are available in the key of E minor. Use chord symbols and Roman numerals.   EXERCISE

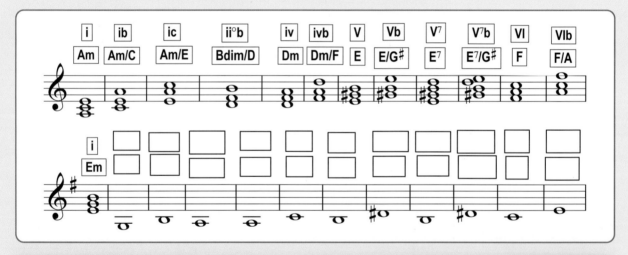

Identifying chords in different position in the key of A minor

The first chord below contains the notes DFA, so it is the chord of D minor. The F is the lowest note so the chord is D minor, 1st inversion. This is written Dm/F. In the key of A minor, it is chord **ivb**. **Now work out the others.**

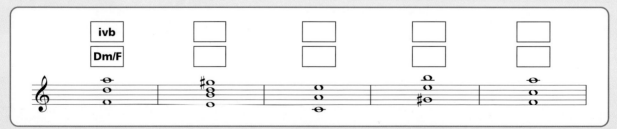

©Higgins & Higgins

Chord Bank: Minor Key

This type of chord bank appears on the Leaving Cert exam paper. Learn how to fill it in. Pay particular attention to the sharps, flats, minor chords (m), diminished chords (dim) and augmented chords (aug).

Key: A minor							
Notes of chord	E C A	F D B	G♯ E C	A F D	B G♯ E	C A F	D B G♯
Chord symbol	**Am**	**Bdim**	**Caug**	**Dm**	**E**	**F**	**G♯dim**
Roman numeral	**i**	**ii°**	**III⁺**	**iv**	**V**	**VI**	**vii°**

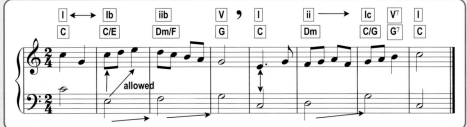

SECTION 5: INVERSIONS (MAJOR AND MINOR)

Inversions are useful if you wish to avoid using the same position of a chord in two consecutive boxes. They make the harmony flow smoothly but should not be overused.

- Chord **vi** should almost always be in root position
- Never double the leading note or any other major 3rd

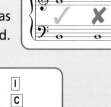

In the following eight-bar phrase, the melody-line was given and was harmonised. Notice how, why and where inversions were used and avoided.

Bar 2	• C/E is useful as it allows the same chord to be used in two consecutive boxes
	• The chord of **vi** could also be used as it produces a falling 3rd in the bass
Bar 3	• It is good to approach and quit first inversions by step (in the bass part)
Bar 4	• **iib** going to **V** is a strong cadential progression
Bar 5	• C/E could not be used in bar 5 as the major 3rd would be doubled (with E in both the treble and bass parts)
Bar 6	• Although doubling the minor 3rd is allowed, **ii** is used instead of **iib** because the rising 4th it produces in the bass line is good
Bar 7	• **ii** cannot go to **I**. However, **ii** can go to **Ic** provided **Ic** goes to **V**
	• An alternative ending would be **V-V⁷-I**
	• **V** can go to **V⁷** but the reverse is unacceptable
	• In **V⁷**, the 7th does not have to appear in the melody or the bass part
	• The second last box could not be **Vb** as the leading note would be doubled and the cadence **Vb-I** is not as strong as **V-I** or **V⁷-I**

©Higgins & Higgins

SECTION 6: BASS LINE BASICS

EXERCISE

In the following example, the melody line was given. Backing chords have been chosen and a bass line was added. Most of the problems in this solution are caused by non-chord notes in the bass line. **Can you improve on this attempt?** Consider these points:

- The bass note below the chord box must reflect accurately the chosen chord eg. Dm/F means that the note F is in the bass part below the box
- Passing notes make the bass line more interesting but these must be musical. Do not jump from a passing note. Check also that there are no unresolved clashes.
- In the key of C, if E is in the melody, do not use the chord C/E. (Doubled major 3rd)
- As this bass moves mainly in crotchets the notes are quite easy to position and have been correctly aligned with the treble part here

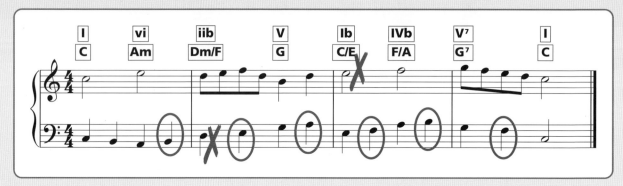

Improved attempt:

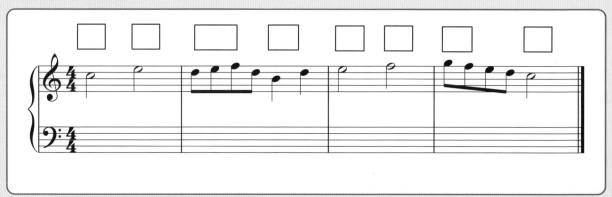

EXERCISE

Correct this bass line:

©Higgins & Higgins

CHORD PROGRESSIONS

EXERCISE

In the following exercises, two sets of chord progressions have been supplied to harmonise some short phrases. In each case choose the harmonisation that you think is stronger and give two reasons for your choice. *(Note: It will be easier to read the progressions if you first write in the Roman numerals.)*

Ex 1
Harmonisation 1

Harmonisation 2

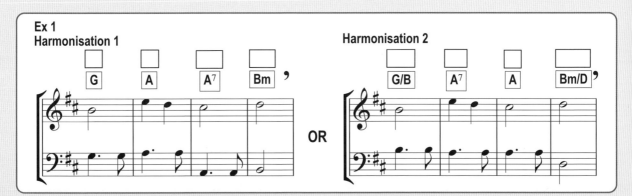

OR

Harmonisation _____ is stronger. Reasons: _____

_____

Ex 2
Harmonisation 3

Harmonisation 4

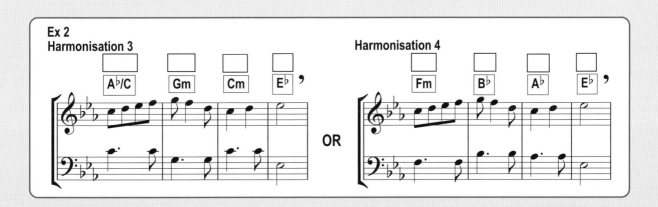

OR

Harmonisation _____ is stronger. Reasons: _____

_____

Ex 3
Harmonisation 5

Harmonisation 6

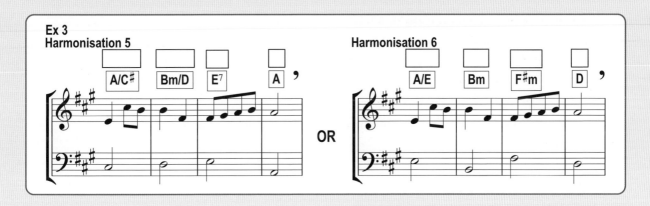

OR

Harmonisation _____ is stronger. Reasons: _____

_____

©Higgins & Higgins

SECTION 7:
HL Q4: Composing melody and bass notes from a set of chords

Sample Question

In this question, you are asked to compose a melody and bass part to fit a set of given chords. The melody and bass must be in the style of the given opening.

Process

1.   Write chords **I – ii – IV – V(')** and **vi** in the key of C major in the chord bank.
2.   Do not omit the suffix 'm' for minor chords when writing chord symbols.
3.   Add the 7th note to chord **V** to form the dominant 7th.

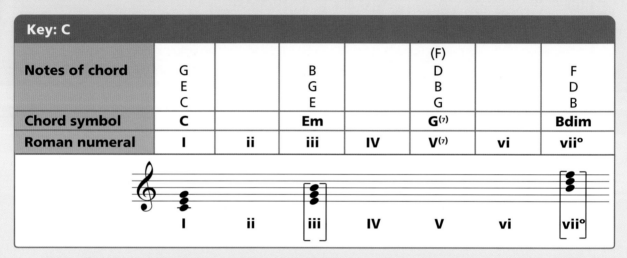

Key: C							
Notes of chord	G E C		B G E		(F) D B G		F D B
Chord symbol	C		Em		G⁽⁷⁾		Bdim
Roman numeral	I	ii	iii	IV	V⁽⁷⁾	vi	vii°

4.   Fill in the bass notes directly below the chord boxes. Chord C means that the note C goes into the bass. Chord C/E means that E goes into the bass and so on.
5.   Make the rhythm of the bass line similar to the given bass part.
6.   Avoid leaps of a 7th, rising 3rds and falling 4ths in the bass part. Avoid repeating a bass note over the barline – leap an 8ve if necessary.
7.   Go through the given chords and work out where you think the cadences are. Write the word 'cadence' over those bars. This may prompt you to use a long note in the melody.
8.   It is easier to sing the given phrase by using tonic solfa names. Elements of this melody should be developed and used in your other **A** phrases eg. quavers or unusual leaps.
9.   Do not restrict yourself to the notes of the given chord. In order to make the melody sound smoother, move by step, using passing notes.
10. Try to include a sequence or a sequential passage, especially in the **B** phrase. Awkward leaps (eg. major 7th or a diminished 5th) can sound quite musical as part of a sequence.
11. Syncopation may sound out of character if it is not already used in the given phrase.
12. Observe the cadence at the end of each phrase. Ending a phrase on any note from chord **V** (tonic solfa names: *soh – te – ray*) produces an Imperfect cadence.
13. Where is the climax of your tune going to be?
14. Stretch the range of the tune slightly and do not meander around the same few notes for more than a bar or two.
15. In a minor key, the augmented 2nd may be avoided by approaching and quitting the raised 7th with the upper tonic or any note from chord **V**.
16. Features of the opening are highlighted in the sample question (*No. 1 on the next page*). Guidelines for composing a tune and bass part in the other systems have also been added.

©Higgins & Higgins

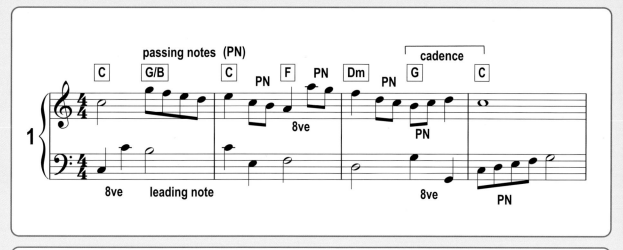

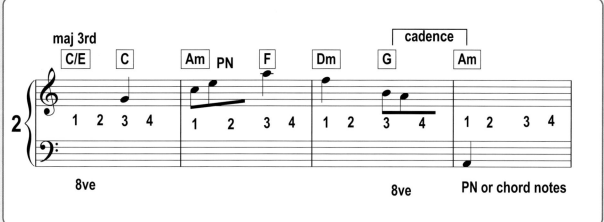

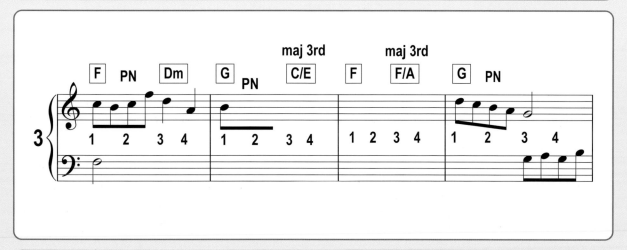

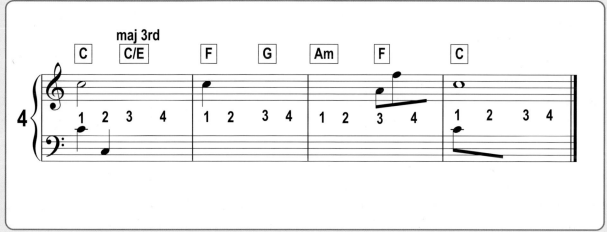

©Higgins & Higgins

SECTION 8:
HL Q5: Composing Bass notes and Chord indications to a given tune

Sample Question

EXERCISE

In this question the melody is given. You are asked to provide suitable backing chords and a bass line in the style of the given opening. The same chord cannot be used in the same position in consecutive boxes. Write Roman numerals or chord symbols in the boxes, but not a mixture of the two.

Process

1. Write chords **I – ii – IV – V** and **vi** in the key of F major in the chord bank.
2. Remember to write the note B♭ (not B) in chords **ii** and **IV**.
3. Do not omit the suffix 'm' for minor chords when writing chord symbols.
4. Use lower case when writing minor chords in Roman numerals.
5. Add the 7th note to chord **V** to form the dominant 7th.

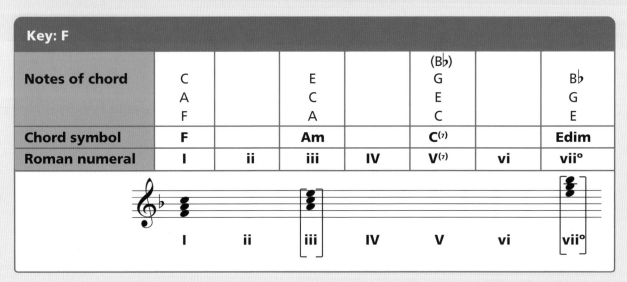

Key: F							
Notes of chord	C A F		E C A		(B♭) G E C		B♭ G E
Chord symbol	F		Am		C⁽⁷⁾		Edim
Roman numeral	I	ii	iii	IV	V⁽⁷⁾	vi	vii°

I   ii   iii   IV   V   vi   vii°

6. Sing the melody and write the word 'cadence' over the final two chords in each phrase.
7. Write the available chords over each box, remembering that the chord you choose must be able to harmonise the tune until the next chord is sounded.
8. Notes that leap usually have to be harmonised.
9. Passing notes are non-chord notes and tend to move by step.
10. Sometimes there are several possible chords for one box. From these chords, choose the one that produces the best progression with the chords before and after it.
11. Actively look for stock progressions that work well eg. **I-vi-ii-V** or **I-IV-V-vi**
12. Supply a bass line, making sure that the bass note directly below the chord box reflects the chord position (eg. in this key, **iib** = Gm/B♭, so B♭ is used in the bass).
13. The bass line should be musical. Avoid awkward leaps (eg. a 7th or an augmented 4th).
14. Use inversions to make the bass line smoother; otherwise stick to root positions.
15. Do not double the major 3rd of a first inversion chord.
16. In the sample question that follows, the beats (1, 2, 3, 4) have been added to help you align the bass and treble notes.
17. For some boxes, no choice of chords has been written in as there is only one possible solution.

©Higgins & Higgins

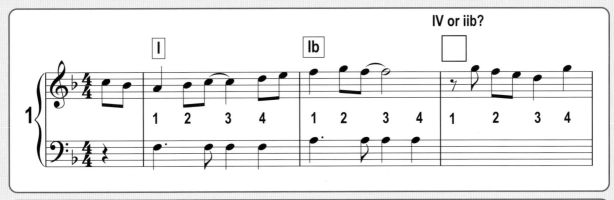

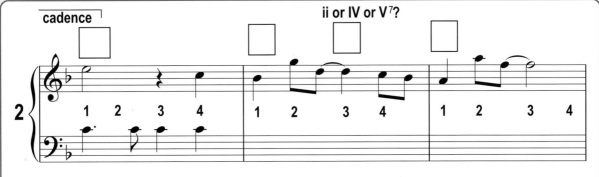

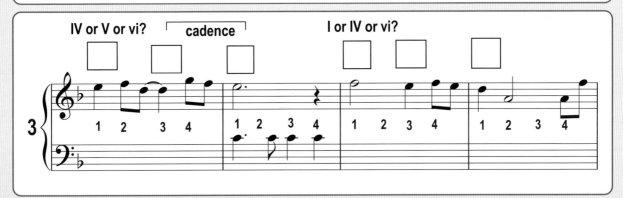

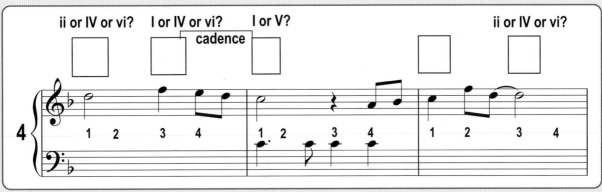

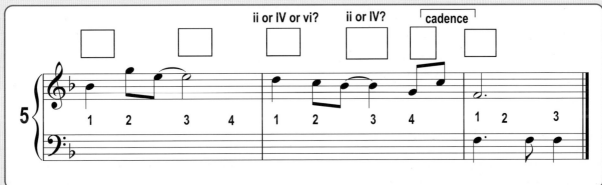

©Higgins & Higgins

SECTION 9:
HL Q6: Adding a Countermelody or Descant with Chordal Support to a given Melody

Sample Question

In this question you write a descant part over a given melody. It is an exercise in **counterpoint**. Both parts are written on the treble clef. Backing chords are also requested.

Process

1. Write chords **I – ii – IV – V⁷** and **vi** in the key of G major in the chord bank remembering to write the note F♯ (not F). Do not omit the suffix 'm' for minor chords when writing chord symbols. Use lower case when writing minor chords in Roman numerals.

Key: G							
Notes of chord	D B G		F♯ D B		(C) A F♯ D		C A F♯
Chord symbol	G		Bm		D(⁷)		F♯dim
Roman numeral	I	ii	iii	IV	V(⁷)	vi	vii°

I   ii   iii   IV   V   vi   vii°

2. Sing the melody and write the word 'cadence' at the end of each phrase.
3. Choose chords that produce the strongest chord progressions.
4. Do not double the major 3rd of any major chord.
5. Use and develop elements from the given descant part and try to use a sequence.
6. Contrary motion and imitation between the parts give a sense of independence.

Before you begin, examine some problems that must be avoided in contrapuntal writing:

- Consecutive 5ths and 8ves are not allowed
- The interval of a 4th between the two parts sounds weak as it produces the effect of a 2nd inversion (6/4) chord.
- Homophony: Do not use a full bar of identical rhythm in both parts simultaneously.

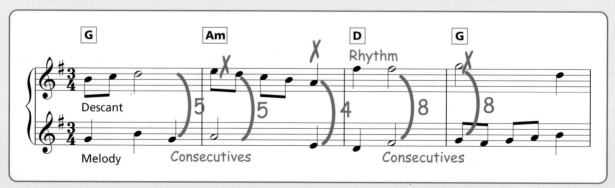

In the sample question that follows, a suggested rhythm has been supplied as well as some suitable chords. Notice that the position of the chord does not have to be stated. The cadence points have also been written in for you.

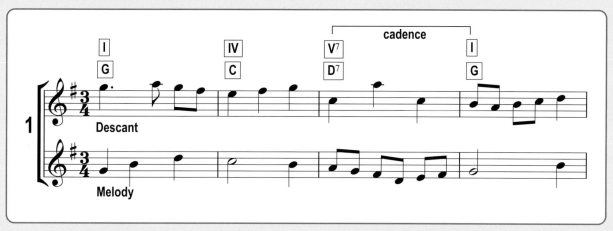

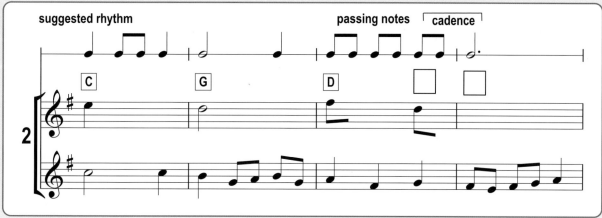

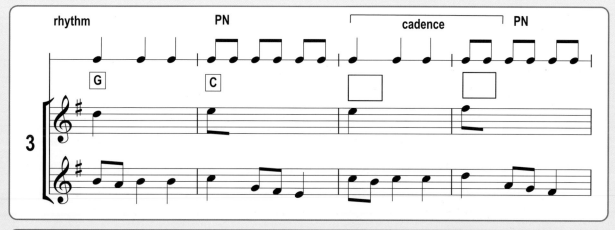

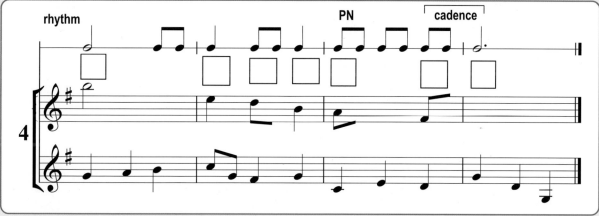

©Higgins & Higgins

SECTION 10:
OL Q4 : Composing Melody and Bass Notes from a set of Chords

EXERCISE

Sample Question

- Study the following piece of music
- Using the given rhythms, add melody and bass notes to compose the cadences and approach chords as follows:
  (i)   At A, a PLAGAL cadence (**vi-IV-I**).
  (ii) At B, an INTERRUPTED cadence (**ii-V-vi**).
  (iii) At C, an IMPERFECT cadence (**IV-I-V**).
  (iv) At D, a PERFECT cadence (**ii-V-I**).

Progress

1. Write out the scale of G on the stave below:

2. Plot the chords available in this key (**I, ii, IV, V, vi**) in the chord bank grid below:

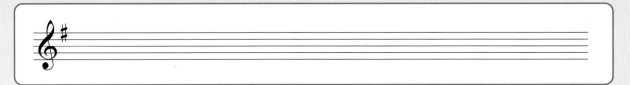

Key: G							
Notes of chord	D B G		F# D B				C A F#
Chord symbol	G		Bm				F#dim
Roman numeral	I	ii	iii	IV	V	vi	vii°

3. Write the Roman numerals for each cadence under the spaces allocated for them.

4. Use the chords in the chord bank to help you work out the chords.

5. The first note in each chord goes into the bass (Chord **vi** = EGB so place the E in the bass; Chord **IV** = CEG, so place C in the bass and Chord **I** = GBD, so put G in the bass).

6. From the remaining two notes in the chord choose a melody note.

7. Make the melody note flow smoothly from the previous melody note.

8. Do not have awkward leaps in either the bass or the melody part.

9. In Perfect and Interrupted cadences, the leading note (the middle note in Chord **V**) moves up a step to the tonic. (In this key, the leading note is F#. It rises a step to G.).

Cadence A below has been completed as an example. Now, using the given chords and rhythms, compose bass and Melody notes at B, C and D.

©Higgins & Higgins

SECTION 11:
OL Q5: Adding Bass Notes and Chord Indications at Cadence Points

EXERCISE

Sample Question

- Study the following piece of music which is in the key of B♭ major
- Add suitable bass notes and chord indications to complete the cadences at A, B, C and D.
- You may use either chord symbols or Roman numerals as you wish

Progress

1. Write out the scale of B♭ on the stave below:

2. Plot the chords available in this key (**I, ii, IV, V, vi**) in the chord bank grid below:

Key: B♭							
Notes of chord	F D B♭		A F D				E♭ C A
Chord symbol	**B♭**		**Dm**				**Adim**
Roman numeral	**I**	**ii**	**iii**	**IV**	**V**	**vi**	**vii°**

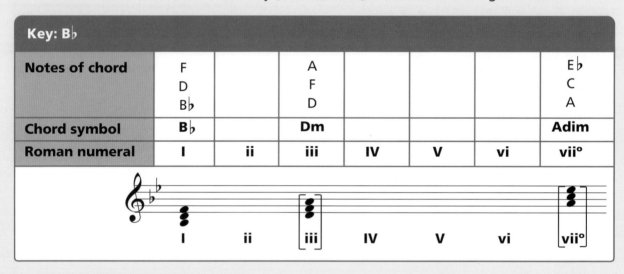

3. The melody notes are given at the cadence points. You must supply bass notes that fit.
4. Every melody note belongs to three possible chords.
5. Work out the chords in the chord bank. Cadence A has been done as an example.
6. The available three chords are written under each note, using Roman numerals.
7. Which chords give the best solution? Choose chords that form cadences.
8. In Cadence B, the following are NOT cadential progressions: **ii-I; ii-IV; ii-vi; IV-IV; IV-vi; vi-I; vi-IV; vi-vi**. The only possible choice is **IV-I** (a Plagal cadence)
9. The first note in each chord goes into the bass part (In the key of B♭ chord **IV** = E♭GB♭ so place the E♭ in the bass; Chord **I** = B♭DF, so place B♭ in the bass.

©Higgins & Higgins

Cadence A has been worked out below. Complete the cadences at B, C and D by choosing suitable cadential progressions and by adding in the bass notes.

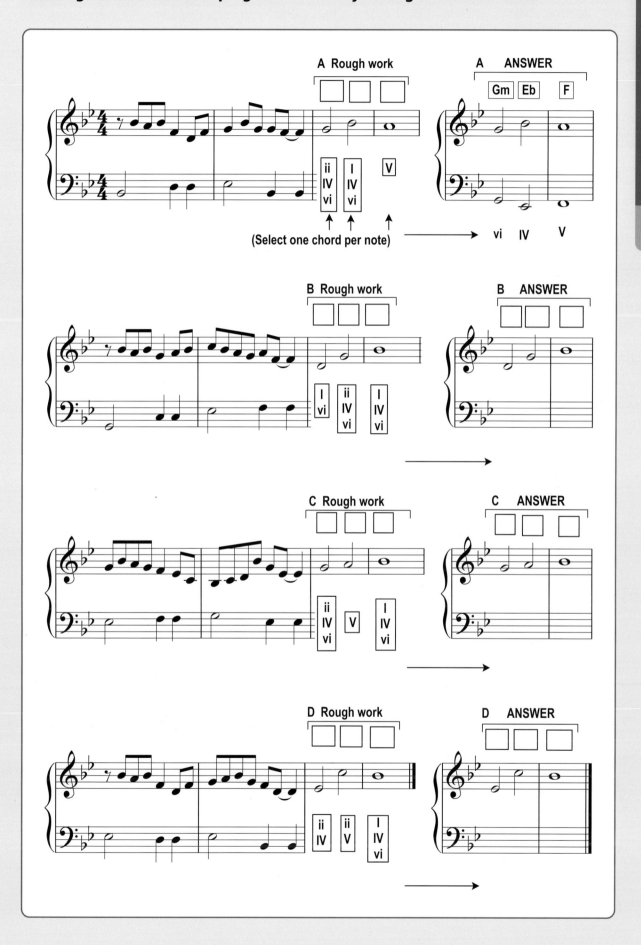

©Higgins & Higgins

SECTION 12:
OL Q6: Adding Descant Notes and Chord Indications at Cadence Points

Sample Question

EXERCISE

- Study the following piece of music which is in the key of C major
- Complete the phrase endings by adding suitable cadence chords and descant notes at A, B, C and D
- You may use either chord symbols or Roman numerals

Progress

1. Write out the scale of C on the stave below:below:

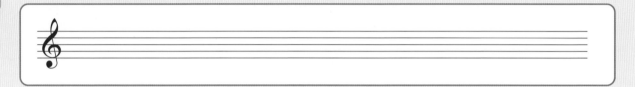

2. Plot the chords available in this key (**I, ii, IV, V, vi**) in the chord bank grid below:

Key: C							
Notes of chord	G E C		B G E				F D B
Chord symbol	C		Em				Bdim
Roman numeral	I	ii	iii	IV	V	vi	vii°

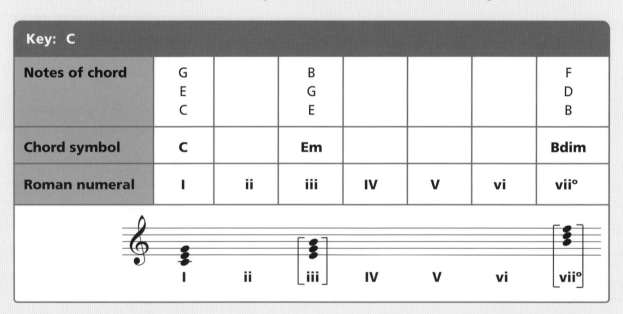

3. Assume that the three chords at each cadence are in root position so look at the bass note to help you work out their names.
4. Write the chord symbols in the boxes provided.
5. Using a pencil, write on the stave the chord notes that could play the descant part.
6. Sing the given descant part and supply the missing notes over the final three chords of each phrase. The aim is to write a nice tune, without awkward leaps.
7. The rhythm could be exactly the same as the given parts. However, passing notes make the tune more interesting.
8. Do not leap from a non-chord note.

©Higgins & Higgins

Cadence A has been completed. Now add chord symbols and descant notes to complete cadences B, C and D. You could use passing notes (as in cadence A below) or long notes (as in cadence B below) in the descant part to make it flow more smoothly.

©Higgins & Higgins

HL Q5: Composing chords to a given tune.

EXERCISE

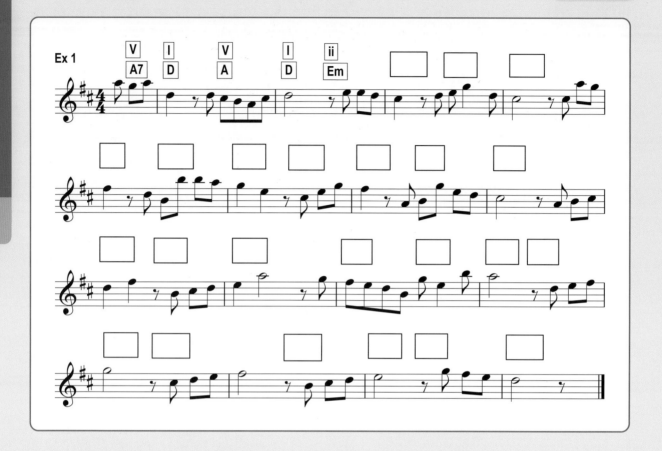

HL Q4: Composing a melody from a set of chords.

EXERCISE

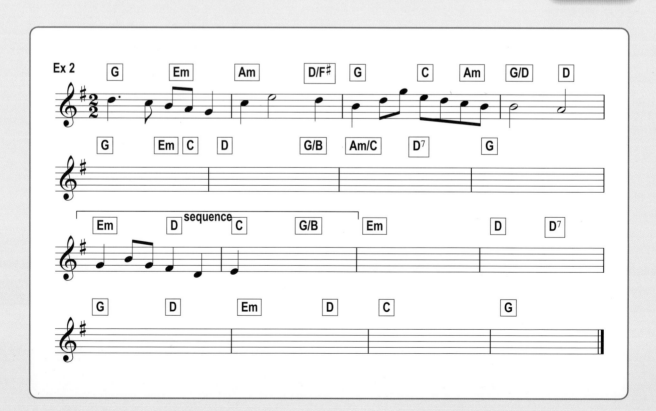

Harmony

48

©Higgins & Higgins

Chapter 3 – Aural Skills

Contents

This chapter, AURAL SKILLS, is illustrated with Musical examples on
CD1, TRACKS 1 to 54

Contents

SECTION 1: INSTRUMENTAL TECHNIQUES

Legato, Staccato, Pizzicato

The following phrase from *Gypsy Air* (Sarasate) is played on violin FOUR times. Unless otherwise instructed, string players play **arco**.

Track 1 – Legato
Track 2 – Staccato
Track 3 – Pizzicato

Track 4 – Left-hand pizzicato on the indicated notes:

Track 5 – Single pizzicato note followed by Bartok pizzicato, also on a single note.
(See page 216)

Legato, Double stopping, Harmonics

Listen to the following phrase from *Czardas* (Monti) played on violin THREE times.

Track 6 – Legato

Track 7 – With double-stopping

Track 8 – With artificial harmonics **(see page 146)**

51

Aural Skills

©Higgins & Higgins

Senza vibrato, Vibrato, Tremolo, Vibrato con Sord

This phrase from *Nessun Dorma* (Puccini) is played four times on violin, as follows:

Track 9 – Senza vibrato
Track 10 – Vibrato
Track 11 – Tremolo
Track 12 – Vibrato con sord

Other String Techniques played on Violin

Track 13 – Scale of G, then scale of G divisi in 6ths
Track 14 – Scale of G, using double-stopping in 6ths

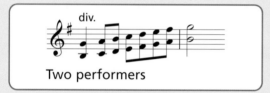

Two performers

One performer

Track 15 – Glissando
Track 16 – Col legno battuto (with wooden part of bow)
Track 17 – Open and stopped string E

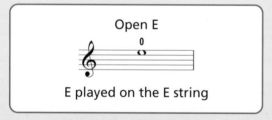

Open E

E played on the E string

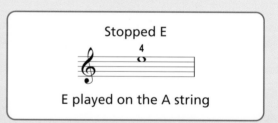

Stopped E

E played on the A string

Some Guitar Techniques

Track 18 – Finger picking
Track 19 – Strumming
Track 20 – Power chords **(See page 163)**
Track 21 – Riff, then Riff with added Lick

Some Drum Techniques

Track 22 – Backbeat (4 types)
Track 23 – Drum fills (6 types)

©Higgins & Higgins

SECTION 2: COMPOSITIONAL TECHNIQUES

TRACKS
24-40

Repetition and Sequences

Track 24 – An excerpt from *Arrival of the Queen of Sheba* (Handel) will be played. A single-line score is partially written out below. The music contains several examples of (i) repetition and (ii) sequence. One example of each technique is already marked on the score. **Which of these techniques is used at the end of bar 8 and at the end of bar 13? Write your answers on the score in the spaces provided (marked *).**

EXERCISE

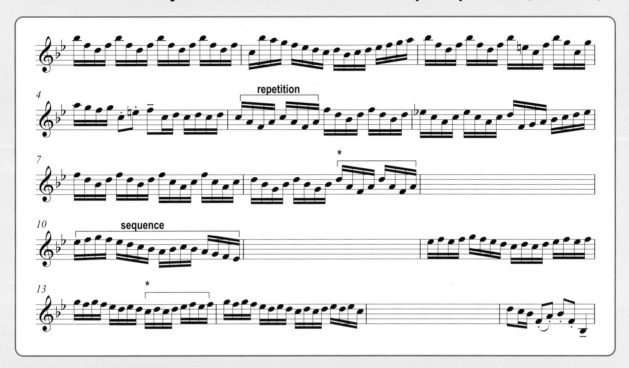

Listen carefully to the excerpt again and identify the missing notes in bars 9, 11 and 15 by writing the correct bar number over each of the bars below:

Bar ____   Bar ____   Bar ____

EXERCISE

Here is another short extract from the same work, but not on the CD. It is the first part of a sequence, starting on the note E♭. **Write the next part of the sequence on the stave, beginning on the note D (fourth line). Use the given rhythm pattern as a guide. Then play your sequence.**

©Higgins & Higgins

Imitation, Imitative entries, Polyphonic texture

Track 25 – Listen to the main theme of a fugue from *Violin Sonata No 3* (Bach). Although there are no singers involved, we refer to the different entries of the main subject in a fugue as 'voices'.

Track 26 – The two voices overlap when the second voice enters in imitation. The texture is polyphonic (or contrapuntal). In this extract one violin plays both voices requiring the violinist to use double-stopping.

Check the intervals between the first two notes of the theme in both voices. **EXERCISE**
Does the second voice enter on the same note as the first voice? Is the second voice an exact canon?

Theme and Variations

Track 27 – Listen to this short melodic phrase from *The Surprise Symphony* (Haydn).

Track 28 – The theme is varied by using a minor key instead of a major one:

Track 29 – Here the theme is varied rhythmically:

Apart from variations in tonality and rhythm, different instruments might take **EXERCISE**
the theme, the harmony might change, the range of the melody could be extended and a higher or lower register may be used. Retrograde and inversion are other possibilities. **Use the stave below to vary the theme in one of these ways.**

©Higgins & Higgins

Alberti Bass

Track 30 – Broken chords in a 'sewing machine' rhythm characterise an Alberti Bass accompaniment. This was popular during the Classical period and was often used in the left hand of piano music. Listen to this example.

Arpeggio Figures

EXERCISE

In an arpeggio, all four notes of a chord (root, 3rd, 5th, upper root) are sounded one after the other, ascending and descending. **Identify the following four arpeggios:**

Arpeggio: | Arpeggio: | Arpeggio: | Arpeggio:

Track 31 – Now listen to the way these arpeggios are incorporated into the music in the following excerpt from *Solfeggietto* (CPE Bach). They are called 'arpeggio figures'.

Broken Chords

EXERCISE

Track 32 – Listen to an extract that illustrates a typical 'ballad style' accompaniment. It consists of the notes of chords sounded successively and, in this instance, is almost like a series of arpeggios (but not quite). **Work out the four chords used below and write down the chord progression, using Roman numerals.**

Chord: | Chord: | Chord: | Chord:

©Higgins & Higgins

Block chords

EXERCISE

Track 33 – Here is a short excerpt from a piano sonata (Op 14, no 1) by Beethoven. The melody is in the treble stave and the left hand accompanies the tune with block chords. **Listen to the music, identify these chords and give their positions (eg. root position, first inversion).**

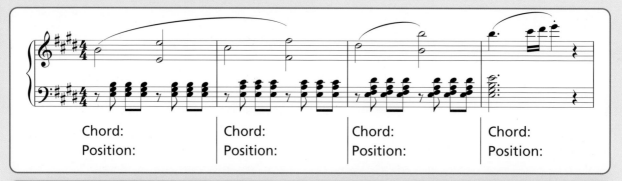

Chord: Chord: Chord: Chord:
Position: Position: Position: Position:

8ves (1)

Track 34 – In Beethoven's *Moonlight Sonata* (Op 27, no 2) the left hand moves smoothly in 8ves.

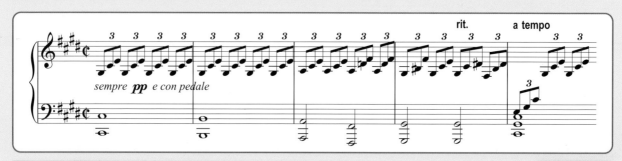

EXERCISE

What is the key of this piece? Pick out the tonic and dominant chords in the extract. Explain the following musical instructions: (i) *sempre pp e con pedale* **(ii) rit. (iii) a tempo (iv) triplet quavers**

8ves (2)

Track 35 – In his *Pathétique* piano sonata (Op 13), Beethoven drives the music forward by writing broken 8ves for the left hand. **How does he also create a pedal effect in the first few bars?**

©Higgins & Higgins

Changing Time Signatures

EXERCISE

Track 36 – In the following extract from *Il Ritorno di Ben* (Cane-Marrone), played here on MIDI-generated xylophone, the strong beats occur at different time-distances from each other due to the changing time signatures

Fill in the ten missing time signatures on the score above.

Changing Key Signatures

Track 37 – Many pop songs modulate to the key a tone higher in order to give the music a 'lift' and to maintain interest. The example below is from a well-known Christmas song.

EXERCISE

Identify both keys, then listen to the extract. Explain how the music modulates from the first key to the second by describing the boxed chord above.

Ostinato / Ground Bass / Repeated Figure

EXERCISE

Track 38 – *Pachelbel's Canon* is a good example of a piece built on a constantly repeating four-bar motif called a ground bass or ostinato. **Listen to this extract and work out the chord progressions.**

©Higgins & Higgins

Pedal / Drone

Track 39 – In Irish traditional music a drone is produced by the uilleann pipes and is used to add harmonic interest and texture to a tune. In art music, composers sometimes place a sustained tonic or dominant pedal at an important juncture in the music to lead the ear towards a particular key. Although the notes being played by the other instruments may not have any direct harmonic relationship with these pedals, the effect is not jarring or dissonant.

The following extract is adapted from a keyboard prelude (Book 1, No 23) by Bach and is played here by flute and cello.

Name the pedal note used here and say whether it is a tonic or a dominant pedal in this key. EXERCISE

12-bar Blues Pattern

EXERCISE

Track 40 – In Jazz, individual band members often break into an improvised solo during a group piece. The other instruments provide harmonic support by playing a series of pre-arranged chords. Listen to a 12-bar set of chord progressions in which only the tonic, dominant and subdominant chords are used. You will hear the chord pattern followed by an improvisation based on it. **Which of the following patterns do you hear? Tick one box only**.

☐	I – I – I – I
	IV – IV – I – I
	V – IV – I – I

☐	I – I – V– I
	I – I – IV – I
	I – I – V – I

☐	I – I – I – I
	IV – IV – IV – IV
	V – V – V – I

Identify chords I, IV and V in the following keys:

Key C:	I = C	IV = F	V = G
Key G:	I =	IV =	V =
Key F:	I =	IV =	V =
Key D:	I =	IV =	V =
Key B♭:	I =	IV =	V =

©Higgins & Higgins

SECTION 3: STUDIO EFFECTS

TRACKS 41-46

Reverberation

Track 41 – Reverberation is the reflection of sound waves from a solid surface to our ears. The time between these random repetitions of the sound is imperceptible. Reverb locates the music in a specific acoustic space – the longer it takes a sound to decay, the larger and more hard-surfaced the room is perceived to be.

Delay

Track 42 – Short **delays** of between 15 and 35 milliseconds help to create ambience. One particular delay effect, **chorusing** can make a couple of voices sound like a large choir in a cathedral. An **echo** is a perceptible sound repetition (after 50 milliseconds). Studios and concert halls try to eliminate echoes when these inhibit sonic clarity.

Flanging

Track 43 – Putting a finger on the **flange** or rim of a tape reel (so that one tape gradually slips out of sync with another tape that is playing the same sound) causes a swooshing effect. **Flanging** occurs when a direct sound and a slightly delayed version of the same sound are combined with continuously varying time relationships of between 0 and 20 milliseconds

Distortion

Track 44 – Distortion can be created in the studio but to achieve an electric guitar's aggressive sound, distortion is induced with an amplifier. Also known as **overdrive**, it can be applied to bass guitars and other amplified instruments such as synthesisers and the Hammond organ.

Panning

Track 45 – Panning passes the sound from one speaker to another, setting up a stereo field to create a sense of space. The term is derived from 'panorama', the panning action used by movie cameras.

Overdubbing and Multitracking

Track 46 – Overdubbing is a technique used to add a supplementary recorded sound to a previously recorded performance. Musicians can overdub a mistake in an otherwise good 'take'. During **multitracking**, multiple musical instruments and vocals can be recorded one at a time onto individual tracks, allowing them to be processed individually, before the final mix-down.

For links to sites that explain these terms more fully, go to:
http://www.leavingcertmusic.com

©Higgins & Higgins

SECTION 4: SONGS AND INTRODUCTIONS

'The Beginning' – Introduction

EXERCISE

Answer the following questions about the introduction:

Question 1

Write down the order in which the following instruments appear in the introduction. If two instruments come in together give them the same number.

☐ lead guitar   ☐ drums   ☐ piano   ☐ bass guitar

Question 2

Which THREE of the following features do you hear in this melodic passage? Tick three boxes.

☐ chromatic movement   ☐ trills   ☐ range of a 4th

☐ minor scale   ☐ syncopation   ☐ leap of a 4th

Question 3

This is the bass line heard in the third phrase of the introduction.

Using the given rhythm as a guide, show how it changes in the fourth phrase by writing the missing notes on the stave below. *(Clue: The final three chords are **ii-V-I**)*

©Higgins & Higgins

'The Beginning' – Bridge leading to the Chorus

TRACK
48

EXERCISE

The lyrics of this section are written here. Answer the questions which follow.

> 1. *When we started out I remember a time*
> 2. *When you didn't mind if I held your hand in mine*
> 3. *Since, when it's all been too much*
> 4. *Well, we just don't seem to touch any more*
> 5. *Now I'm believing that*
> 6. *If we could both pretend that it's the beginning*
> 7. *Maybe it doesn't have to end, oh no...*

Question 1

Which THREE of the following musical features can you hear in this section? Tick three boxes.

☐ compound duple time ☐ minor key ☐ ornamental piano figure

☐ walking bass ☐ block chords ☐ ascending chromatic passage

Question 2

In which line does the vocal harmony begin? _____

'Breaking the Rules' – Introduction

TRACK
49

EXERCISE

Answer the following questions about the introduction:

Question 1

Which ONE of the following can you NOT hear in the introduction. Tick one box only.

☐ castanets ☐ wind chime ☐ TV test tone

☐ triangle ☐ reverse cymbal ☐ guitar

☐ shakers ☐ piano ☐ synth. pad

Question 2

What is the piano playing in the introduction? Tick one box only.

☐ ascending broken chords ☐ one repeated note

☐ descending chromatic scale ☐ trills

☐ different inversions of chords in the right hand ☐ rapid scales

©Higgins & Higgins

'Breaking the Rules' – Verses 1 and 2

TRACK 50

EXERCISE

Verse 1
1. I know you lied to me,
2. I know you lied to me
3. Baby can't you see,
4. I know that you've been breaking the rules

Verse 2
5. They say you've done the cruellest thing
6. But friends don't have to tell me you're with him
7. Oh, cos I feel it in your touch, feel it in your kiss
8. That you've been breaking the rules.

Question 1

Write down one difference you hear between the musical treatment of verse 1 and verse 2.

_____

_____

Question 2

Listen to the main melody and write the four missing notes on the stave below. *(Clue: The upward leap is greater than the leap in bar 1).*

'Take it Easy' – Introduction

TRACK 51

EXERCISE

Question 1

Listen to the 'ah' being sung in the introduction. Write the missing notes for this descending melodic phrase on the stave below, using the given rhythms as a guide.

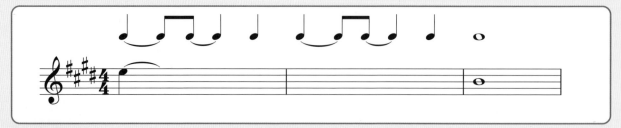

Question 2

There are hand claps in the introduction. Which one of the following indicates most accurately (with >) where the hand claps are heard? Tick one box.

©Higgins & Higgins

'Take it Easy' – Chorus

TRACK 52

EXERCISE

The chorus lyrics are written below. Answer the question that follows.

> *Take it easy, no need to rush*
> *Take a little extra time, when it's all too much*
> *Take it easy, no need to rush*
> *Take a little extra time, when it's all too much.*
> *Cos time will wait for us.*

Question

Which of the following drum rhythms accompanies the singing during the chorus? Tick one box.

'Don't take the Train' – Introduction

TRACK 53

EXERCISE

Listen to the introduction to the song. The sounds are heard in the following order:

1. Train sound.   1. _____

2. Sustained note on Synth. Pad.   2. _____

3. Panned Spanish guitar with   3. _____
   delay effect.

4. Harmonica.   4. _____

5. Power chords, Drums/Cymbal   5. _____
   and Shaku Flute.

6. March-like Rhythm.   6. _____

7. Piano Figures.   7. _____

8. Scale on Spanish Guitar.   8. _____

Question 1

Listen again and familiarise yourself with the individual sounds. Then, cover the list and write down the sounds in the correct order, while you listen to the extract again.

©Higgins & Higgins

Question 2

Listen to the opening melodic phrase, which is repeated several times. Insert the missing notes in the score below. *(Clue: The notes are all descending.)*

Question 3

Which of the following piano figures can you hear? Tick one box.

'Little Thing Called Love' – Introduction

TRACK
54

EXERCISE

Answer the following questions about the introduction to this song:

Question 1

The following instruments play the introduction. Write down the order in which they appear.

☐ hammond organ   ☐ bass guitar

☐ piano   ☐ splash cymbal (rattly sound)

☐ drums and synth. brass   ☐ electric guitar

Question 2

Which one of the following rhythms is played at the very end of the introduction? Tick one box.

©Higgins & Higgins

Chapter 4 – Irish Music

Contents

This chapter, IRISH MUSIC, is illustrated with Musical examples on
CD1, TRACKS 55 to 70

TRACK LIST:

55. **Reel:** *Boys of the Lough*
56. **Hornpipe:** *Cooley's Hornpipe*
57. **Double Jig:** *Cherish the Ladies*
58. **Slip Jig:** No name
59. **Single Jig:** *Sergeant Cahill's Favourite*
60. **Slide:** *Pádraig O'Keeffe's*
61. **Slow Air:** *The Banks of the Suir*
62. **Planxty:** *O'Connor's*

63. **Polka:** *The Lakes of Sligo*
64. **Mazurka:** *Sonny's Mazurka*
65. **March:** *Fáinne Geal an Lae*
66. **Ornament:** Cran
67. **Ornament:** Roll
68. **Ornament:** Triplet
69. **Ornament:** Grace note
70. **Ornament:** Slide

Contents

According to the D.E.S. Leaving Certificate Music syllabus (2.3.3), *'students should have sufficient experience of listening to Irish music to enable them to understand, identify and describe from aural and visual perception the range and variety of Irish music heard today'* as well as *' Irish musical idioms and influences'*. In addition, Higher level students must be able to *'perceive aurally and describe traditional and modern-day performing styles and the contribution Irish music has made to folk music in other countries, especially in North America'*.

Students identify aspects of Irish music played for them in the exam and they must also write a short essay on one topic related to the tradition.

It is ESSENTIAL for students to refer to music they have heard in relation to each of the following topics. Relevant internet links may be found at:
http://www.leavingcertmusic.com

SECTION 1: INSTRUMENTS

Fiddle

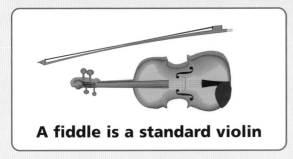

A fiddle is a standard violin

G B D

Range of Irish Fiddle

The style of playing, rather than the instrument itself, makes the fiddle sound Irish. Traditional fiddlers play generally in the first position and this gives them a range of just over two 8ves from the note G below middle C to the B above the treble clef. (Some players use second position on the top string to reach C, C♯ and D.)

Unlike violinists, they do not have to grip the instrument firmly between the chin and shoulder as they do not need to move their left hand very far up and down the fingerboard. Unlike violinists, they may use their left wrist to help support the instrument. Fiddlers may hold the instrument under their chin or against their chest, shoulder or upper arm. Traditional players tend not to use the full bow and a very light grip is needed for fast bowing decorations. The exception to this is the East Galway style of playing which favours the use of the full bow. The four main regional styles in fiddle playing are from Clare, Donegal, Sliabh Luachra and Sligo. These styles are distinguished mainly by their bowing variations. In the Donegal style, short strokes are used, changing direction with each note. Vibrato is not a feature of Irish fiddle playing. The fiddle probably dates back to the mid-16th century. It is likely that a lot of our dance tunes, particularly the reels, were composed by fiddle players.

Ornamentation on a Fiddle

The main fiddle decorations are the **roll**, the **cut**, **trebling**, **triplets**, **droning** and **sliding**.

Roll

This uses the melody note and the notes directly above and below it. There are five notes in all.

Another example of a roll

A quick flick of the 3rd finger on the fingerboard and a brief lifting of the first finger produces this roll:

It is not possible to do a roll like these on an open string as it would require crossing onto the lower string at speed. Other forms of the roll are played by fiddlers, depending on the notes involved.

Cut

Cuts or grace notes are useful for separating repeated notes. The third finger is the most usual cutting finger.

©Higgins & Higgins

Trebling

Changing the bow direction can turn a crotchet into three even notes and this is called trebling. A more difficult version, restricted to slow airs and hornpipes is called a double treble.

The treble

The signs above the notes indicate the direction of the bow.

A double treble

This is less commonly used.

Triplets

These are often used for filling in the interval of a third between two notes or to decorate a main note by an upper or lower auxiliary note.

Droning

The bow is drawn across two strings while only one of them is being fingered. The most common drone is the fourth below the melody note, especially at the end of a phrase.

Sliding

The pitch of a note is changed by no more than a semitone by sliding the finger upwards along the string. Sliding often occurs from the open string E to the note F natural using the first finger.

Describe how the fiddle is used in Irish traditional music, mentioning performers you have heard.

EXERCISE

Regional Styles of Fiddle Playing

Purists complain that a very plain session style of playing has become prevalent in Irish traditional music due to travel, the media and CDs, all of which encourage players to imitate styles of playing from outside their own region. Some legendary players, such as **Tommy Potts**, have a personal style and play unusual versions of tunes with their own unique interpretation.

Sligo Style

The Sligo style has a brisk pace, with a 'lift' to the playing and smooth bowing. In the ornamentation, rolls are used more than trebles. The style is showy. The fiddle music from Sligo is well known because of the playing of **Michael Coleman**, Paddy Killoran and James Morrison who all emigrated to the USA between 1915 and 1925 and made recordings in New York up to the 1940s. Many fiddlers back in Ireland tried to imitate the style they heard on these 78 rpm records. Current players of the Sligo style include **Kevin Burke**.

©Higgins & Higgins

Donegal Style

The main feature of Donegal fiddling is the use of single-note bowing, with short bow-strokes. The style has a staccato-like effect, helped by fast tempos. The bow-hand carries out most of the ornamentation so there are more trebles and bowed triplets than rolls in Donegal-style fiddling. The Scottish influence is evident in the repertoire, which includes highlands and strathspeys and in the drone effect used by some players. Many Donegal tunes are in the key of A. **The Glackin brothers** (from Dublin) and the fiddlers in Altan, **Mairéad Ní Mhaonaigh** and **Ciarán Tourish** are exponents of the Donegal style.

Clare Style

The Clare style has a more relaxed tempo, allowing the fiddler to concentrate on the beauty of the tune. There is great use of rolls. The bowing is more rhythmical but less slurred than in Sligo. The type of tune and the slower speed make the Clare style sound different from the others. **Martin Hayes** and his father **P.J.** (of the Tulla Céilí Band) are the best-known fiddlers in the Clare style.

Sliabh Luachra Style

Often called the Cork-Kerry style, it favours polkas and slides, played at a fast tempo and geared towards dancing. The left hand provides the ornamentation, while the bow-hand produces characteristic rhythmic effects, such as drones (ie. when an open string is struck simultaneously with a fingered string). In fact this is probably the most rhythmical style. The fiddler leans hard on the bow and this can make the tone sound rough. There are also many slow airs in this region. **Matt Cranitch** is an exponent of this style of playing.

Performers and Tunes

Martin Hayes from Co Clare and living in the USA, has recorded the reel, *The Morning Dew*, the jig, *I buried my wife and danced on her grave* and the *Galway Bay Hornpipe*. He collaborates with the guitarist Dennis Cahill. **Nollaig Casey** is from Co Cork and is both a classical violinist and a traditional fiddler. She has played on the soundtrack of over twenty feature films and she has recorded the slow airs *Caoineadh Eoghain Ruadh* and *Cape Clear*. She now performs and records with the guitarist Arty McGlynn. Other well-known fiddlers include **Liz Carroll**, **Frankie Gavin**, **Eileen Ivers**, **Seán Keane**, and **Tommy Peoples**.

TIN WHISTLE

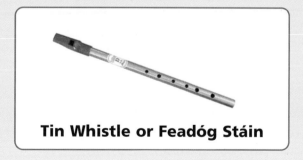

Tin Whistle or Feadóg Stáin

There is evidence that the tin whistle existed in Ireland in the 12th century and possibly earlier. It is a small end-blown flute normally made of tin, brass, wood or plastic. It has six holes on which a major scale can be played. Its range is just over two 8ves. The Clarke whistle is made of rolled metal with a wooden fipple or plug. Air is blown through a narrow channel against a sharp edge. Clarke style whistles tend to have a breathy tone. Most players today use the Generation style cylindrical instrument which has a plastic mouthpiece and a clearer tone. Tin whistles are available in a number of keys, D and C being the most popular. A lot of traditional music is played in keys of one or two sharps, so the D whistle is favoured for group performance. The folk revival of the 1950s led to a big surge of interest in the tin whistle.

Tin Whistle Ornaments

These include **cuts**, **rolls**, **slides** and **crans**. Playing techniques include the use of **tonguing** and vibrato.

A **cut** is a grace note that can (a) separate two notes or (b) accentuate the note that follows it.

A **double cut** or **casadh** is when you insert two very quick notes before the principal note, one of the notes being the principal note and the other involving a quick flick of the finger.

The **long roll** consists of the main note, a cut on that note, a tap on the note directly below it and back to the main note.

The **short roll** is used on crotchets, mainly in reels. It starts with the cut on the main note. It needs to be tongued to achieve the effect.

The **cran** is an uilleann pipes ornament. It is similar to a roll, but with cuts and no taps. It is used on a tin whistle when a roll cannot be played eg. on the lowest note. **(See page 75)**

Tin whistle players usually do not **tongue** all of the notes in a tune, but some notes can be made to sound more defined than others by using this technique. The player makes a 'tuh' sound when blowing on that note by putting the tongue behind the upper teeth. This produces a percussive attack.

Vibrato can be achieved by opening and closing an open hole or by varying the breath pressure.

Performers

Mary Bergin is known for the virtuosity and the fast fluid pace of her playing. She uses her tongue to punch out the rhythm and the fingers for ornamentation. Among the tunes she has recorded is the reel, *The Drunken Landlady* and the expressive slow air, *Mo Mhúirnín Bán*. The *Stack of Wheat* is an example of a hornpipe and is found in **Geraldine Cotter's** tin whistle tutor. Beginners quickly learn to play tunes such as the march *Roddy McCorley* (also called *Seán South from Garrowen*), *Fáinne Geal an Lae* (also called *Raglan Road*), *Kerry Polka* and the patriotic *Oró Sé Do Bheatha Abhaile*. Many pipers play the whistle.

EXERCISE

Show that you have heard at least one well-known performer on the tin whistle by describing TWO or THREE tunes from a CD, or from a live performance.

©Higgins & Higgins

LOW WHISTLE

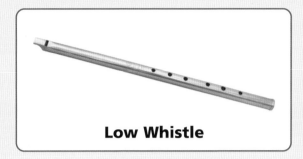

Low Whistle

The low whistle appeared in the early 1970s and was made from aluminium tube. It is usually tuned to D, an 8ve below the usual D tin whistle and is twice as long (about the same size as a flute). The most popular models are not tuneable. It is especially effective for slow airs. The piper, **Davy Spillane**, played the low whistle in *Riverdance*.

FLUTE

Irish Flute or Feadóg Mhór

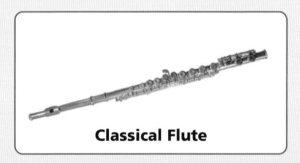

Classical Flute

It is unlikely that the flute appeared in Ireland before the 18th century, but it is not possible to be exact about this. The traditional Irish flute is a crosswind flute, made from boxwood or ebony, and is about 55cm long. It has an embouchure (mouth-hole) and six holes and can be played in the keys D and G without difficult cross fingerings. This suits a large variety of traditional Irish melodies. The key of A major is also manageable as there is only one half note (G♯) to contend with, the F♯ and C♯ already taken into account on a D flute. By adding four metal keys, mounted to wooden blocks, this flute becomes a fully chromatic instrument. On a fully-keyed instrument, it can be difficult to slide into the note or roll a note, so many players stick to the basic model. It has a range of more than two 8ves, one less than the classical flute, but it has a mellower tone. The open finger hole design allows the flute player to use musical decorations such as cutting, rolling and cranning (which is a piping ornament). Indeed, many of its stylistic features are influenced by the piping tradition. Since tonguing does not apply in Irish piping, many Irish flute players do not use it, preferring to articulate the notes by using grace notes. Tonguing occurs when the player utters the syllables 'tack-a-ta' to achieve an effect. Performers also use a strong attack in the lower register. Unlike Classical flautists, they do not use breath vibrato. However, finger vibrato occurs as an ornament. The staccato of the Classical flautist has not been adopted by traditional players who prefer legato-playing and who aim for a full, rich, mellow sound with a clear melodic line. Tempo and dynamics remain even.

©Higgins & Higgins

Flute Ornaments

A **glottal stop** is produced when the syllable 'ah' is used to articulate instead of 'ta'.

The **cut** is a short, very quick note above the note it ornaments. Cuts are generally used to separate notes of the same pitch. A **tap** or a **flick** is a cut from below the melody note. **Rolls** are a way of breaking up long notes and of keeping the rhythmic beat of the music going. The **long roll** breaks up a dotted crotchet into quavers by inserting first a **cut**, then a **tap**. A **short roll** is applied to a crotchet to divide it into two quavers.

Long roll   **Short roll**

As it is the lowest note on the pipes, it is not possible to play a **roll** on D, so it has its own ornament, called the **cran**. The idea of the cran is to break up a long D by inserting two or three cuts, each with a different finger. The finger and the order of the cuts depend on the individual player. The important thing is for the rhythm of the ornament to be as precise as possible. Flute players now use the cran too.

Long cran   **Short cran**

Styles

The main distinguishing features of the different styles involve rhythm and the use of decoration. **Sligo** performers tend to play quickly, with long phrases and lots of descending rolls and triplets. **Leitrim** and **North Roscommon** playing is less ornate and more rhythmical, players tending to articulate with the tip of the tongue and to use shorter phrases. The **Belfast style** deserves mention. The music is shrill and energetic and is heavily influenced by fife and drum bands.

Performers

Matt Molloy has played in many groups, including the Bothy Band and has made some solo CDs. He is now a member of the Chieftains. Originally from Roscommon, he has a highly developed personal style which many young players try to emulate. It is thought that he was the first to popularise cranning on the flute. Although he uses piping decoration, he plays evenly, with a very subtle use of rhythm and lots of slides, cuts, triplets and rolls. He sometimes emphasises important parts of a phrase by bending a note. In his recording of *Jenny's Chickens* he introduces a flattened B into a B minor reel to unexpected and dramatic effect. He plays some of his own compositions as well as standard traditional tunes like *The Mason's Apron* (reel).

Listen to music played by Matt Molloy, Fintan Vallely, Seamus Tansey or Catherine McEvoy, and describe their style.

EXERCISE

©Higgins & Higgins

FREE-REED INSTRUMENTS

Melodeon

Button Accordion

Piano Accordion

Concertina

Harmonica

Melodeons, **accordions** and **concertinas**, informally called the **squeezebox** or **box**, are free-reed instruments. This means that the sound is produced as air flows past a vibrating reed in a frame. The air pressure is generated by bellows.

The **melodeon** is diatonic. It is a single-action instrument which means that it produces a different note by pushing and pulling the bellows. It has one row of ten buttons on the treble (right) side, producing twenty notes in one major key. There are four reed-engaging stops over the right side. There are two spoon-shaped levers on the bass (left) side, which give the tonic and dominant chords in that key only. The melodeon is effective for playing dance tunes because of its rhythmic push-pull action. **Johnny Connolly** from Galway has recorded *Harvest Home* hornpipe and *The Irish Washerwoman* jig on the *An tOileán Aerach* album (1991)

The **button accordion** is also a single-action instrument. The basic model has a second row of buttons, tuned a semitone above the first set, giving a fully chromatic instrument. As traditional music is mostly diatonic, the second set of keys is used mainly for ornamentation such as **rolls**. It also has more bass buttons than a melodeon. **Joe Burke** is the master of accordion playing. He originally included *The Dawn Reel* on a 78 rpm record in 1959 and he re-released it along with other standards such as *The Shaskeen* hornpipe and the more unexpected *Carolan's Concerto*. He is known for his effortless playing and for not allowing overly-complicated ornamentation to obscure the melody. **Tony MacMahon** is best known for his rendition of slow airs on the button accordion. Dynamic contrast is important in his playing and he uses bass buttons and chords to achieve dramatic drone effects. An example is *Caoineadh Eoghan Rua*. His marches achieve a truly martial feel eg. *The Battle of Aughrim*. **Sharon Shannon's** playing is innovative and is influenced by Ethnic music from Finland (*Butterflies*), by Reggae

©Higgins & Higgins

(*Bjorn Again Polka*) and even by the Classical minuet (*The Duke of York's Troop*).   She also plays concertina and fiddle.

The **piano accordion** has a piano keyboard for the melody on the right side and bass buttons for the chords on the left. It is a double-action instrument. This means it produces the same note on press and draw. It is a popular instrument in Northern Ireland. Scorned in the past in the rest of the island, it was confined mainly to Céilí bands. It has been promoted in recent years, however, by the playing of **Alan Kelly** from Roscommon and is now accepted in all settings. He has recorded the slow reel, *The Duke of Leinster* and the hornpipe, *The Harp and Shamrock*.   The piano accordion is also heard in the Folk tradition of other countries.

The **concertina** is a small, hexagonal accordion. There are two types, the **English** which is a double-action chromatic instrument and the **Anglo** or **German** which is a single-action diatonic instrument. The Anglo is the most widely used concertina in Ireland and is tuned to C / G. There are three rows of five buttons on the left side of the bellows and three rows on the right. The melody is divided between both hands. The concertina arrived in Ireland at the end of the 19th century. It is most popular in Clare where several regional styles emerged, most of which were associated with set dancing, for example polkas and slides played by fiddlers from Kerry and Limerick crept into the repertoire of south west Clare concertina players. Some players opt for simple melodies, others emphasise dance rhythms. Techniques such as **double-noting** (ie. playing two 8ves together) and **chording** add depth to the music. Piping techniques such as **droning**, **cranning** and **cutting** have been adapted for the instrument. **Triplets** are also used to ornament tunes. **Mrs. Crotty** (1885-1960) was probably the most gifted and well-known concertina player of her time. Such talented performers are widely imitated and in recent years this has resulted in technically superb playing in no particular regional style. Present-day players include **Noel Hill** (*Ask my Father* and *Boys of Bluehill)* and **Niall Vallel**y (*Muireann's Jig*).

The **harmonica** is the smallest and simplest of the free reed instruments, but the tone and pitch of each note can be dramatically altered by the player. It is more expressive than the bellows-blown instruments, which are limited to playing notes of a set pitch. While not used in Irish sessions since the 1950s, the harmonica has its own category in Fleadh Cheoil na hÉireann. The **diatonic** harmonica (also called a **mouth organ** or a **blues harp**) has ten holes which can produce 19 notes (not 20, due to a repeated note) in a three-8ve range. Each hole has two reeds – one plays when breath is exhaled and the other when inhaled. It is played in a single key. Pitch bending (or note bending) makes it suitable for blues music. Irish tunes such as the set dance, *The Blackbird* and *Chief O'Neill's Hornpipe* contain both a 7th and a flattened 7th and sound effective on the harmonica. Bent or blue notes are called long notes in Ireland. The **chromatic** harmonica is like two diatonic harmonicas in one instrument, allowing the musician to play in any key desired. It has a sliding bar. Chromatics are probably the best suited to play modern jigs and reels that have chromatic passages or ornamentation. The tremolo harmonica has two reeds per note. One reed is tuned a bit sharp and the other a bit flat. This gives a wavering sound. **Octave** harmonicas have two reeds per hole which are tuned to the same note a perfect 8ve apart. They can play the melody and a chordal accompaniment.   Harmonica players ornament their tunes with triplets, grace notes and note bends. Rolls are used in slow airs. Performers include Brendan Power and Phil Murphy.

EXERCISE

Listen to music performed by Brendan Power (eg. his bluesy arrangement of *The Rights of Man*) or Phil Murphy (eg. his vamping technique in reels and jigs). Comment on their style.

©Higgins & Higgins

UILLEANN PIPES

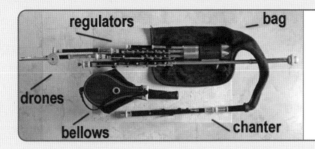

Uilleann Pipes
(image courtesy of Na Píobairí Uilleann)

Labels: regulators, bag, drones, bellows, chanter

A set of uilleann pipes is made up of bellows, bag and seven pipes – the chanter, three drones and three regulators. Pipers pump the bellows with one elbow to keep the bag filled with air while they play the tune on the chanter with both hands. They lean the heel of their hand on the keys of the regulators giving a sort of vamping, chordal accompaniment while also keeping a drone going. Uilleann pipes have a range of two full 8ves including semitones. The bottom note is D. The tenor, baritone and bass regulators may be played singly or together to create chords. The tenor, baritone and bass drones may be switched on and off. The chanter and regulators have double reeds and the drones have single reeds. The two styles of piping are legato (open-fingering) and staccato (close-fingering). Unlike Scottish war-pipes, uilleann pipes are played sitting, not standing; they are played indoors, not outdoors; they are a social not a military instrument; the chanter has a range of two 8ves, not just nine notes; unlike war-pipes, they have regulators and of course, they use a bellows instead of a blowpipe.

The uilleann pipes arrived in the 17th century, became popular at the end of the 18th century (when harping was in decline) and lost popularity a century later (due to the easier availability of the melodeon). Public interest fluctuated during the following decades until the traditional Irish music revival in the 1950s, followed by the founding of pipers' clubs in the 1960s and the success of groups such as Ceoltóirí Chualann and the Chieftains. The description **union** is used in relation to Irish pipes but has no musical significance.

Uilleann Pipes Ornaments

Crans, **pops**, **rolls** and **triplets** are used to decorate piping tunes.

Cran

A cran occurs on the bottom D and E notes. It is useful for separating repeated notes in fast tunes. The chanter must be lifted from the knee and the D and E are graced from a higher A, G and F#.

D Cran   **E Cran on the beat**

Cut

A cut splits a note into two or separates repeated notes. The grace notes are not random. D, E, F# and G are graced by A, A and B by C# and C# by D.

Cuts on the notes D, A and C#

©Higgins & Higgins

Rolls

A short roll consists of cut-note-pat-note and a long roll consists of note-cut-note-pat-note. This style of playing is called close or tight playing. An open or legato-style roll uses a note above and below the main note.

Short roll   Long roll   Open roll

Pop

Popping is unique to the uilleann pipes. Notes on the upper 8ve are accentuated when the chanter is lifted off the knee just as they begin to sound. This adds volume and changes the pitch slightly.

Pat

In a pat, a note is played and is then closed off briefly resulting in a rhythmic silence. It can also refer to the ornamental note below the melody note.

Performers

Triplets, vibrato and sliding as well as regulator-use and individual approaches to chanter-fingering contribute to a piper's playing style. Famous 20th century pipers included Willie Clancy, Johnny Doran and Seamus Ennis. Present-day pipers include **Liam O'Flynn**, who has recorded over fifty albums including solo work with orchestras (Shaun Davey's *The Brendan Voyage*, 1980), film scores and collaborations with John Cage, Mark Knopfler, Nigel Kennedy and the poet Séamus Heaney. **Paddy Moloney** is a founder member of the Chieftains, who have collaborated with film makers, Rock and Chinese musicians alike. **Davy Spillane** was a member of Moving Hearts and is a featured soloist on some of Bill Whelan's works.

Describe the uilleann pipes. Refer to any well-known performer.

EXERCISE

OTHER INSTRUMENTS

Irish Bouzouki

Bodhrán

Banjo

Mandolin

©Higgins & Higgins

BODHRÁN

The bodhrán came to prominence in the 1960s thanks to Seán O'Riada and his Ceoltóirí Chualann. It is a shallow, untuned drum usually covered with goatskin. It is held sideways in one hand and played with a beater or tipper or by using the back of the fingers of the free hand. There are no apparent regional styles, but differences can be heard between individual players. The direction of the stroke (down or up) is one of the factors that make the accompaniment interesting.

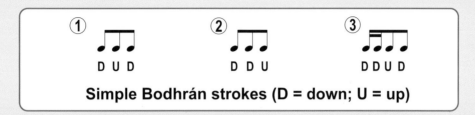

Simple Bodhrán strokes (D = down; U = up)

Players vary their method of beating the drum, sometimes using the two-sided stick style or the hand style. They also change the tone colour by beating the wooden part or rim of the drum from time to time. The palm of the non-playing hand can be pressed against the inside face of the skin. This dampens the volume and causes a less lingering 'boom'. Pitch can be changed slightly by moving the position of the pressing palm and the position of the beating stick or hand on the outer face of the skin. Well-known bodhrán players include **Mel Mercier**, **Tommy Hayes** (the jig, *The Three Sea Captains*) and **Kevin Conneff**, who also sings with the Chieftains.

BONES AND SPOONS

Animal **bones** can be used as a percussion instrument in traditional Irish music. Taken from the ribs of a cow or a sheep, they consist of two curved pieces of bone, around 12cm long. They hang down vertically from the hand, between the thumb, index and middle fingers. The wrist is shaken as the arm moves away from the player and back again. Both hands may be used. This produces a clicking accompaniment of single strokes, triplets and syncopated figures all of which blend well with the bodhrán in the music of the Chieftains and Micheál O'Súilleabháin, among others. Two kitchen **spoons**, usually dessert spoons held back to back, can provide suitable accompaniment for an Irish tune. One hand holds them and beats them against the player's lap, while the other drags across them, rattling them, ensuring maximum variety in tone colour.

DRUM KIT

The Céilí band drum kit consists of woodblock, snare drum and bass drum. The drummer is expected to be disciplined and cannot permit the snare or bass drum to drown out the other instruments. Drummers have their own competition at Fleadh Cheoil na hÉireann and also play in marching and pipe bands where they can express themselves more.

BOUZOUKI, BANJO and MANDOLIN

Banjo: The first commercial recording of an Irish banjo player was in 1916. The present-day tenor banjo has four strings, tuned GDAE, an 8ve below the fiddle. It is a melody instrument. The tone is brittle as the strings vibrate for less time than a guitar. Single-note trebling is a suitable embellishment in banjo music. In the 1960s, **Barney McKenna** of The Dubliners was the best-known banjo player in Ireland. **Gerry O'Connor** recorded *Funk the Cajun Blues* (1992).

Bouzouki: A Greek instrument introduced in the mid 1960s by Johnny Moynihan and made popular by **Dónal Lunny**.   The Irish version has a flat back and four double strings.

Mandolin: Although dating back to the 16th century in Europe, the American version did not appear until the late 19th century. This flat-backed model is tuned to GDAE, like the fiddle, and is effective in groups. **Andy Irvine** plays mandolin.

EXERCISE

Write a short essay on the use of percussion instruments in Irish traditional music, referring to well-known performers.

PIANO

Although a non-traditional instrument, the piano has its own competition at Fleadhanna for melody with accompaniment. **Micheál O'Súilleabháin** plays it on his many recordings, usually in a fusion with Classical or Jazz music. **Mary Corcoran**, a former member of Templehouse Céilí band is an exponent of the vamping piano which is used in Irish Céilí music as an accompanying instrument, useful for maintaining a steady beat and providing a bass line to the predominantly treble line-up. Basically, a single note is played in the left hand on the beat and an off-beat chord is played by the right hand. The choice of chord progressions depends on the player's knowledge of the tunes and a descending (sometimes chromatic) bass line is a feature of many pianists' style.

EXERCISE

Write out any Irish dance on the staves below and sketch in the chords that could be used by a piano or guitar player.

Tune with Vamping Piano: *Cooley's Reel*

Piano part by John Cooney

©Higgins & Higgins

Irish Music

80

SECTION 2: HARP

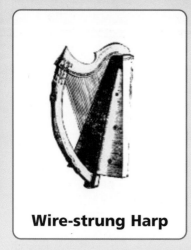
Wire-strung Harp

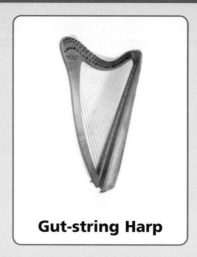
Gut-string Harp

Orchestral Harp

Old Irish/Bardic Harp

This was a wire-string instrument, with brass strings. It had a bell-like sound. Harps varied in height over the centuries and the number of strings ranged from 30 to 45. It was a heavy instrument with a willow soundbox. It was held on the knee, leaning against the left shoulder. The shorter treble strings were played with the left hand; the long bass strings with the right. This may be a link with the tradition of men sitting on the right side of the church and the fireplace and women on the left. It was played with long fingernails. The strings vibrated for longer so the player had to be able to dampen them frequently to keep the notes clear. Harpers used a lot of ornamentation but not a lot of harmony. There was a good range of dynamics. The wire-harp was tuned to the Mixolydian, and later the Ionian mode in G. It was almost impossible to play accidentals adequately. Pentatonic tunes allowed the harper to use several different modes and avoid certain strings. **The Brian Boru Harp**, portrayed on Irish coins, dates back to the late 14th century. It has 29 strings and is 70 cm high. **Cruit** and **Cláirseach** are the Irish words for harp.

Modern Irish/Neo-Irish Harp

John Egan built a neo-Irish type in the 1820s. The present-day Irish harp is a gut-string instrument, with 34 nylon strings. It has a mellow tone. Harps are now taller, thinner and lighter and have a round, not a square, sound box. They are played with the fleshy part of the fingertips. The pitch of each string can be raised a semitone by means of brass levers along the neck. The modern Irish harp is smaller than the orchestral harp.

THE HARP IN SOCIETY: Main developments

Role of the Harper in Ancient Times

Up to the 14th century harpers were associated more with the aristocracy than with the 'ordinary people'. They played music, accompanied a bard's poetry and songs, chanted their benefactor's praises and performed at family ceremonies in return for privileges such as rent-free land. Traditional dances were not usually part of their repertoire. From the 14th century, there were strict laws discouraging the landed English gentry from adopting Irish culture.

©Higgins & Higgins

Blind Harpers

It was commonplace for people who became blind to take harping lessons in order to earn their living as entertainers. The well-known tune *Tabhair dom do lámh* was composed by **Rory Dall O'Catháin** (1570-1650) an itinerant harper who emigrated to Scotland. **Turlough O'Carolan** (1670-1738), also a blind travelling harper, included Baroque features in many of his compositions, most notably *Carolan's Concerto*. His music was well received in the 'big houses'. His planxties (eg. *Madam Maxwell* and *Planxty Irwin*) were composed in honour of a person or a family.

Attempts at Reviving the Tradition

Several harping festivals took place in Granard, Co. Longford, towards the end of the 18th century. In a last-ditch attempt to revive the old style of harp playing, some patriotic citizens organised the Belfast Harp Festival in 1792. Its aim was to note the music, poetry and oral traditions of Ireland. **Denis Hempson** (1695-1807) was the only harper who played in the old style, using long fingernails, at the festival. Bunting managed to save some tunes (eg. *An Chúilfhionn*). He also wrote down the performing techniques he observed. As the instrument was incapable of embracing modern musical requirements and became impractical the old style of playing was not revived. The piano became fashionable in the 19th century just as the harp was falling out of favour.

EXERCISE

In the latter half of the 20th century, Seán O'Riada attempted to replicate the sound of the old wire-strung harp when he played harpsichord with Ceoltóiri Chualann. The Chieftains included the harper, **Derek Bell** in their line-up. Several other fine soloists and innovators emerged including **Paul Dooley**, **Máire Ní Chathasaigh**, **Laoise Kelly** and **Gráinne Yeats**. Some of these players are now developing new techniques for playing the old Irish harp. **Write an essay on present-day harping. Expand on some of these ideas.**

TURLOUGH O'CAROLAN (1670-1738) (the 'O' is often dropped)

Background

When he was a child, Carolan's family moved from Meath to Roscommon where his father's employers, the McDermott-Roes, took care of his education. He was blinded by smallpox at 18, then took harp lessons and at 21, he became a travelling harper. He earned his living by teaching, composing and performing harp music. Mrs McDermott-Roe remained his most important patron throughout his life. Even though he lived during the Penal Times, a grim period in Irish history, he was accepted by all sides of the political and social divide, composing for both Protestants (eg. the Irwins) and Catholics (eg. the Plunketts).

Tunes

Around 200 of his compositions have been saved and published, including his first composition, *Sí Bheag, Sí Mhór*. The **planxty**, a type of harp tune composed in honour of a person, is associated with him and is recognisable by the patron's name in the title, for example *Madam Maxwell*, *Elizabeth McDermott-Roe*, *Fanny Power*, *Eleanor Plunkett*, *Planxty Irwin* and *Planxty O'Rourke*. It has no specific form or metre, although many of Carolan's planxties are in 6/8 time.

Style

Carolan's music shows three main influences:

(a) The old tradition of harp playing, inherited from the Irish bards and itinerant musicians, for example *Carolan's Farewell to Music*.

(b) The traditional songs and dances of the Irish people, for example *Carolan's Favourite Jig*.

©Higgins & Higgins

(c) The art music of contemporary Italian composers such as Corelli, Vivaldi and Geminiani. Baroque features are obvious in *Captain O'Kane* and *Carolan's Concerto* which have elegant melodies, sequences, ornaments, running scale passages and strong cadence points

Legacy

Although not part of the dance and slow air repertoire usually heard at pub sessions, Carolan's music has been arranged for both Irish and Classical instruments and manages to retain its unique appeal. Some of his pieces were played at the Belfast Harp Festival in 1792, over 50 years after his death. Robert Burns, the Scottish poet, set a song called *Louis, What Reck I By Thee* to a Carolan tune (*Gracie Nugent*). The Irish composer, Thomas Moore, used several of Carolan's melodies for his own songs, for example *Fly not yet (Planxty Kelly)* and *The Wandering Bard (Planxty O'Reilly)*. Seán O'Riada and Ceoltóirí Chualann helped to revive an interest in Carolan during the 1960s and his music has been recorded by modern-day harpers such as Laoise Kelly, Máire Ní Chathasaigh and Gráinne Yeats, as well as by groups such as The Chieftains, The Irish Film Orchestra and The Douglas Gunn Ensemble. Gerald Barry has even used *Sí Bheag, Sí Mhór* as the basis for the first part of his *Piano Quartet no 1*, composed in 1992.

Carolan: *Captain O'Kane*

Carolan's Favourite Jig

Carolan's Farewell to Music

Carolan: *Sí Bheag, Sí Mhór*

These tunes may be heard in full at
http://www.leavingcertmusic.com

©Higgins & Higgins

BELFAST HARP FESTIVAL and the COLLECTOR, EDWARD BUNTING

Aim of the Festival

The Belfast Harp Festival took place in July 1792. It was organised by patriotic citizens such as Dr James McDonnell and members of the United Irishmen including Henry Joy McCracken. They hoped it would revive the ancient music and poetry of Ireland and preserve the remnants of the Gaelic harp tradition for posterity.

Participants

Ten Irish harpers played at the four-day event – Charles Byrne, William Carr (the youngest at 15), James Duncan, Charles Fanning and six blind harpers, Dan Black, Denis Hempson (the oldest at 96), Hugh Higgins, Rose Mooney, Arthur O'Neill and Patrick Quinn.

Bunting's Role at the Festival

Edward Bunting (1773-1843), an organist from the age of 11, was employed to notate the airs. While the harpers played, he sketched the outline of the music and went back over them later, filling in the gaps. Some of the tunes are notated in keys that would not have been possible to use on the harp. He sometimes added notes and features that would be more suited to classical instruments. His transcriptions are speckled with accidentals for which there were no strings, for example the tune called *The Princess Royal*, which he collected from Arthur O'Neill and which he published in the key of F minor. It is not fair to be too critical, however, because he saved tunes from extinction and gave us important information about the harpers and their style of playing. The 40 tunes he collected at the Festival included *Sí Bheag Sí Mhór*, *The Fairy Queen*, *Eibhlín a Rún* and *Lord Mayo*.

March: *Lord Mayo* or *Tiarna Mhaigh Eo*

Bunting's Publications

Spurred on by his experience at the Festival, Bunting toured Connaught and Ulster to gather more tunes. He was the first Irish collector that we know about who visited musicians in their own area. The blind harper, Arthur O'Neill (1734-1816), even dictated his memoirs to him.

Bunting published almost 300 tunes in three volumes.

- **1796:** *A General Collection of the Ancient Irish Music* contains 66 tunes adapted for the piano. It includes *Carolan's Concerto*.
- **1809:** *A General Collection of the Ancient Music of Ireland* contains 77 tunes in romantic piano arrangements, some with specially written songs in English. He also describes how the harp had developed. This volume includes *Planxty Irwin*.
- **1840:** *The Ancient Music of Ireland* is the most important historical source for the

techniques used by the old Gaelic harpers. In the introduction, Bunting lists the fingering and damping techniques used by each hand. The book contains just over 150 tunes arranged for the piano, including *Tabhair dom do lámh*.

In 1819, Bunting moved to Dublin where he continued working as an organist. He died there in 1843. His manuscripts are now housed in Queen's University, Belfast.

Bunting's Importance

Despite the inaccuracy of his transcriptions, Bunting is important because he was the first collector to collate the tunes in a systematic and informative way. The material which he collected is unique and has been used as the basis for other composers' works (for example, in some of the songs of Thomas Moore).

MAP OF IRELAND

EXERCISE

On the map below, mark the areas that are relevant to the study of traditional Irish music. Include the following:

Belfast (Harp festival); Cúil Aodha (O'Riada); Gaeltacht areas; Sliabh Luachra (on the Cork/Kerry/Limerick border); Clare (concertina-playing) and Sligo (home of the master fiddlers).

COLLECTORS

Composers of Classical music use notated scores to transmit their work. Folk music, being an oral tradition, is transmitted through performance. Thousands of Irish traditional tunes that have survived to the present day may have been lost forever were it not for the forward-thinking music collectors who began, in the 18th century, to note down what they heard.

1724: John and William Neale (father and son) printed the first collection of Irish Music, *A Collection of the Most Celebrated Irish Tunes*. This consisted of around 50 tunes including Carolan's *Gracey Nugent* and *Luke Dillon*. Also found in this collection are *Táimse im Chodladh*, *Ceann Dubh Dílis* and *Thugamar féin an Samhradh Linn*.

1796, 1809 and **1840: Edward Bunting** published three volumes of tunes taken down directly from performers at the Belfast Harp Festival and on his subsequent trips in Ulster and Connaught. **(See page 83)**

1855: George Petrie knew Bunting and helped to set up the *Society for the Preservation and Publication of the Melodies of Ireland*. Like the collector, **Eugene O'Curry**, he worked for the Ordnance Survey Commission. Petrie's *Ancient Music of Ireland* contains nearly 200 melodies as well as song texts in Irish and English and detailed notes about the sources of the songs and pieces. The piano accompaniments written by his daughter for the melodies were stylistically inappropriate, so the republished collection (2002) has returned the tunes to their original melodic format.

1873, 1888 and **1909: Patrick Weston Joyce** was encouraged by Petrie to note down the music that he himself remembered from his early days in Limerick and these are authentic renditions of the tunes. The songs he published were the first to actually match words and music. 842 songs and airs appeared in the *Old Irish Folk Music and Songs* (1909), some of which were taken from manuscripts and collections by **William Forde**, **John Edward Pigot** and **John Goodman**.

1903 and **1907: Francis O'Neill** is considered by traditional musicians to be the most important collector of dance music. *O'Neill's Music of Ireland* has 1850 tunes, including jigs, reels, hornpipes, marches, airs and O'Carolan tunes. *The Dance Music of Ireland* has 1001 dance tunes and is referred to as 'The Book'. These were the first collections compiled by and aimed at Irish music performers. O'Neill had a colourful life, running away from Co. Cork at the age of 16, working as a cabin boy, surviving a shipwreck, becoming a shepherd and a schoolteacher, eventually joining the police force in Chicago, where he was shot by a gangster before becoming Chief of Police in 1901. He and a colleague, James O'Neill, collected the tunes from Irish immigrants in Chicago. Some tunes were duplicated but they still managed to publish 2,500 different tunes altogether and these are an invaluable source for performers.

Modern transport and recording technology have enabled **20th century** collectors to travel further, to make more accurate recordings and to bring the music more directly to a wider public by means of radio and television broadcasts. **Séamus Ennis** was a piper employed by the Folklore Commission to collect music all around Ireland. He began this work in the 1940s. He made programmes for the BBC and RTE. **Breandán Breathnach** was a civil servant who collected around 7000 tunes. His *Ceol Rince na hÉireann* series was published in five volumes between 1963 and 1999. **Ciarán MacMathúna** made recordings in authentic locations around Ireland. *Mo Cheol Thú*, his best-known radio programme, aired on RTE from 1970 to 2005. Although not himself a collector, **Aloys Fleischmann** professor of Music at U.C.C., spent 40 years cataloguing every traditional tune found in previous collections in his *Sources of Irish Music* project, published posthumously in 1999.

©Higgins & Higgins

SECTION 3: IRISH DANCE MUSIC

Reel (*Cooley's Reel*)

The reel was brought to Ireland from Scotland at the end of the 18th century and is now the most common type of tune here. It is a lively dance in 4/4 time  consisting mainly of quavers, with an accent on the first and third beats of the bar. Most reels are in **AABB** (binary) form, although some have more sections. The **A** section is called the **tune** and consists of eight bars which are repeated. The **B** section, also lasting eight bars, is in a higher register and is called the **turn**. It, too, is repeated. This 32-bar round is played twice or three times before another reel is played. The dancer wears soft shoes.

Hornpipe (*Rights of Man*)

The hornpipe also dates back to the end of the 18th century and probably came from  England. The dancing masters adopted it as a show piece. It is a slow dance in 4/4 time, beginning on an upbeat (or anacrusis) and characterised by a dotted rhythm with some triplets. The dotted notes usually get less value than implied in a written score. Hornpipes usually end on three crotchets. The first and third beats of each bar are accented. The dancer wears hard shoes and performs intricate steps. It follows the same structure as outlined above for the reel (a 32-bar round in **AABB** form).

Double Jig (*I buried my wife and danced on her grave*) and Single Jig (*Off She Goes*)

The jig has been in Ireland since the 17th century   and may have come from Italy through the harpers. Like reels and hornpipes, jigs often have 32 bars in **AABB** form. They are danced with soft shoes. Double jigs are lively and in 6/8 time. They consist mainly of quavers, grouped in threes. Single jigs are in either 6/8 or 12/8 time and differ from double jigs by their crotchet-quaver rhythm.

Slip Jig (*Drops of Brandy*)

The slip jig is in 9/8 time and the 8-bar sections are not repeated. It is danced in soft shoes, usually by women.  There are three main beats per bar, each grouped into three quavers. There may be some crotchet-quaver movement.

Slides (*Denis Murphy's Slide*)

Slides are fast single jigs ending with two dotted crotchets (whereas single jigs end with three quavers followed by a dotted crotchet).

Polkas (*Kerry Polka*)

Polkas arrived in Ireland at the end of the 19th century from Bohemia, via England. They are associated with the Sliabh Luachra region. They are in 2/4 time and consist mainly of quavers with some semiquavers. They are bouncy and are played for group set-dances.

Mazurkas (*Shoe the Donkey*)

Mazurkas originated in Poland. They are in 3/4 time. A typical bar has a crotchet followed by four quavers.

©Higgins & Higgins

Reel: *Cooley's Reel*

Hornpipe: *Rights of Man*

Double Jig: *I Buried My Wife and Danced on her Grave*

Single Jig: *Off She Goes*

©Higgins & Higgins

Slip Jig: *Drops of Brandy*

Slide: *Denis Murphy's Slide*

Polka: *Kerry Polka*

Mazurka: *Shoe the Donkey*

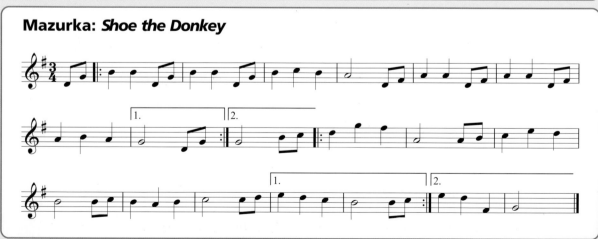

©Higgins & Higgins

SECTION 4: THE SINGING TRADITION

General characteristics of Sean-Nós singing

The term sean-nós is used to describe unaccompanied solo singing, usually in the Irish language. Words and music are of equal importance. Songs are sung with free rhythm, and the singer speeds up and slows down to suit the words, some of which may sound distorted when the syllables are elongated or clipped. Dynamics are not used. To convey emotion, the singer ornaments the tune. No two performances of a song by the same singer will be identical.

Regional styles

The three regions associated with sean-nós singing are Donegal, Connemara and Munster. These are Gaeltacht areas and each has its own distinctive spoken dialect. In the Donegal style of sean-nós singing rhythm tends to be regular and melodic ornamentation is sparse and restrained. In Connemara, the songs themselves tend to have a narrow range and the ornamentation used by singers is very florid. The Munster style is the closest to 'Classical' singing with many singers using vibrato. The range of the songs is wide, so there is more intervallic variation.

Ornamentation in Sean-Nós singing

Melodic ornamentation can be (a) 'melismatic' where a note is replaced or decorated by a group of adjacent notes or (b) 'intervallic' in which additional notes are used to fill an interval between two notes of the tune. The interval between two notes might even change when a phrase is repeated. **Rhythmic** variation involves the lengthening or shortening of notes.

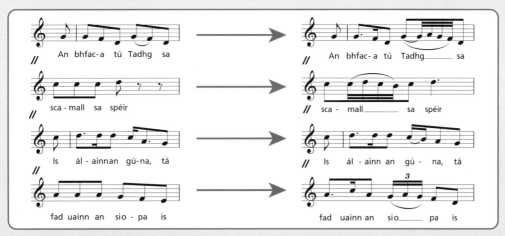

Characteristics of the Singing

The singer may have a nasal tone quality. Some singers use their chest voice only; others prefer their head voice. Some females pitch their voices high and sound strained to the uninitiated listener. The singer may take short breaks between phrases but some try to ensure continuity by linking the end of a phrase to the start of the next. Glottal stops are heard when the singer interrupts the flow of air through the windpipe. The singer may slide onto a melody note from an interval of less than a semitone. Often the consonants *l*, *m*, *n*, and *r* are accentuated and this may create a drone effect. Extra meaningless syllables are sometimes introduced, eg. '*Thug (a) mé*'. Some singers end a phrase with the consonant *m*, *n* or *ng*. Some singers slow down at the end of a song while others speak the final line.

Performers

Present-day singers include **Seosaimhín Ní Bheaglaioch** (Kerry), **Iarla O'Lionaird** (West Cork), **Josie Sheáin Jeaic Mac Donncha** (Connemara) and **Sailí Gallagher** (Donegal).

Describe a performance of sean-nós singing that you have heard.   EXERCISE

©Higgins & Higgins

IRISH SONG TYPES		
TYPES	**COMMON FEATURES**	**EXAMPLES**
LOVE SONGS	Expressive. Often sad.	• *Una Bhán* • *Bríd Og Ní Mháille*
LAMENTS	About loss, death, emigration, eviction. They describe a tragic event or pine for better times.	• *Anach Chuain* • *Seán O'Duibhir an Ghleanna* • *An Mhaighdean Mhara*
PATRIOTIC SONGS	Aislingí – dreams in which Ireland is represented by a beautiful woman. Rebel songs and Famine songs describing the abuse of the system of land tenure by absentee landlords.	• *Táimse im' Chodladh* • *Róisín Dubh* • *Slieve Gallen Braes*
WORKING SONGS	For repetitive tasks in a forge, kitchen or a field where a steady rhythm is needed.	• *Ding Dong Déderó* • *Amhrán na Cuiginne*
RELIGIOUS SONGS	Most are sorrowful, focusing on the Crucifixion. Mary, in grief, is depicted not as a stoical, silent woman but as an angry, keening mother. Christmas Carols.	• *Caoineadh na dTrí Muire* • *Wexford Carol* • *Don Oíche Ud i mBeithil*
LULLABIES and DANDLING SONGS	Steady rocking rhythm in lullabies. The onomatopoeic expression 'seoithín seo' frequently occurs. In dandling songs, a child is bounced on the mother's lap.	• *Dún do Shúile* • *Déirín Dé* • *Is Trua gan Peata an Mhaoir Agam*
HUMOROUS SONGS	Light-hearted and lively. The listeners may join in when there is a refrain.	• *An Poc ar Buile* • *Lanigan's Ball*
DRINKING SONGS	Celebratory and lively	• *Preab san Ól* • *Níl sé 'na Lá*
MACARONIC SONGS	Bilingual songs, some of which carry embedded patriotic messages in the Irish text.	• *One Day for Recreation (Is gan éinne beo im chuideachta)* • *Siúil a Rún*
BALLADS	Narrative poems set to music, with several verses. Themes include rebellion and love. Some begin with the words 'Come all ye'.	• *Spancil Hill* • *The Fields of Athenry* • *Kevin Barry* • *The Wind that Shakes the Barley*

©Higgins & Higgins

SECTION 5: OTHER ESSAY TOPICS

GENERAL CHARACTERISTICS OF IRISH MUSIC

Aural tradition

Performers learn traditional Irish music by ear. A tune may have different titles (eg. the jig, *Over the water to Charlie* is known as *Lads Of Tipperary* as well as *Mrs Casey* and *The Silken Wallet*). There could be several versions of a tune due to errors in the learning, to a personal interpretation of what was heard and to different language dialects. Articulation, phrasing and tempo vary from performer to performer and even from verse to verse.

Tunes

The range of Irish tunes and songs is often wider than an 8ve. The last note in a section is sometimes repeated, as is the final tonic. Apart from the '*doh*' mode tunes may be in the '*lah*' mode, the '*ray*' mode (eg. *Cooley's Reel*), or the '*soh*' mode The seventh note of the scale is flattened in some tunes (eg. *She Moved Through the Fair*) and in others the fourth and/or the seventh notes of the scale are omitted (eg. *Kerry Polka*). The structures are usually simple. Many tunes are in **AABA** (eg. *The Last Rose of Summer*), **ABBA** (eg. *Roddy McCorley*) and **AABB** form (eg. many reels, jigs and hornpipes).

Variation

Irish music is melodic rather than harmonic. Subtle and complex ornamentation as well as melodic variation are favoured over chords and harmony. However, traditional instruments such as harp and accordion can provide a chordal accompaniment and pipes have drones and regulators. As variation is important, solo performance allowing personal expression, is deemed to be closer to a pure traditional style than group performance. Soloists have greater options for embellishing a tune. Such melodic and rhythmic variation includes triplets, grace notes and sliding, depending on the instrument, the regional style, the possibilities within a tune and of course, the ability and preference of the musician.

Styles

Different regional styles exist and the most prevalent are from Donegal, Sligo, East Galway, East Clare, West Clare and Sliabh Luachra (connecting the borders of Cork, Kerry and Limerick). Sean-nós singers from Connemara produce a very florid line, compared to a less decorated and more 'Classical' style in Munster and a sparsely-ornamented style in Donegal. Fiddling styles are recognized by the different bowing techniques used. In recent times, however, a musician's place of birth does not determine their chosen style of playing, such are the influences of radio, recordings, concerts, sessions, competitions and travel.

Instrumental Music

Most of the instrumental music is dance music: reels, hornpipes, jigs, slip jigs, slides, polkas and mazurkas. Slow airs are played in free rhythm like an instrumental version of a slow song. Planxties were composed for harp in honour of someone and although many are in 6/8 time, they are not dances. Piping features have been adopted for fiddle and flute and virtuoso playing has become more evident. Some players add 8ves, fifths and fourths for embellishment. Non-traditional elements that now occur include syncopation, polyphony and expressive dynamics. Orchestral, popular, electronic and ethnic instruments from other countries are also used.

MODES

The pattern of tones and semitones between consecutive notes in a scale determines its mode. The major scale or *doh* mode has the pattern of intervals Tone-Tone-Semitone-Tone-Tone-Tone-Semitone. G and D major are the most common keys in Irish instrumental music. D minor, E minor and A minor are also popular. Modes were used in old Church music (eg. plainchant) and in the Folk music of many countries. Although traditionally unaccompanied, there are harmonic implications in modal melodies. Pipers must know modes in order to use the regulators effectively. The most common modes used in Irish music are the *doh* mode, the *ray* mode, the *soh* mode and the *lah* mode. Examples of tunes in these modes include *Denis Murphy's Slide* (*doh*), *Drowsy Maggie* (*ray*), *Rakish Paddy* (*soh*) and *Teahan's Favourite* (*lah*).

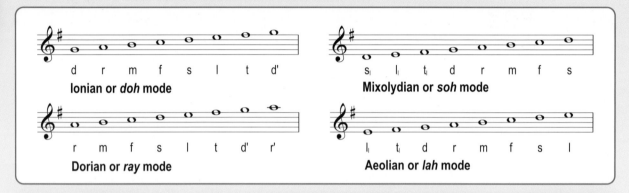

Ionian or *doh* mode — d r m f s l t d'

Mixolydian or *soh* mode — s, l, t, d r m f s

Dorian or *ray* mode — r m f s l t d' r'

Aeolian or *lah* mode — l, t, d r m f s l

EXAMPLE of a MODAL TUNE

EXERCISE

Sing or play the tune, Anach Chuain. Then carry out the following tasks.

1. Work out the key and write the tonic solfa names below the notes.
2. The final note is E. How many Es are there in the piece altogether?
3. What is the mode of the tune? Is it the *doh*, the *ray*, the *soh* or the *lah* mode?
4. Using letters, write down the form of the tune.
5. Find the lowest and highest notes. Then calculate the range of the tune.
6. Circle one instance of melodic variation or ornamentation on the score.
7. How many leaps of a 7th can you find?
8. Apart from the wide range of the tune, the modal tonality and the use of melodic variation, write down one feature of Irish traditional music you hear and see in this piece.

Anach Chuain

INFLUENCE OF IRISH MUSIC ON THE MUSIC OF NORTH AMERICA

The Irish traditional music scene is vibrant all over the USA and Canada today. Hundreds of thousands of Irish immigrants arrived in North America and Canada in the early 18th and 19th centuries and influenced the Folk music in the Appalachian Mountain regions, Newfoundland, Nova Scotia and Cape Breton, as well as on the West coast. Frontier life was tough and their musical traditions were respected, being a link with home. In Newfoundland, people still have Waterford surnames and speak with Waterford accents.

Shared Repertoire

A shared repertoire now exists between Irish, American and Canadian Folk performers. *Rosey Connolly*, collected by Edward Bunting in 1811 in Derry, became *Rose Connolly*, an American folk song. An English version of another song, *Siúil a Rún*, appeared in Wisconsin. *St Anne's Reel* is French-Canadian and *Fred Finn's Polka* is American, yet both resemble Irish tunes in their structure and style. Versions of *Haste To The Wedding*, *Soldier's Joy* and *The Fisher's Hornpipe* have been played by Native Americans for the past two hundred years. *The Contradiction* is a four-part reel that is more than two centuries old. It was called *Miss Gunning's Delight* when it first appeared in England, then as it travelled through Scotland, Ireland and America, it became more elaborate and attained a new title, *The Contradiction*. The tune, collected by O'Neill, worked its way northward to Cape Breton where it has been recorded by their traditional musicians eg. **Ashley MacIsaac** and **Joe Cormier**. Several countries now lay claim to the tune.

Native Americans

The slip jig called *Drops of Brandy* now exists with different time signatures in the **Métis** fiddling tradition in Canada. During the Klondike Gold Rush in the 1890s, Irish fiddlers and pipers shared tunes with their fellow prospectors. Similarities still exist today between Irish and **Athabaskan** dance music, in Alaska and North West Canada. Athabaskans practise tunes by lilting them before attempting them on instruments. (In Ireland there are lilting competitions in the Fleadh Cheoil every year.) Set dancing is popular in both traditions. The Athabaskan fiddler, **Bill Stevens**, also ornaments his dance music with double-stops and slides.

Appalachian Music

Ballads and dance tunes brought over by Irish, Scottish and English immigrants were the basis for much **Appalachian** music. Tunes were modal. Singers adopted techniques such as vocal improvisation, ornamentation and a nasal tone. Fiddlers began to use double-stopping possibly in an attempt to reproduce a piping-style drone. Appalachian music was a precursor to Bluegrass, Rock, Country and Blues, all of which display characteristics of their Folk origins.

Sligo Fiddling Style, Nova Scotia and Cape Breton

In the 1920s and 30s, the recordings of Sligo fiddler, **Michael Coleman**, inspired performers on both sides of the Atlantic and his fiddling style can be heard in **Nova Scotia**. Many tunes were also borrowed from Irish piping and mouth music traditions. Although their main influences are Scottish, there are also double jigs dating back to Irish settlers in **Cape Breton** and their fiddle players still ornament their jigs, reels, marches and slow airs with grace notes, trebling and double-stopping.

EXERCISE

Write a short essay on the influence of Irish music on the music of North America. Show that you have listened to the music you mention.

©Higgins & Higgins

CHANGES FROM WITHIN

Regional Styles

As a result of travel, recordings and the Fleadh Cheoil, performers now imitate players from outside of their own geographical region. Consequently, players often adopt styles other than their own regional style. The brothers **Paddy**, **Kevin** and **Séamus Glackin** are from Dublin but are exponents of the Donegal style of fiddling. Paddy learned the air *Paddy's Rambles Through the Park* from John Doherty, the great Donegal fiddle player. On the CD *Paddy Glackin: In full spate* (1991) the Donegal influence is very evident.

Performing Skills

As Irish musicians began to make a living from performing, standards inevitably rose. Imitating virtuoso performers on studio-enhanced recordings leads to a quest for perfection. This sometimes hinders improvisation and naturally-occurring variations in amateur playing.

Instruments

Instrumental techniques have also developed because of the improved quality of the instruments and the availability of chromatic notes. This has had an impact on the music itself, allowing performers to try ideas that would not have been possible on older, more limited instruments. The bodhrán became an integral part of the tradition in **Ceoltóirí Chualann**, in the 1960s.

Interaction Between Instrumentalists

Musicians now attempt to create the sounds made on other instruments. **Matt Molloy** is credited with adapting the cran, a piping ornament, for the flute. Piano and accordion players are now using the fiddle technique of playing a triplet on a single note. They strike the same key rapidly with three fingers in succession. **Mícheál O'Súilleabháin** ornaments tunes in this fashion on the piano in *Woodbrook* (*Between Worlds*, 1995). Flute players achieve a similar effect through triple tonguing. This stylistic crossover has resulted in interesting new playing techniques.

Performing Context

The setting for Irish music continues to evolve, originally centred on the home, moving to the dance-hall, into the pubs and onto the stage and the studio. Professional and semi-professional Irish musicians give concerts, record albums and participate in sessions. Some tutor in Summer schools. These include the fiddler **Martin Hayes**, the concertina player **Noel Hill**, the tin whistler **Mary Bergin** and the accordionist **Joe Burke**. Their music is for listening to, not just for accompanying dancers and it has continued to adapt to its diverse environments.

Groups

The Bothy Band (1974-79) has had a big impact on present-day musicians. Each member was a virtuoso traditional player – Paddy Keenan (pipes), Kevin Burke (fiddle), Matt Molloy (flute), Dónal Lunny (bouzouki and bodhrán), Tríona Ní Dhomhnaill (keyboards and vocals) and Mícheál O'Domhnaill (guitar and vocals). By blending their individual styles they made an original sound. Lilting airs and songs were interspersed with driving dance tunes played at top speed. They brought Irish traditional music to a younger audience, introduced elements of Jazz, Rock and Classical music, created an international interest in it, performed it all in a sophisticated manner and sparked off new ideas in others.

Discuss the changes that have occurred in Irish music in recent years. Show evidence of personal research.

EXERCISE

©Higgins & Higgins

Fusions

Irish performers borrow elements from other styles (eg. instruments and tunes) and merge them with their own music. The most common fusions occur between Irish traditional and **Classical** (eg. Shaun Davey, *Granuaile*), **Rock** (eg. Horslips, *Dearg Doom*), **Jazz** (eg. Micheál O'Súilleabháin, *Oíche Nollag*), **Pop** (eg. Corrs) and other **Ethnic** traditions (eg. Afro-Celt Sound System).

Literacy

Many Irish performers are musically literate and are able to recall or learn tunes by using tonic solfa or alphabetic, graphic, numerical or staff notation. They now have access to tunes which might otherwise have been lost. Published collections such as O'Neill's *Dance Music of Ireland* (1907) have added a huge number of tunes to those already in circulation. When orally transmitted, tunes may be altered beyond recognition so it is useful to have a written record of them in their original form. Although the ear is still the primary form of transmission, notation skills allow more people to be taught by a single teacher.

Internet

The Internet affords immediate access to MIDI versions of tunes with online discussions about techniques, for example at **http://www.thesession.org**

Music for Dancing

Céilí bands are modelled on American dance bands during the early part of the 20th century. Large dance halls with no amplification shaped the nature of their music and its performance, given that the dancers needed to hear a strong, steady beat. Irish-American songs from that era are still heard today, including *The Stone Outside Dan Murphy's Door* and *My Irish Molly-O*. The Irish Céilí bands of the 1940s and 1950s were made up of similar instruments – fiddles, flutes, a button accordion, a banjo, a concertina, a vamping piano, but no saxophone or piccolo. The **Kilfenora** and **Tulla** Céilí Bands from Co Clare are the best-known Céilí bands in Ireland.

Music for Listening

Apart from Céilí bands, Irish traditional music has been a solo art in Ireland. In the 1960s **Seán O'Riada** introduced the concept of group playing for listeners, instead of dancers. His Ceoltóirí Chualann played dance tunes and planxties (eg. *Planxty Johnston*). In an attempt to reproduce the sound of the wire harp, O'Riada introduced harpsichord into the group as well as the bodhrán. Different soloists were featured and different textures were produced within a single piece – this is how Jazz bands play. There was a mixture of dance types within a single set.

Worldwide Audience

Nowadays group playing of Irish traditional music has led to the involvement of musicians from different genres. **The Chieftains**, for example, have recorded with Chinese musicians, Country singers such as Lyle Lovett and many Rock and Pop stars including the Rolling Stones, Sting, Elvis Costello and Van Morrison. Concerts, CDs, DVDs, film and TV promote the music, so a worldwide audience is now enthusiastic about the folk music of a small country, Ireland.

Discuss the changes that have occurred in Irish music, due to outside influences. Show evidence of personal research.

EXERCISE

©Higgins & Higgins

THE CÉILÍ BAND

The term **céilí** means 'a gathering of people for dance'. The function of the céilí band is to provide music for dancers. It should be loud enough to be heard by a crowd of dancers in a large hall. It needs to be rhythmic. All the melody instruments play the tune in unison. Drums are used to provide a backbeat ie. to keep the time. The piano adds a bass line and harmony and keeps an even tempo. A bodhrán or guitar would not be as effective in a packed hall with no amplification, so these are not used.

Music

At a **Fíor-Céilí** only dance-tunes considered to be of Irish origin are accepted (eg, *The Walls of Limerick* and *The Siege of Ennis*) so waltzes and polkas are not played. A **Céilí and Old-Time Dance** caters for waltzes in between the Irish dances. In Northern Ireland the tempo is laid back and leisurely whereas further south, a faster tempo is preferred by dancers.

Instruments

In a standard céilí band there are ten players. For a good blend, a band employs the maximum number of families of instruments. Brass is not generally accepted in this tradition although the saxophone has appeared from time to time. A typical line-up would be one accordion, one concertina, one set of pipes, one banjo, two fiddles, two flutes, drums and piano.

Reed	String	Woodwind	Percussion
2 or 3 players	*3 or 4 players*	*2 players*	*both players*
Accordion	Banjo	Fife	Drums
Concertina	Fiddle	Flute	Piano
Harmonica	Mandolin	Tin whistle	
Uilleann Pipes			

On Stage

The position of the instruments on stage is crucial for an ideal balance. Fiddles and flutes are at the front. Banjo is a little behind them and the accordion and concertina are further back as they have greater volume. Drums and piano are the furthest away from the dancers.

Dates

The Gaelic League organised the first Irish céilí in London in **1897**. The music included jigs, quadrille sets and waltzes. Long rows of dancers faced each other, a practice that continues to this day. The Tara Céilí Band inspired the present-day line-up when they played in London in **1918**. Fr Tom Larkin set up the Ballinakill Céilí Band in **1926** at a time when the clergy wished to rid Ireland of Jazz music. He chose tunes that suited the delicate blend of flute, fiddle and piano. Other bands rated themselves against the Ballinakill whose recordings remained influential for thirty years. When new village halls sprang up in the late **1930s**, after house dances had been banned, many céilí bands were formed, including the Tulla and the Kilfenora in Co Clare. In the **1930s** and **40s** céilí music was broadcast on Irish radio and in the **1950s**, it was kept popular not only by the Fleadh Cheoil but also by Irish-made recordings. In the **1960s**, Seán O'Riada condemned céilí bands for their lack of individual expression. However, despite their critics and despite competition from other types of entertainment, céilí bands remain busy today.

EXERCISE

Listen to a Céilí band and describe the performance.

©Higgins & Higgins

SEÁN Ó RIADA (1931-71)

Career

Born John Reidy in Cork, Seán O'Riada graduated with a B Mus degree in 1952. As a young man he played piano in Jazz and dance bands. He was Assistant Director of music in Radio Eireann for two years until he left for Paris in 1955, where he made some programmes for *Radiodiffusion Télévision Française*. In 1957 he became Music Director of the Abbey Theatre in Dublin. His 15-part radio series, *Our Musical Heritage*, was broadcast by Radio Eireann in 1962. From 1963, he lectured in the Music department at UCC where one of his students was Micheál O'Súilleabháin. He moved from Dublin to the Irish speaking village of Cúil Aodha (Coolea) in Co. Cork. As a musician, O'Riada was:

(a) a performer and an innovative arranger of Irish traditional music,
(b) a composer of European art music and
(c) an educator and a broadcaster.

Ceoltóirí Chualann: Style

O'Riada criticized céilí bands, whose playing he likened to 'the buzzing of a bluebottle in an upturned jam jar'. He hoped to create a popular audience for traditional music to give it the dignity it deserved, so he formed a 'folk orchestra', Ceoltóirí Chualann, in 1960. The musicians wore dress-suits, one factor which helped to place this folk art on a par with other art forms in urban Ireland. Using traditional instruments, the group interspersed solos, duets and trios with the full ensemble sound, an idea borrowed from Jazz bands. Their imaginative arrangements involved interweaving melodies and Classical-style harmonies.

For centuries the bodhrán was treated as a primitive rhythm instrument used as a noisemaker by mummers and wren-boys. When O'Riada included it in Ceoltóirí Chualann, it became a mainstream traditional Irish music instrument in many groups. Virtuoso bodhrán-playing has since become the norm. O'Riada also wanted to revive 18th century Irish harp music – pieces such as *Carolan's Concerto* – so he played the harpsichord in order to replicate the sound of the wire-string harp.

Ceoltóirí Chualann: People

Despite not giving many concerts, they had a big following, thanks to two series of radio programmes, *Reachaireacht an Riadaigh* and *Fleadh Cheoil an Raidió*. Darach O'Catháin, a sean-nós singer from Connemara, featured with the group in some of these programmes.

Harpsichord	Seán O'Riada	**Bodhrán**	Peadar Mercier
Pipes	Paddy Moloney	**Flute**	Michael Tubridy
Tin Whistle	Seán Potts	**Accordions**	Sonny Brogan,
Fiddles	John Kelly, Martin Fay,		Eamon de Buitléar
	Seán Keane	**Singer**	Seán O'Sé, famous for
Bones	Ronnie McShane		*An Poc ar Buile*

Ceoltóiri Chualann's last performance was recorded on the album *O'Riada sa Gaiety*. When the group broke up in 1969, some of them joined The Chieftains, whose style was greatly influenced by O'Riada.

Carolan's Concerto

©Higgins & Higgins

Compositions: Soundtracks, Incidental and Religious Music

The evocative use of traditional airs (eg. *Róisín Dubh*) and patriotic tunes (*A Nation Once Again*) in his orchestral scores made O'Riada a national celebrity during the 1960s. These works reinforced the Irish nation's pride in its cultural identity at a time when the country was celebrating the 50th anniversary of the Easter Rising of 1916, a pivotal event in Irish history. His soundtracks and incidental music include:

- *Mise Eire* and *Saoirse* (film documentaries by George Morrison about the foundation of the Irish Free State) – 1959 and 1960
- *The Song of the Anvil* and *Honey Spike* (plays by Brian McMahon) – 1960 and 1961
- *The Playboy of the Western World* (film version of the play by JM Synge) – 1963
- *Rhapsody of a River*, *Pobal* and *An Tine Bheo* (short films directed by Louis Marcus) – 1966

As well as using traditional tunes as the basis for hundreds of arrangements, he drew connections between Celtic and Indian music. He formed and directed a community choir for which he wrote a number of liturgical works. The well-known *Ag Críost an Síol* is sung during the Offertory in *Ceol an Aifrinnn* (1965) and is long associated with Cór Cúil Aodha, together with his other Mass, *Aifreann 2* (1968) and a *Requiem* (1970).

Compositions in European Classical style

He wrote choral works, a symphony, pieces for solo instruments and chamber groups, including

- *Nomos 1 – Hercules Dux Ferrariae* (8 movements for string orchestra) – 1957
- *Nomos 2* (for baritone, SATB choir and orchestra) – 1957
- *Nomos 4* (for solo piano and orchestra) – 1958
- *Nomos 6 – Triptyque pour Orchestre Symphonique* – 1960 (for orchestra)
- *Five Epigrams from the Greek Anthology* (for SATB choir, flute and harpsichord) – 1958
- *Four Holderlin Songs* (for voice and piano) – 1964
- *Hill Field* (for voice and piano) – 1965
- *Sekundenzieger* (for voice and piano) – 1966

EXERCISE

What are the Main points you would give in a short essay about Seán O'Riada in the Leaving Cert exam?

20TH CENTURY TIMELINE – PART 1: 1900-1950

This timeline offers a backdrop for an essay on the development of traditional Irish music in the 20th century. It is by no means complete. In the Leaving Cert exam students should not quote every detail mentioned here. Instead they should pick out the overriding mood of each decade, citing or adding names and events that they consider to be the most relevant for their answer.

The most significant decade of the century in the area of traditional Irish music is the 1950s. A typical essay could trace the progress of the music under these headings:

(a) Up to the 1950s (b) 1950s and 1960s (d) 1970s and 1980s (e) 1990s.

Mention the effects of society and the economy; the influence of media (especially radio and recordings), travel, emigration, immigration, instruments, technology and education.

1900s	• Captain O'Neill publishes 1850 Irish tunes in 1903 and 1001 more tunes in 1907.
1910s	• In 1916, a banjo and accordion duo, Eddie Hebron and James Wheeler, become the first Irish performers in America to be recorded on 78rpm, playing dance music. They play *The Stack of Barley*.
1920s	• American dance halls draw huge numbers to their Irish dances. Bands start to use tenor banjos, saxophones, drums and guitars to add volume and variety. • Live Irish music is played on the Irish radio (2RN). Due to broadcasting time constraints, dance tunes are now restricted to a few minutes. • The records of New York-based fiddlers Michael Coleman, James Morrison and Paddy Killoran greatly influence Irish musicians back home. Coleman's virtuoso playing reshapes old tunes into masterpieces (eg. *Jenny's Chickens*). • There is a campaign to rid the Irish countryside of Jazz in 1926. • The Ballinakill Céilí band (in Galway) is set up by a priest, Father Larkin, to safeguard the morality of his parishioners. Flutes, fiddles and a piano are used.
1930s	• Traditional players are auditioned by classically-trained music directors for radio These know little about traditional Irish music and expect musical literacy. • Commercial recordings are already changing the geography of Irish dance music. Musicians are influenced by the different regional styles they hear on records. • The Irish Dancing Commission creates strict rules for music and dances in 1930. • With the Public Dance Halls Act in 1935, clergy and police enforce strict morality. House dances are banned but supervised céilís flourish in parish halls right up to the 1950s. The Kilfenora and Tulla Céilí bands are popular. • The Gaelic League bans set dances from céilís due to their foreign origins (quadrilles). • In 1935 EMI Records set up a recording studio in Dublin.
1940s	• Traditional Irish music has a low status in comparison with Classical and Pop music. Traditional musicians who participate in the Feis Ceoil are told to learn how to play properly by 'informed' adjudicators. Morale is low • The BBC employs the piper Séamus Ennis to collect traditional music in Ireland. He is able to learn tunes after one hearing. Starting in 1947, he gathers 2000 tunes in five years.

20TH CENTURY TIMELINE – PART 2: 1950-2000

1950s	• The first Fleadh Cheoil (held in Mullingar in 1951) is organised by Comhaltas Ceoltóirí Éireann to give traditional musicians an appreciative audience. It becomes a major annual cultural event. It standardises the repertoire and has an impact on regional styles and techniques. • Gael-Linn is founded in 1953 to promote the Irish language and its heritage. It produces a series of 78rpm records, focusing on solo accordionists. • Ciarán MacMathúna broadcasts authentic recordings made in people's homes.
1960s	• RTÉ television is launched. It broadcasts Irish music programmes. • Ceoltóirí Chualann is formed by Seán O'Riada. Includes harpsichord and bodhrán. Arrangements have solo and ensemble playing. Old harp music is revived. • The economy begins to boom. Traditional players are paid to play in pubs. Repertoire changes from jigs and reels to imported country and western music, waltzes and ballads. • The first of Breandán Breathnach's volumes of collected tunes is published (1963). • The folk revival in America causes a ballad boom. The Clancy brothers appear on prime-time television in the US. They add a new vitality to songs and avoid sentimentality. The Dubliners reach the UK charts with *Seven Drunken Nights*. The Wolfe Tones sing rebel songs. • People flock to dance halls to be entertained by showbands (eg. Miami and Royal).
1970s	• In 1975 The Chieftains sell out The Albert Hall, London, on St Patrick's Day. They continue to introduce global audiences to Irish music up to the present day. • Celtic Rock emerges with Horslips who are urban, middle-class and educated. They play electric fiddle, guitar and drums in hit tunes such as *Dearg Doom*. • A trad Irish song, *Whisky in the Jar*, is a hit for Progressive Rock group, Thin Lizzy. • The bouzouki, clavinet, pipes and guitar are played by the Bothy Band. This music is energetic and hugely influential. After their break-up, Donal Lunny joins Planxty.
1980s	• The instrumental version of *Hey Jude* (Beatles) by De Danann turns into a hornpipe and a reel. They also experiment with *The Arrival of the Queen of Sheba* (Handel) . • Irish music blends with other styles. Fusion occurs with Rock (Moving Hearts), with Jazz (Micheál O'Súilleabháin) and with Classical music (Shaun Davey). • Clannad sings a song with Irish lyrics (*Theme from Harry's Game*) on Top of the Pops (1982) and provides the incidental music for a BBC series, *Robin of Sherwood*. • Enya uses overdubbing and synthesisers to achieve a Celtic sound. • The economy is very weak. A new wave of emigration hits Ireland. • The Pogues, who fuse trad with Punk rock, record *Fairytale of New York* (1987). • Revival of Céilí bands, céilís and set dancing.
1990s	• There is a return to regional roots eg. Altan (Donegal) and Dervish (Sligo). • The RTÉ programme, *Bringing it all back home* (1991), explores Irish music in the US. Emigration is no longer an issue as the economy is booming. Celtic tiger arrives. • *Riverdance* (1994) has an Ethnic/Jazz mix. Anúna provides Celtic choral harmonies. • Kila experiments with Eastern European, Japanese, Latin and Jazz fusion. • African and other Ethnic drums become commonplace in Irish trad settings. • Technology is used on stage to add studio-type effects eg. Afro-Celt Sound System. • Irish music becomes a compulsory part of Junior and Leaving Cert Music courses. • There is an ongoing debate about continuity versus change and purism versus innovation. The popularity of Irish music is unprecedented.

©Higgins & Higgins

ESSAY-TYPE QUESTIONS

Each of these essays must show evidence of personal research:

1. **Ornamentation in traditional Irish Music.** Mention singing and playing on different instruments, quoting examples of ornaments and giving the names of performers and tunes.

2. **Tonality in traditional Irish Music.** Deal with modes, pentatonic scales, capability of different instruments to play different keys and give examples of tunes.

3. **Non-traditional elements found in traditional instrumental Irish Music.** Write about instruments, playing styles and techniques, fusions and repertoire.

4. Using the given timeline, describe the main **developments** in traditional Irish music in the 20th century. Mention musicians, music and styles.

5. Referring to specific features, performers and pieces, explain four types of **fusion** involving traditional Irish music as one of the elements.

6. Describe the structure of a piece of **fusion** you know in which one of the styles is Irish traditional music. Outline the general features of the work and explain how the performer(s) you name deal with the various aspects you mention.

7. Write a note about the **Céilí Band**. Mention how it developed, naming the instruments, well-known groups and their playing style.

8. Describe a **performance** of a piece of traditional Irish Music you have heard. Outline the general features of the tune, including its structure and explain how the performer(s) you name dealt with the tunes. Consider using *Riverdance* (Bill Whelan), *Drowsy Maggie* (Chieftains) or *Woodbrook* (Mícheál O'Súilleabháin). Choose a piece that has been recorded and that is available to purchase. Your description has to be verifiable.

9. **Seán Ó'Riada** has contributed much to music in Ireland. Support this statement by describing the different roles he had and by naming some of his works.

10. Discuss the importance of **Mícheál Ó'Súilleabháin** in making Irish traditional music accessible to a wide public. Describe at least one of his works and name three others giving details of instrumentation and stylistic features.

11. Write an account of **any Irish composer**, apart from Mícheál O'Súilleabháin, working in the area of traditional Irish music in the 21st century. Mention style, works, instruments, recordings and collaborations (if any).

12. Write a note about how Irish traditional music has been influenced by the music of other **European** countries. Mention dances, instruments and styles and name some of the repertoire we may have inherited. Use the Internet to find resources.

13. Explain the format of the dances as well as the type of tunes used for **group set dancing**. Name dances (eg. *The Caledonian*) and tunes. Compare set and céilí dancing music.

14. Describe how the **accordion*** (and its family) is used in traditional Irish music. Refer to the instrument itself, performers and tunes.

   You could also do a similar essay about other instruments.

©Higgins & Higgins

MAP OF USA AND CANADA

On the map below, mark the areas mentioned in the essay on page 93.

On the map below, mark the areas mentioned in the essay on page 93.

EXERCISE

©Higgins & Higgins

Course A – Bach

Contents

1600 – 1750 BAROQUE PERIOD

The Baroque period dates roughly from 1600 to 1750. The term 'Baroque' was used to describe the ornate and dramatic architecture of the 17th and 18th centuries and was adopted to describe the elaborate music of this time also. After the upheaval of the Reformation and the Counter Reformation, Europe was divided in two, with the Protestants in the north (Germany) and the Catholics in the south (Italy). The religious differences were evident in the artistic creations of the period – with the exhuberant, florid, grand buildings and statues of Rome in contrast with the more sober German art forms.

Musical patronage was important to composers in this period and it was usual to seek employment as a court or church musician, or composer. Art music was primarily the domain of the nobility and wealthy upper class. The composer's musical output depended on what was demanded of him by his patron and his compositions correspond to the positions he held during his lifetime.

Baroque Style

Texture: Textures used include monophonic (a single line), homophonic (a single line with harmonic support) and polyphonic (two or more melodies weaving together). The most important feature however was the presence of the continuo (basso continuo) which provided a continuous harmonic support. Compositional techniques influenced the texture – imitation and canon, both contrapuntal techniques, were common in this period.

Melody: Baroque melody was elaborate and ornate and often had irregular phrase lengths. Both instrumental and vocal melodies featured decorations (trills, grace notes and turns) and sequences (a motif repeated at a different pitch in the same voice). Arias used melismas (a single syllable with many notes), while recitatives were syllabic (each syllable had only one note). Both featured word painting (a word or a meaning highlighted by the music).

Instruments: Along with the obligatory continuo, strings were the main component of orchestras and ensembles. String instruments were smaller in size and more limited than those of today. The wind family was made up of just flute (originally a type of recorder) and oboe, with bassoon joining later. The brass section consisted of trumpets and horns. Neither had valves so they were limited in their capabilities. The timpani were used occasionally. Church vocal music was written for full SATB choir (soprano, alto, tenor, bass). The performers were all male, with boys providing the higher voices.

Form: Many orchestral, instrumental and vocal forms were developed during these years, such as the suite, concerto grosso, cantata, oratorio and opera.

Features: Contrasts were important. These appeared in dynamics (loud versus soft with few crescendos), solo versus tutti, high versus low and fast versus slow (a fast section after a slow section or a fast moving part against a slow moving part). The diatonic tonal system had been established – major and minor – and this led to a strong relationship between keys. The main modulations were from the tonic key to its five related keys of dominant (5th), subdominant (4th) and all three related minors. Cadential points were now also more pronounced.

Contemporaries include: Claudio Monteverdi (1567 – 1643 Italy), Heinrich Schütz (1585 – 1672 Germany), Dietrich Buxtehude (1637 – 1707 Denmark), Henry Purcell (1659 – 1695 England), Alessandro Scarlatti (1660 – 1725 Italy), Domenico Scarlatti (1685 – 1757 Italy), Antonio Vivaldi (1678 – 1741 Italy) and George Frideric Handel (1685 – 1759 Germany).

©Higgins & Higgins

BACH'S LIFE

Johann Sebastian Bach was born in Eisenach, Germany, in 1685 and was orphaned at the age of ten. Living with his older brother, he studied klavier and organ and sang in the church choir. From 1703 to 1707 he worked as a church organist. He married in 1707 and this marriage produced six children, two of whom became composers. A year later he became organist in Weimer where he stayed until 1717, writing mainly church and organ music. In 1717 he became the kapellmeister to Prince Leopold in Cothen where he wrote mainly secular music – some for teaching. His wife died in 1720 and he married Anna Magdalena in 1721. This appears to have been a happy time for him and he and Anna produced a number of children, two more of whom achieved fame as composers.

In 1723 he became Kantor at St Thomas's School in Leipzig. This was a prestigious appointment and the job carried with it a heavy workload. Bach was required to take responsibility for the music in the city's four churches where regular cantata performances with orchestra and choir were necessary. He had to supervise and compose for special occasions like weddings and funerals, as well as the regular Sunday services. He was also required to train the senior choir and teach at the school. He travelled a lot within Germany, during his time in Leipzig, inspecting organs and performing. He died in 1750.

His works are catalogued in BWV numbers (*Bach Werke-Verzeichnis*) which are not necessarily in chronological order but according to genre. His compositions include sacred choral music (passions, masses and over 200 cantatas), orchestral music (6 Brandenburg concertos and numerous suites), chamber music, organ music and keyboard music (including 48 preludes and fugues and many other pieces).

BACH'S STYLE

Bach was a virtuoso organist and a prolific composer. He was a devout Lutheran and placed his sacred compositions at the centre of his repertoire. The chorale hymn tune was the basis for many of his compositions and the music mirrored the sense of the words when possible. He liked using wind instruments and enjoyed experimenting with instrumental combinations. His music is contrapuntal in style and his output includes a large number of pieces for teaching purposes which he wrote for his wife, his children, his students and some of his patrons. They vary in difficulty and are an invaluable source for all students and teachers today.

Features:

(i) He enjoyed word painting in his chorales and often highlighted the meaning of the words by adding a dissonance, a chromaticism, or other musical technique.

(ii) His textures are rich and contrapuntal.

(iii) His melodies can be played on different instruments (depending on availability).

(iv) He modulated to related keys

©Higgins & Higgins

BAROQUE FORM

Ritornello

Ritornello form is based on a recurring idea. In vocal music, the ritornello (recurring idea) would be played by the instruments, sometimes in different keys, as an interlude between verses.

Recitative

A recitative is declamatory or speech-like singing used especially in opera, oratorio and cantata. The words are an important feature and recitatives are usually syllabic – one note per syllable.

There are two types of recitative:

(i) **Recitative secco** accompanied by bare chords and simple bass. The melody follows the rhythm of the words.

(ii) **Recitative accompagnato** or **stromentato**, with more involved accompaniment

Aria

This is a vocal piece from an opera, oratorio or cantata written for solo or duet singing. The melodic lines are elaborate and ornate and have melismatic sections – many notes per syllable. Da Capo arias are in **ABA** form where the second **A** is an exact repeat of the first.

Chorale

A chorale is a simple hymn tune used in Lutheran church services and sung by the congregation.

Cantata

A cantata is music for solo and chorus with orchestral accompaniment. Written with either sacred or secular text, it consists of a number of arias separated by recitatives. In Germany, chorale cantatas became important devotional works used on Sundays and other festive occasions and usually consisted of an opening chorus, two or three arias – or maybe a duet in place of one – and a closing chorale all linked by recitative.

Continuo

The basso continuo (continuo for short), provides support and harmony. It consists of a continuous line of music, usually steady and even, to be played by a bass instrument from the viol family (nowadays a cello or double bass) and a chord-playing instrument (usually an organ or harpsichord) from the keyboard family. The keyboard player plays from a **figured bass**.

Figured Bass

This is a line of music in the bass with added numbers beneath the staff to indicate what chords to play.

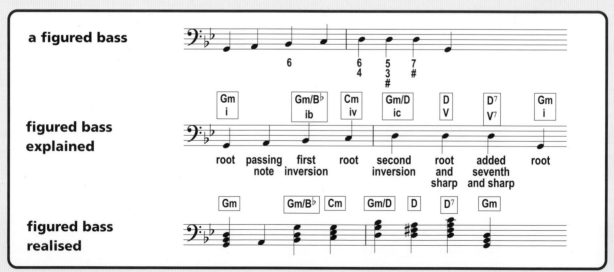

©Higgins & Higgins

Ground Bass

This is a form which features a recurring phrase (an ostinato) in the bass.

Chaconne

A chaconne is a form which uses a ground bass that passes into upper parts.

COMPOSITIONAL TECHNIQUES

Canon

This is the strictest form of contrapuntal imitation. The voices repeat a melody at a specific time and pitch interval and they overlap and imitate each other note for note. Occasionally, the imitating voice may alter an opening interval to suit the harmony.

Imitation

This is a compositional device whereby a voice repeats a melody *almost* note for note at a specific pitch and time interval. The entries overlap.

> # Cantata – Jesu, der du meine Seele BWV 78
> # Jesus, by Thy Cross and Passion

BWV 78 belongs to a group of chorale cantatas composed during Bach's years in Leipzig. It was composed for the fourteenth Sunday after Trinity in the Lutheran liturgical calendar and probably received its first performance on September 10, 1724. The gospel for the day tells the story of the ten lepors. The text is based upon a 1641 hymn by Johann Rist and also contains some material from the Gospel of St. Luke.

The theme of the whole cantata is that leprosy destroys the body as sin destroys the soul. As humans, we are weak and commit sin. Through the Bible, God offers us hope. We ask him to help us not to sin again and we hope for life ever after in heaven.

There are seven movements in this cantata:

Movement	Form	Voice	Key	Time	Track
Chorus	Chaconne/Ritornello	SATB Choir	G min	3/4	1
Duet Aria	Da Capo Aria	Soprano and Alto	B♭ maj	¢	2
(T) Recitative	(Rec) Secco	Tenor	–	¢	3
Tenor Aria	Dal Segno/**ABB¹**	Tenor	G min	6/8	4
(B) Recitatitive	(Rec) Accompagnato	Bass	E♭ maj – F min	¢	5
Bass Aria	**ABA¹**	Bass	C min	¢	6
Chorale	**AABC**	SATB Choir	G min	¢	7

©Higgins & Higgins

Instruments

Four solo voices: Soprano, Alto, Tenor and Bass with Choir	
Violins I and II (VI)	1 Flauto traverso (Fl)
Violas (Vla)	2 Oboes (Ob)
Violone (double bass) (Viol)	Horns (Cor)
Continuo (Cello and Organ) (C)	

The horn indicated by Bach was a slide horn and he dispensed with it in later writings. The flauto traverso (play across) indicates that the flute should be used and not a recorder There are a number of performed ornaments that do not appear on the score.

The first movement is an arrangement of the chorale hymn used in the final movement. For this analysis we will begin with the seventh movement.

SEVENTH MOVEMENT   Chorale   G Min (verse 12 of original hymn)

Summary of text

Lord, I believe. Do not let me give up hope. Make me strong when I'm about to sin. I will meet you in heaven.

All the vocal parts are doubled by the instruments as follows:

Soprano	Flute, Oboe I, Horn and Violin I
Alto	Oboe II and Violin II
Tenor	Viola
Bass	Continuo

The tenor voice sounds an 8ve lower than written.

There are sixteen bars divided evenly into 4 x four-bar phrases. The form is **AABC** and the texture is homophonic. Repeated notes are a feature and there is a cadence every two bars as follows:

Section A Bars 1 - 4		Section A Bars 5 - 8	
Bar 2	Perfect cadence (**V-i**) in G min	**Bar 6**	Perfect cadence (**V-i**) in G min
Bar 4	Imperfect cadence (**i-V**) in G min	**Bar 8**	Imperfect cadence (**i-V**) in G min
Section B Bars 9 -12		**Section C Bars 13 -16**	
Bar 10	Perfect cadence (**V-I**) in F maj	**Bar 14**	Imperfect cadence (**ivb-V**) in G min
Bar 12	Perfect cadence (**V-I**) in B♭ maj (relative major)	**Bar 16**	Perfect cadence in G min with a *Tierce de Picardie* (the minor 3rd of the tonic is raised a semitone giving a final major chord).

©Higgins & Higgins

Chorale   16 Bars   G Min – F Maj – B♭ Maj – G Min

FIRST MOVEMENT   Chorus G Min   (verse 1 of original hymn)

Summary of text

Jesus, through your death you have saved my soul from hell...in your word I find refuge.

This movement is in **ritornello form**, having a recurring orchestral section between sung sections. It occurs seven times in different keys and is not always played in its entirety. This orchestral ritornello is made up of a number of different themes.

Ground Bass Theme (the Chromatic or Ostinato Theme)

Although the Ground Bass Theme is played mainly by the continuo, it appears in the upper instruments also and is hinted at by the alto, tenor and bass. Therefore, the movement is a Chaconne. The important feature of the theme is the descending chromatic pattern. The remainder of the theme is sometimes altered.

- descending chromatic line representing the suffering of Christ
- descends over an interval of a 4th (from G down to D)
- Perfect cadence

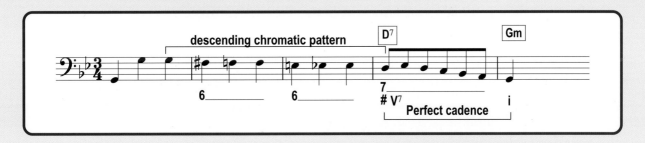

©Higgins & Higgins

Grief Motif (the Syncopated Theme)

The important feature of the Grief Motif is the syncopated rhythm. The end of the theme is sometimes altered.

- syncopated and dotted rhythm (dotted crotchet on second beat)

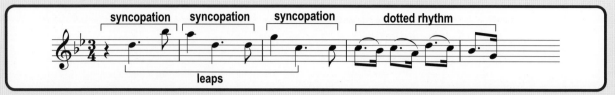

Joy Motif (three-note idea)

This is a rising three-note idea –
two semiquavers and a quaver –
and is a happy contrast to the Grief Motif

Chorale Melody

Chorale melody in 3/4 time; sung by the soprano using eight lines of verse 1 text.

- repeated notes
- rhythm and length of each phrase has changed in order to fit the melody

Instruments

SATB Chorus with the following instruments:	
Violins I and II (Vl)	1 Flute (Fl)
Violas (Vla)	2 Oboes (Ob)
Violone (double bass) (Viol)	Horns (Cor)
Continuo (Cello and Organ) (C)	

The soprano sings the Chorale Theme, doubled by horn. The flute doubles an 8ve higher. The alto, tenor and bass sing in imitation or in canon throughout the movement. The order of voices changes – sometimes ATB and sometimes TAB. The texture is mainly polyphonic.

Section	Key	Bar	Track
Orchestral Ritornello	G min	1	8
Chorale lines 1 and 2	G min – C min – G min	17	9
Orchestral Ritornello	G min	37	10
Chorale lines 3 and 4 and Ritornello	G min – C min – G min – D min	49	11
Chorale line 5 and Ritornello	D min – F maj	73	12
Chorale line 6 and Ritornello	F maj – G min – B♭ maj – G min	89	13
Chorale line 7 and Ritornello	G min – C min – F maj B♭ maj – G min	107	14
Chorale line 8 and Ritornello	G min	129	15

©Higgins & Higgins

Orchestral Ritornello   Bars 1 – 17   G Min

Bar 1   Four bars on continuo, wind and strings.

- Chromatic Theme on continuo
- Syncopated Theme on flute, first oboe and first violin
- second oboe, second violin and viola accompany
- Perfect cadence at bars 4 – 5

Bar 5   Four bars repeated with variations.

Bar 9   Four bars on strings and oboes with no continuo or flute.

- first oboe has Chromatic Theme
- unison scale passage on strings

Bar 13   Four bars on strings and oboes with no continuo or flute.

- second oboe has the Chromatic Theme
- oboe sequence in bars 13 and 14
- string sequence in bars 14 and 15
- oboe trill in bar 16

Chorale lines 1 and 2   Bars 17 – 37 G Min – C Min – G Min

Bar 17   Four bars as alto, tenor and bass enter imitatively, at different intervals, with a version of Chromatic Theme. Soprano enters in bar 21, a beat before the bass.

- Joy Motif in continuo
- canon on the oboes
- staccato strings

(compare and contrast with bars 1 and 2 of chorale hymn)

Bar 21   Five bars as soprano and flute enter with first line of chorale hymn.

- Chromatic Theme on continuo and bass voice
- first violin and first oboe have version of Syncopated Theme
- syncopated rhythm in accompaniment
- Perfect cadence at bars 24 – 25

©Higgins & Higgins

Bar 25 Eight bars as alto, tenor and bass enter imitatively at different intervals, alto and tenor singing an inversion of the Chromatic Theme (ascending) and bass sings it descending in C minor (subdominant).

- mirror canon on oboes (first oboe ascends while second oboe descends).
- trills on the tenor
- quavers on continuo
- oboe sequences in bars 30 and 31
- G minor in bar 32

(compare and contrast with bars 3 and 4 of chorale hymn)

Bar 33 Four bars as soprano and flute enter with second line of the chorale hymn.

- Chromatic Theme on the continuo
- version of Syncopated Theme on first violin
- trills on flute and viola
- syncopated accompaniment rhythm
- vocals stop on chord **V** in bar 36
- Perfect cadence at bars 36 – 37

Orchestral Ritornello   Bars 37 – 49   **G Min**

(compare and contrast with bars 5 – 8)

Bar 37 Repeats the music of bars 5 – 8.

Bar 41 Eight bars of Chromatic Theme with accompaniment.

- Chromatic Theme on second violin bar 41
- Chromatic Theme on first violin bar 45
- sequences in bar 45 – 47

Chorale lines 3 and 4   Bars 49 – 68   G Min – C Min – G Min

(compare and contrast with bars 17 – 36)

Bar 49 Repeat of the music of bar 17.

- oboe and violin swap parts from bar 17
- third line of chorale hymn in bar 53
- C minor in bar 61, G minor in bar 65
- fourth line of text in bar 65

Orchestral ritornello   Bars 69 – 73   G Min – D Min

Bar 69 Four-bar instrumental passage.

- Chromatic Theme on the first violin
- tonic pedal D on the continuo
- Perfect cadence in D minor at bars 72 – 73

©Higgins & Higgins

| Chorale line 5 | Bars 73 – 85 | D Min – F Maj |

Bar 73   Four bars as tenor, alto and bass enter imitatively with a new rising idea.

- Joy Motif on continuo
- imitative entries in oboes
- version of Chromatic Theme on strings

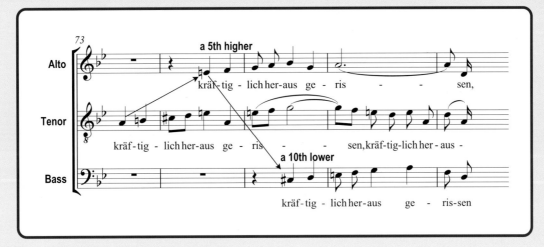

Bar 77   Four bars vocal counterpoint.

- Chromatic Theme on continuo and bass voice
- sequences in bars 78 and 79
- version of Syncopated Theme on oboes
- Perfect cadence in D minor at bars 80 – 81

Bar 81   Five bars as soprano and flute enter with fifth line of chorale in F major

- Chromatic Theme on continuo and bass voice
- sequences in bars 82 and 83
- imitative entries on word *heraus* (away) with tenor answered by alto

| Orchestral Ritornello   Bars 85 – 89 | F Maj |

(compare and contrast with bars 1 and 4)

Bar 85   Four bars of orchestral interlude repeating the two main themes.

- Perfect cadence in F major at bars 88 – 89

| Chorale line 6 | Bars 89 – 99   F Maj – G Min – B♭ Maj |

Bar 89   Six bars as alto, tenor and bass enter imitatively with a new idea based on a rising 4th and featuring the rising three-note Joy Motif.

- Joy Motif on the continuo
- staccatos on oboe
- G minor in bar 90

©Higgins & Higgins

Bar 95   Five bars as soprano and flute enter with sixth line of chorale in B♭ major.

- Chromatic Theme on continuo and bass voice
- Perfect cadence in B♭ major at bars 98 – 99

Orchestral Ritornello   Bars 99 – 107   **B♭ Maj – G Min**

Bar 99   Eight-bar instrumental passage.

- Chromatic Theme on continuo
- version of Syncopated Theme in other instruments
- Perfect cadence in B♭ major at bars 102 – 103
- sequences in bars 103 – 106
- dialogue bars 103 and 104 and bars 105 and 106
- parallel 10ths on continuo and second violin in bars 104 and 106

Chorale line 7   Bars 107 – 121   G Min – C Min – F Maj – B♭ Maj – G Min

Bar 107   Eleven bars as tenor, alto and bass enter imitatively using the Chromatic Theme.

- second oboe answers first oboe a 5th lower (bar 109)
- first violin answers continuo a 4th higher
- continuo and bass voice have Chromatic Theme in C minor (bar 111)
- first oboe (bar 112) answers the second oboe (bar 110)
- second oboe (bar 112) answers the first violin (bar 110)
- second oboe, second violin and tenor have Chromatic Theme in F major (bar 113)
- first oboe, first violin and alto have Chromatic Theme in B♭ major a 4th higher (bar 115)

Bar 118   Four bars as soprano and flute enter with seventh line of chorale in G minor.

- Chromatic Theme on continuo and bass voice
- Syncopated Theme on first violin and first oboe

Orchestral Ritornello   Bars 121 – 129   **G Min**

Bar 121   Four-bar instrumental passage.

- dominant pedal (D) on continuo
- Chromatic Theme on second oboe imitated canonically a 5th higher on flute and first oboe
- parallel 3rds on violins

Bar 125   Four bars of dialogue and sequences.

- Joy Motif on viola and continuo

Chorale line 8   Bars 129 – 140   G Min

Bar 129   Seven bars as tenor, alto and bass enter imitatively at a two-bar distance.

- Joy Motif in sequence on continuo
- viola doubles continuo in 3rds and 6ths alternately
- syncopated rhythm on violins answered by oboes

©Higgins & Higgins

Bar 136 Five bars of main themes and eighth line of chorale .

- Chromatic Theme on continuo and bass voice
- Syncopated Theme on oboe and strings
- eighth line of chorale (bar 137)
- Perfect cadence in G minor at bars 139 – 140

Orchestral Ritornello   Bars 140 – 144   G Min

(compare and contrast with bars 5 and 8)

Bar 140 Final statement of the orchestral ritornello.

- **ic – V – I** Perfect cadence
- final chord of G major as the Bb in second violin is raised to a B♮ (Picardy 3rd)

1. **Fill in the missing notes from the Chorale and Chorus on the staves below.** **EXERCISE**

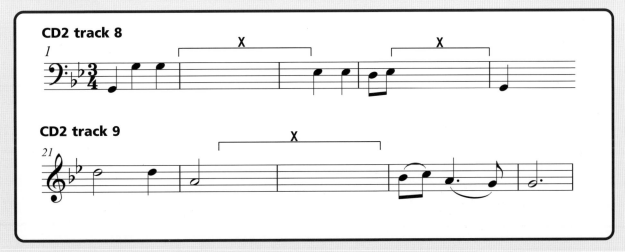

2. **In your answer, outline TWO similarities and THREE differences between the setting of the text in movements 1 and 7. Mention BOTH movements and include time signature, key signature, instruments and form in your answer.**

3. **Realise the figured bass on the stave below.**

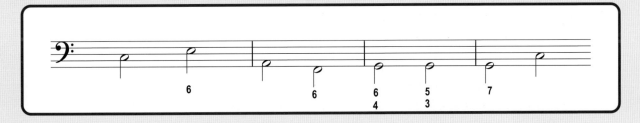

©Higgins & Higgins

SECOND MOVEMENT   Aria Duetto   Bb Maj

Summary of text

We hurry to you, oh Jesus, for help. Hear how we pray for your help. Grant us thy favour.

Instruments

Soprano and Alto with Organ, Cello and Violone (double bass)

This movement is in **ternary form**. It is a Da Capo aria. There is also an Instrumental Ritornello which is heard at the start of the A section for the first time and which recurs throughout the aria.

The continuous quaver and crotchet movement (a walking bass) through the entire aria in the cello and violone (double bass), highlights the feeling of hurrying. The lightness of the staccato and pizzicato aids the happy mood.

The texture is mainly polyphonic. The B section is minor and has slower rhythms with more sustained notes.

Section	Theme	Key	Bar	Track
A	Instrumental Ritornello	Bb maj	1	16
	Vocal and instrumental	Bb maj	9	17
B	Vocal and instrumental	G min – C min – D min – F maj	51	18
A	Exact repeat of **A**	Bb maj	1	16/17

Section A   Instrumental Ritornello   Bars 1 – 8   Bb Maj

Bar 1   Eight bars with upbeat; organ, cello and walking bass on violone (double bass).

- inversions on figured bass
- violone doubles cello harmony
- Perfect cadence; Bb major (bar 8)

Section A   Vocal and instrumental   Bars 9 – 50 Bb Maj

Bar 9   Four bars with upbeat; soprano and alto in canon at the 4th, at two bars distance).

- sequences
- melismatic and rhythmic word painting on *eilen* (hurry)

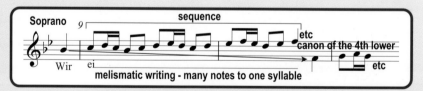

Bar 13   Four bars; continuous movement in accompaniment; parallel 6ths from *Jesu* (bar 14).

Bar 16   Seven bars with alto and soprano in canon at the 4th and at two beats distance.

- sequences and dialogue at '*Jesu*' and '*Meister*'
- bar 19 and 20 parallel 3rds and 6ths
- Perfect cadence in Bb major in the accompaniment at bars 19 – 20

©Higgins & Higgins

(compare and contrast with bars 11 – 16)

Bar 22   Six bars with upbeat, the same as bars 11 – 16 with voices switched.
   • parallel 3rds instead of 6ths in bar 27

(compare and contrast with bars 16 – 19)

Bar 28   Four bars of canon with soprano beginning and alto answering.

Bar 32   Four bars of parallel 6th movement.

Bar 36   Two bars of dialogue followed by two bars of parallel 3rd movement
   • dialogue begins in alto; Perfect cadence in B♭ major at bars 41 – 42

(compare and contrast with bars 1 – 8)

Bar 43   A repeat of the Instrumental Ritornello.

> ## Section B Vocal and instrumental   Bars 51 – 98
> ### G Min – C Min – D Min – F Maj

Bar 51   Ten bars; upbeat; first four on soprano and alto; canon at the 5th, two bars distance.
   • slower rhythms and sustained notes
   • parallel 4ths in bar 59 and Perfect cadence in C minor in bar 60

Bar 61   Four bar Instrumental Ritornello in C minor.

Bar 65   Four bars (2+2) with upbeat.
   • word painting on words *ach! höre* (oh hear)
   • parallel 3rds

Bar 69   Twelve bars of canon in G minor with soprano answering the alto; ends in D minor.
   • soprano answers with a wider leap of a 5th in bar 71; alto had used a 4th
   • Perfect cadence in D minor in bar 80

Bar 81   Two-bar instrumental passage.

Bar 83   Four bars (2+2) of theme sung by alto, answered by soprano a 5th higher

Bar 87   Twelve bars of polyphonic singing.
   • parallel 3rds in bars 87, 91, 95 and 96
   • melisma on word *freulich* (joyful)
   • F major at bar 90 and Perfect cadence in bar 98

*The aria then returns directly to bar 1 and repeats the first 50 bars up to the pause. Ending the **B** section on F major makes this return to B♭ major easy as it moves from dominant to tonic.*

> ## THIRD MOVEMENT   Tenor Recitative

Summary of text

I am a sinner...I cannot resist evil and temptation. I admit my failings and beg for your forgiveness...let my misdeeds not anger you.

Instruments   Tenor and Continuo

This is a **recitativo secco** (dry) which means it has a very sparse accompaniment. The tonality is uncertain, reflecting the despair and feeling of isolation, until the end when it rests on C minor. The melody line is full of wide leaps and augmented intervals to highlight words, and the harmony includes many diminished chords. It is declamatory and full of dramatic speech. Notice too that the vocal part ends its phrases unaccompanied with the continuo cadencing after it each time.

©Higgins & Higgins

- appoggiatura (bar 3)

- wide intervals in (bar 2)

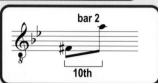

- augmented and diminished intervals (bars 1 and 11)

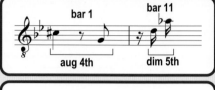

- diminished chord (bars 18)

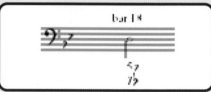

- Perfect cadence in C minor (bar 12) and in F minor (bar 15)
- more active accompaniment from bar 20 onward
- melismatic treatment of the word *erzürnet* (angry)

FOURTH MOVEMENT   Tenor Aria   G Min

Summary of text

Your blood has cleansed me. If the devil wants to fight me, Jesus will stand by my side and make me brave.

Instruments   Tenor with Flute and Continuo

This aria is in ABB[1] form with a recurring Instrumental Ritornello. It is light-hearted and melodic with the flute and tenor interweaving like a duet. It is the only movement in a compound duple time. There is a Dal Segno at the end. This is an instruction to go back to the sign and repeat the music as far as the pause or other mark.

There are a number of appoggiaturas in this movement. An appoggiatura is an ornament which is as important melodically as the note on which it 'leans' and from which it takes, normally, half the time-value. It has two effects – either filling an interval or providing a suspension.

Section	Theme	Key	Bar	Track
A	Instrumental Ritornello	G min	1	19
	Vocal and instrumental	G min – B♭ maj	13	20
B	Vocal and instrumental	B♭ maj – C min – E♭ maj	31	21
B¹	Vocal and instrumental	C min – G min	43	22

©Higgins & Higgins

Bach

Section A Instrumental Ritornello Bars 1 – 12 G Min

Bar 1 Twelve bars with an upbeat on flute and continuo.

- at X (bar 1), the appoggiatura is written out resulting in a passing note
- at Y (bar 12), the appoggiatura is written out forming a suspension
- 8ve leaps in the continuo
- sequences in bars 5, 6 and 7, and 9 and 10
- syncopation (crotchet on off-beat) in bars 5, 6, and 7
- rising semiquaver scales against a descending bass line in bar 11
- Perfect cadence in bar 12

Flute – Instrumental Ritornello (with appoggiatura written out)

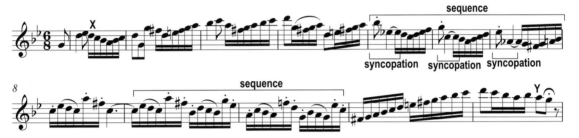

Section A Vocal and instrumental Bars 13 – 30 G Min – B♭ Maj

(compare and contrast with bars 1 – 2 and 9 – 12)

Bar 13 Six bars with upbeat on tenor and flute accompanied by continuo.

- tenor begins and flute finishes the phrase

Bar 19 Eight bars (4 X 2)

- tenor with flute countermelody
- repeated bars (21 and 23); tenor sequence (bars 21 – 24)
- descending repeated notes on continuo
- performed appoggiatura on last note that is not on the score (bar 26)
- Perfect cadence in B♭ major in bar 26

Bar 27 Four bars of Instrumental Ritornello with upbeat.

Section B Vocal and instrumental Bars 31 – 42 B♭ Maj – C Min – E♭ Maj

Bar 31 Twelve bars in C minor and E♭ major.

- sequences in bars 33 – 36 on flute
- 8ve leaps and a melisma on word *Streite* (fight)
- 8ve leaps on the bass at bar 35
- sequences on both flute and continuo in bars 39 and 40
- upward leap on the word *beherzt* (brave) in bars 39 and 40
- Perfect cadence in bar 42 in E♭ major

©Higgins & Higgins

Section B1 Vocal and instrumental   Bars 43 – 61

The same text from Section B is used and treated similarily.

Bar 43   Two bars of Instrumental Ritornello with upbeat in C minor.

Bar 45   Eight bars of counterpoint between flute and tenor in G minor.

- repeat of the 8ve leaps in bars 47 and 48 on the word *Streite*
- parallel 6ths in bars 49 and 50
- parallel 3rds in bars 51 and 52
- 8ve leaps on the bass in bars 51 and 52

(compare and contrast with bars 21 – 24 and 39 – 40)

Bar 53   Nine bars

- dominant pedal D on the tenor for the word *stehet* (stand)
- continuo plays the tenor part (from bars 21 – 24) in sequence in G minor
- flute repeats bars 21 – 24 in G minor; bars 59 and 60 similar to 39 and 40
- Perfect cadence in bar 61

The Dal Segno sends the music back to bar 1 and it plays the Instrumental Ritornello up to the pause in bar 12 which brings the movement to a close.

---

1.   **1 Fill in the missing notes from the arias in movements 2 and 4 on the staves below**

EXERCISE

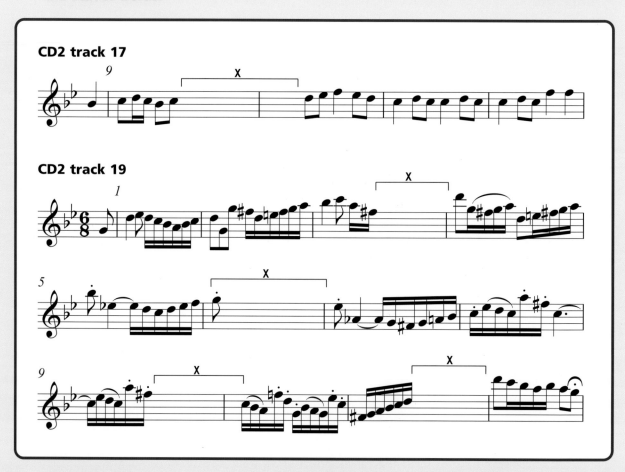

2.   **Compare and contrast the 2nd and 4th movements under the following headings accompaniment, key, time, tempo, melody, instruments and voice.**

©Higgins & Higgins

FIFTH MOVEMENT   Bass Recitative
E♭ Maj – G Min – F Min

TRACK
5

Summary of text

The wounds, nails, crown and grave that made the Saviour suffer are now a sign of his victory and give me strength. I feel no pain or torture because of your love... and I now return this love to You, Jesus Christ.

Instruments   Bass with Strings and Continuo

This is a **recitativo accompagnato** which means there is an active accompaniment. There are big contrasts in tempo, texture, mood, tonal centre and accompaniment throughout this movement. It is typically syllabic until the final section where it becomes more ornamented and melismatic.

- pedal E♭ for the opening two and a half bars

- augmented, wide and diminished intervals

- ornamentation including the appoggiatura in bar 13 and the many trills in the final ten bars

- Perfect cadences in bar 7 (E♭ major) in accompaniment after vocal line, bar 16 – 17 (A♭ major) and bar 27 (F minor) in accompaniment after vocal line
- changing tempi reflecting the mood: *vivace* (fast), *adagio lento* (slow) and *andante* (steady)
- chromatic descending line on the continuo from bar 13

EXERCISE

3. **Compare and contrast the 3rd and 5th movements under the following headings: accompaniment, key, time, tempo, melody, instruments, voice.**

4. **Give THREE Baroque features Bach uses in this cantata. Explain each.**

©Higgins & Higgins

Bach

SIXTH MOVEMENT Bass Aria   C Min

Summary of text

I will not seek revenge because your word promises hope. If we believe in you, nobody can steal us from your hands.

Instruments   Bass Voice with Strings, Continuo and Oboe

This aria is written more in a concerto style than the familiar aria styles of the 2nd and 4th movements. It uses a recurring Instrumental Ritornello Theme and an elaborate, free flowing oboe solo. When the bass voice is added, it is noticeable how many times the parts overlap.

The form is ABA[1] but the material in both the A and B sections is similar. The key is C minor with the A♭ written in the score along with the required B♮.

Recurring Instrumental Ritornello Theme

The opening recurring idea is accompanied homophonically. Notice the trill which is used repeatedly in this movement. This theme usually begins on either the 1st or 3rd beats (with upbeat).

Recurring oboe solo

The oboe solos use flowing semiquavers, sequences and scales. This example ends on the dominant (Imperfect cadence). It links up seamlessly with the Ritornello Theme, one flowing into the other. The oboe solo doesn't always begin on the same beat.

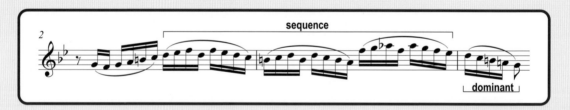

Section	Theme	Key	Bar	Track
A	Instrumental Ritornello	C min	1	23
	Vocal and instrumental	C min – E♭ maj – G min	9	24
B	Vocal and instrumental	G min – F min – C min	33	25
A[1]	Vocal and instrumental	C min	44	26

Section A   Instrumental Ritornello   Bars 1 – 8   C Min

Bar 1   Eight-bar instrumental passage; upbeat; Ritornello Theme and oboe solo.
          • Perfect cadence in bar 8

©Higgins & Higgins

Section A Vocal and instrumental Bars 9 – 32
                                        C Min – E♭ Maj – G Min

TRACK 24

Bach

123

Bar 9   Four bars on bass voice accompanied by oboe and continuo.

- bass voice melody is similar to the Ritornelo Theme
- oboe plays its solo above the bass voice from bar 10 onwards (polyphonic texture)
- semiquaver – crotchet rhythm in the continuo
- parallel 3rds in bar 11
- Imperfect cadence in bar 12

Bar 12   Five bars of Ritornello Theme and oboe solo.

Bar 17   Five bars with voice, oboe and Ritornello Theme overlapping.

- bass voice part repeats the music of bars 9 – 11
- oboe plays over the bass voice from the start
- semiquaver-crotchet rhythm on continuo used in dialogue with strings in bar 18
- parallel 6ths in bar 19
- key change and Perfect cadence in E♭ major in the instrumental parts in bar 21

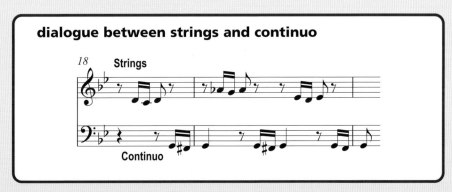

dialogue between strings and continuo

Bar 22   Five bars; bass and oboe continue; Ritornello Theme joins for cadence in G minor.

- ovarlapping themes
- Perfect cadence in G minor (bars 25 – 26)

Bar 26   Seven bars of oboe solo and Ritornello Theme brings this section to a close in bar 32 with a Perfect cadence in G minor.

Section B Vocal and instrumental Bars 33 – 44
                                       G Min – F Min – C Min

TRACK 25

Bar 33   Ten bars of new music with some similarities to previous section.

- sequence in bars 34-36 in bass and oboe
- Ritornello Theme in F minor overlapping with bass part in bars 36 – 37
- dominant pedal of C held by the bass voice on the word *ewigkeit* (eternity)
- melisma on the word *rauben* (to steal)
- bass finishing in the key of C minor (bar 42)
- Ritornello Theme in C minor to end this section; Perfect cadence (bars 43 – 44)

©Higgins & Higgins

Section A¹ Vocal and instrumental Bars 44 – 53   C Min

This section re-uses the text from section B.

Bar 44   Ten bars of bass and instruments overlapping with themes.

- compare bass voice to bars 9 and 10
- dialogue from bar 18 is used in bars 46 and 47
- dominant pedal of G is held by the bass voice
- Ritornello stops in bar 52 leaving the bass to finish the section with the continuo on a perfect cadence in C minor.

The Dal Segno sends the music back to bar 1 and it plays the Instrumental Ritornello up to the pause in bar 8 which brings the movement to a close.

EXERCISE

1.   **What are the differences between a recitative and an aria? Explain your answer, using points from the 5th and 6th movements as examples.**

2.   **What is a 'figured bass'? Explain.**

3.   **What is the 'continuo'? Explain.**

4.   **List ALL the instruments Bach uses in this Cantata.**

5.   **What are the FIVE related keys of C minor?**

6.   **Explain the following tempo marks:**
     Andante
     Vivace
     Adagio
     Lento

7.   **What is a 'pedal'? Explain.**

©Higgins & Higgins

Course A – Tchaikovsky

Contents

19TH CENTURY RUSSIA AND THE ROMANTIC PERIOD

The word 'romantic' can be used to imply many things from love to imagination. In the arts, it usually means that fantasy and expression are more important than the classical features of balance and symmetry. By the middle of the century, many European countries were becoming increasingly aware of their national identity and traditions. This, along with the political developments where traditional rulers were forced to give way to more democratic forms of government, led to the growth of nationalism.

During this time the conditions for music in Russia improved with the foundation of the Imperial Russian Music Society in 1859, the St. Petersburg Conservatory (1860) and the Moscow Conservatory (1865). Also, in line with what was happening in the rest of Europe, a group of composers known as 'The Five' (Mily Balakirev, César Cui, Alexander Borodin, Modest Mussorgsky and Nikolay Rimsky-Korsakov), sought to write music with in distinctive Russian style.

Romantic style

Texture: This refers to how melodies and harmonies are layered. With the emphasis in Romantic music on dramatic expression, textures often changed quite quickly from section to section. Usually homophonic with melody and accompaniment, there could often be polyphonic sections where main themes combine to illustrate a point in the story. As the the range and power of the instruments increased, so did the variety in tonal colour.

Melody: Long expansive melodies which included unusual modulations, a wide range, dramatic leaps and chromatic moments could be heard on any instrument in the orchestra. Harmonies included chords with added notes as well as previously unused chords and progressions.

Instruments: The 19th century orchestra was big and included a wide variety of instruments. The brass and percussion sections in particular had grown since the 18th century. Interesting combinations of instruments which created different timbres and tonal colours helped the composer to set the required mood. The piano, which had only been invented at the beginning of the 18th century, had developed into the ideal vehicle of Romantic expression.

Form: Composers continued to use the symphony, concerto and sonata of the Classical period. However, the number of movements was no longer restricted to three, the forms were extended and the rules relaxed to allow for increased expression. The importance of the story being told led to the development of **programme music** and the **symphonic poem**. Piano music moved away from abstract pieces to ones portraying particular emotions and the solo song with piano, which became known as the **art song** or **lied**, was developed.

Features: The main features of Romantic music include a wide dynamic range and modulation to non-related keys. The use of a **leitmotiv** – a recurring theme said to represent a particular idea, mood or character – also became common. Large-scale doubling of parts added to the texture of the compositions where necessary and pieces would also feature changing tempi within the movements or sections.

Russian Features: For a long time Russian music existed primarily in two forms – Folk and Religious. Most art music had been imported from the west. As the harmonic vocabulary expanded, the modalities of Russian Folk music and liturgical chant could now be incorporated into compositions. In the 1800s, when nationalism was to the fore in Europe, Russian composers combined Romantic ideas with Folk idioms to create their own style.

©Higgins & Higgins

The visual aspect of the music was important with the choice of key and the direction of the music an aid to the story telling eg. flat keys and downward moving passages used to portray sadness, fear, love or melancholy.

Contemporaries include: Hector Berlioz (1803 – 1869 France), Johann Strauss II (1825 – 1899 Austria), Johannes Brahms (1833 – 1897 Germany), Antonin Dvorák (1841 – 1904 Czechoslovakia), Nikolay Rimsky-Korsakov (1844 – 1908 Russia) and Jean Sibelius (1865 – 1957 Finland).

TCHAIKOVSKY'S LIFE

Peter Ilyich Tchaikovsky was born in a small town in Russia in 1840. He began piano at the age of five and showed a lot of talent. However, at the age of ten, he was sent to boarding school where there was very little music. After school, he studied law and worked as a civil servant for three years. It was not until 1862 that he began his music career in earnest when he enrolled in the newly-opened St Petersburg Conservatory which had been founded by the pianist/composer Anton Rubenstein. When he graduated, he worked as a professor of theory and harmony at the new Moscow Conservatory from 1866 to 1878.

In 1877, Nadezhda von Meck offered him financial support of approximately 6000 roubles a year. This patronage allowed him to give up teaching and concentrate on composing and travelling. His music was well received outside Russia and he conducted many of his major works in Europe. He also visited America and Great Britain in the early 1890s. He died in Russia of cholera in 1893. Compositions include ballets (*Swan Lake* and *The Nutcracker Suite*), a number of operas, chamber music, concertos, overtures and six symphonies as well choral music, piano pieces and songs.

TCHAIKOVSKY'S STYLE

Tchaikovsky's moods often fluctuated between elation and depression with long periods spent in introspective gloom and melancholy. He was typically Romantic, choosing the theme of fatal love as the subject matter of many of his compositions. While he had received support and help as a student from 'The Five', he never identified himself with out-and-out nationalism. He was more influenced by western music, admiring in particular the French. He also had a lifelong passion for the music of Mozart.

Features:

(i) His orchestration was imaginative. His interest in colour and timbre saw him constantly seeking new combinations of instruments.
(ii) He included many scale passages in his accompaniments.
(iii) He wrote beautiful descriptive melodies allowing his themes to grow and develop, using sequences and expressive leaps.
(iv) He used Classical structures like sonata form but expanded on them.
(v) There are contrasting textures, keys and tempi in his music.
(vi) He also used unexpected keys.

©Higgins & Higgins

ROMANTIC FORM

Concert Overture

The overture is a piece of music preceding an opera or oratorio usually referring musically to what follows. It evolved into a one-movement orchestral work composed for the concert-hall and usually had a title which gave a pictorial or emotional clue. The **concert overture** was written as a stand alone piece and was usually in **sonata form**. It would also be regarded as **programme music** – music that tells a story. Mendelssohn's *Hebrides Overture* and Tchaikovsky's *1812 Overture* are other examples of concert overtures.

Sonata Form

A sonata form movement falls into three main sections – Exposition, Development and Recapitulation (Recap). The relationship between the keys is the basis of this form.

Section	EXPOSITION		DEVELOPMENT	RECAPITULATION	
Subject	A (I)	B (II)	A/B (I/II)	A (I)	B (II)
Key	Tonic	Dominant	Various	Tonic	Tonic

The **Exposition** is where we hear the themes played for the first time. They are divided into two groups called subjects (**A** and **B**). There can be any number of themes within these two subject groups. All the themes in subject A are in the tonic or home key. All the themes in subject B are in the dominant key in a major-key work, or the relative major in a minor-key work.

The **Development** uses material from the Exposition. Motives, rhythms or fragments of ideas from either subject group can be developed by changing the texture, the key or the arrangement or by using compositional techniques such as dialogue and sequence. Modulations will be to related keys such as the dominant, subdominant, and the related majors or minors.

The **Recapitulation** restates the music of the Exposition. However, the second subject themes, **B**, will now be in the tonic key thus resolving the 'tension'

The movement may begin with an Introduction which uses unrelated material, and end with a Coda which will refer back to the melodies heard. There may also be a Codetta – a little Coda – to end the Exposition.

Romeo and Juliet Fantasy Overture

Shakespeare's Romeo and Juliet has all the elements which make it appealing to composers – particularly in the Romantic period.

Romeo, a Montague, and Juliet, a Capulet, meet, fall in love and marry. They keep it a secret from their feuding families. Friar Lawrence – Romeo's former tutor and their only confidante – gives Juliet a sleeping drug to make her appear dead. He sends a message to Romeo telling him to take her away but Romeo does not receive the details. He finds her 'dead' and commits suicide by taking poison. Juliet awakes and, seeing what has happened, kills herself with his dagger. The families unite at the end realising that their feuding has caused the tragedy.

©Higgins & Higgins

Other composers who have used this Shakespearian story include Berlioz, who wrote a Romeo and Juliet Symphony in 1839 which contains solo and choral voices, Prokofiev, who wrote a ballet on the story in 1935. and Leonard Bernstein (West Side Story – 1957).

Tchaikovsky wrote his first draft in 1870. Balakirev – one of the 'The Five' – suggested corrections. Tchaikovsky continued to alter the piece and the final version with a reworked ending and a changed Friar Lawrence theme was finished in 1880.

Instruments

Violins I and II (Vl)	Piccolo	4 Horns in F (Cor)
Violas (Vla)	2 Flute (Fl)	2 Trumpets in E (Tr)
Cellos (Vc)	2 Clarinets in A (Cl)	2 Tenor Tromboni (Tbni)
Double Basses (Cb)	2 Oboes (Ob)	1 Bass Trombone (Tbn) (B)
	Corno Inglese* (C.i.)	1 Tuba (Tba)
3 Timpani in E, B, F♯ (Timp)	2 Bassoons (Fg)	
Cymbals (Ptti)		
Bass Drum (Gr C)	(*Corno Inglese is usually called the Cor Anglais)	

This was written as a 'Fantasy' Concert Overture. Tchaikovsky allows us to indulge our imagination when listening to it. It is a one movement work in common time and in B minor. There is an Introduction and a Coda and it is in a modified sonata form.

There are three main themes in this work. Friar Lawrence, Strife and Love. Each has their own specific features.

Friar Lawrence is the peace keeper. He is the mediator and represents the voice of reason and his theme is calm, rising and up-lifting. Through the overture, you will hear how, by altering the instrumentation, pitch and accompaniment, this theme becomes more insistent, agitated and demanding.

The Strife Theme depicts the conflict between the two families. It is a strong and forceful theme which changes very little throughout the overture – showing the immovable presence of the feuding families right up to the end.

The Love Theme is a long expansive melody full of emotion. Tchaikovsky alters this the most, extending it and changing the orchestration. It shows how the love between Romeo and Juliet grows and matures against all the odds, even after death.

Section	Bar	Key	Track
Introduction	1	F♯ min – F min – E min – B min	27–30
Exposition	112	B min – D♭ maj	31
Development	273	F♯ min – G min – B min	32
Recapitulation	353	B min – D maj – B min – C min – C♯ min – B min	33
Coda	485	B maj	34–36

©Higgins & Higgins

INTRODUCTION

It is not usual to have one of the important themes heard in the Introduction but Tchaikovsky has chosen to do that in this overture.

Section	Key	Bar	Track
Friar Lawrence (FL)	F♯ min	1	27
Transition	F♯ min – F min	11	28
Friar Lawrence (FL)	F min – E min	38	29
Link + Friar Lawrence	E min – B min	78	30

Friar Lawrence Theme (FL)   Bars 1 – 11   F♯ Min

TRACK
27

(Andante non tanto quasi Moderato – steady or walking pace not so much like moderate)

Bar 1   Ten and a half bars on first clarinet accompanied by second clarinet and bassoons

- homophonic texture
- low register
- hymn-like quality
- Imperfect cadence at bars 9 – 10

Transition   Bars 11 – 37   F♯ Min – F Min

TRACK
28

Bar 11   Ten bars on strings and horns.

- sustained chords; beginning on low strings; horn added
- enharmonic change – C♯ final note in bar 20 which becomes D♭ in the next bar
- key change down a semitone from F♯ minor to F minor

Bar 21   Seventeen bar link in F minor

- descending four-note idea in 3rds played by the cellos
- D♭ pedal on the double basses and violas
- repeated dialogue between flute and harp from bar 26

©Higgins & Higgins

- aug 4th in bars 26 – 27 on flute
- aug 2nd on flute in bars 31 and 35
- rising series of F minor chords in different positions on harp spread arpeggio-like
- sustained chordal accompaniment on other instruments

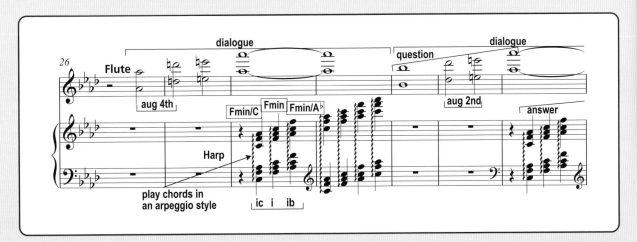

Friar Lawrence and Transition   Bars 38 – 77   F Min – E Min

(compare and contrast with bars 1 – 11)

Bar 38   Three-bar intro followed by FL Theme in F minor on first flute and first oboe accompanied by second flute, clarinets and corno inglese with new idea on strings.

- contrapuntal texture
- descending three-note idea on strings
- pizzicato strings
- high pitch
- scale movement on strings from bar 44
- Imperfect cadence at bars 49 – 50

(compare and contrast with bar 21)

Bar 51   Transition. Repeat of bar 11 music but in F minor and modulating to E minor.

(compare with bar 21)

Bar 61   Seventeen bars repeat of bar 21 material in E minor.

- violas, bassoons and oboes (an 8ve higher); descending four-note idea in 3rds
- pedal C on cellos and double basses
- dialogue is between violins and harp with augmented intervals in same places
- rising harp chords are now in E minor
- entry of the timpani in bar 76 increases the tension

Link and varied Friar Lawrence   Bars 78 – 111 E Min – B Min

(poco a poco string. accel (stringendo accelerando) – little by little increase the speed)

Bar 78   Eight-bar link.

- timpani roll, suspensions on strings and increasing dynamics

©Higgins & Higgins

Bar 86   Eleven bars on wind, accompanied by remaining instruments.

- a.2 means both instruments play same line
- wind instruments play a version of FL Theme in unison or 8ves
- piccolo enters in bar 90
- Allegro – lively at bar 90
- loud dynamic, *marc* – meaning play it out
- tremolo strings
- timpani roll
- two-bar motif from FL Theme on wind with horns and viola imitating at the 4th a bar later (sounds like dialogue)
- whole orchestra stops on an F♯ note – the dominant of B minor – in bar 96

Bar 96   Molto meno mosso – much less movement

- soft dynamic
- B minor chord, 1st inversion heard in dialogue between wind and string (bar 105)
- quickening tempo and increasing dynamics

EXPOSITION

The Exposition has two contrasting subject groups. The first subject has one theme with a lot of linking ideas while the second subject group has two themes.

Section	Key	Bar	Track
Strife (1st subject)	B min	112	37
Transition	B min – D min	115	38
Altered Strife in Canon and Transition	D min – G min – B min	126	39
Strife and Transition	B min	151	40
Love Theme (part 1) (2nd subject)	D♭ maj	184	41
Love Theme (part 2) (2nd subject)	D♭ maj	193	42
Love Theme (part 1) (2nd subject)	D♭ maj	213	43
Codetta	D♭ maj	243	44

First Subject Strife Theme
(Allegro Giusto – lively and strict)   **Bars 112 – 115   B Min**

While the Strife theme is less than four bars long, there are a number of motives that are part of the Strife mood.

Bar 112   Three and a half bars on flutes and first violin in 8ves accompanied by remaining wind, four horns, timpani and remaining strings.

- homophonic texture
- repetition
- syncopated rhythm with quaver rest on 3rd beat
- dotted rhythm

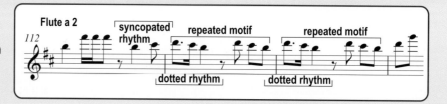

©Higgins & Higgins

Transition   **Bars 115 – 126**   **B Min – D Min**

Bar 115   Four bars of semiquaver scale passages on strings followed by four bars of separate motives.

- descending chromatic scales on low strings
- two-bar sequence built on repeated semitone motif (bar 118)
- Strife idea played twice at bar 120
- four bars of dialogue between the first violin and piccolo, flutes and clarinets
- off-beat rising three-note motif of two semiquavers and a quaver (bar 122) which is a common Folk rhythm
- repeated off-beat crotchet accompaniment on strings at bars 122 – 124
- repeated off-beat crotchet accompaniment on oboes and horns (bars 123 – 125)

Altered First Subject Strife in Canon Bar 126 – 150
                                      D Min – G Min – B Min

Bar 126   Nine bars of altered version of Strife played imitatively by cello and double bass answered by piccolo, flutes and oboes. Accompanied by violin scales.

- polyphonic texture
- D minor bar 126
- G minor bar 130
- imitation at 8ve and double 8ve and at a minim distance

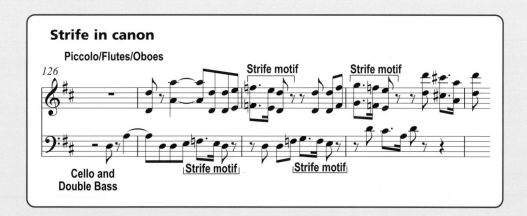

Bar 135   Transition. Eight bars of dialogue between the string and wind.

- repeated three-note motif (two semiquavers and a quaver)
- off-beat crotchet accompaniment
- rushing scales in bar 143 on the strings
- irregular off-beat repeated block chords (stabbing) of B minor in 2nd inversion on remaining instruments from bar 143

©Higgins & Higgins

First Subject Strife Theme and Transition
Bars 151 – 183   B Min – D Maj

TRACK 40

(compare and contrast with bars 112 – 115)

Bar 151   Thirteen bars of Strife on fuller orchestra.

- louder dynamic – *ff*
- trumpet joins the flutes and first violin playing theme
- timpani more involved
- trombones, tuba and bass drum added and cymbals play on 3rd beat when other instruments are silent

Bar 154   Scale passage followed by two-bar sequence and two bars of Strife as before.

- rising scales are played by first flute, first clarinet, violins and viola
- descending chromatic scales on bassoons, cello and double bass
- repeated strings
- two-bar Strife has fuller orchestra

Bar 164   Twenty-bar Transition.

- off-beat three-note motif heard in dialogue and in sequences on wind instruments
- bassoon melody
- repeated A on bottom strings becoming a pedal (dominant preparation)
- 8ve 'A's on cello
- horn chords alternate with off-beat motif on cello and double bass

Second Subject   Love Theme (part 1)
Bars 184 – 192   D♭ Maj

TRACK 41

It is expected that the second subject material should be presented in the relative major key in the exposition. Tchaikovsky prepares for this by having an A in the bass – which is the dominant of the relative major D. However, at the last minute, he slips down a semitone and presents the theme in D♭ major.

Bar 184   Nine-bar melody on corno inglese and viola accompanied by bassoon, horns, double bass and cello.

- homophonic texture
- syncopated accompaniment on horns
- wide leaps
- pizzicato low strings
- *con sordini* (mutes) on viola
- rising harp arpeggio at end of theme

Love Theme *(as written)*

©Higgins & Higgins

Love Theme *(at concert pitch)*

Second Subject Love Theme (part 2)
Bars 193 – 200 and 201 – 212   D♭ **Maj**

Bar 193   Eight bars (2x2 + 2x2) with upbeat on first violin accompanied by remaining strings.

- homophonic texture
- strings are divided and muted
- wide leaps
- repeated D♭ chord on viola (like a pedal)

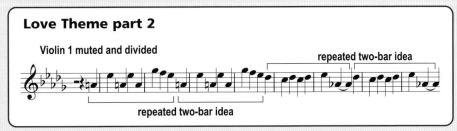

Bar 201   Eight bars repeated and extended with added cello, double bass and bassoon.

- motif is developed sequentially
- bassoon and double bass double each other playing harmonic support
- harp in bar 211
- rising scale on flutes and oboes leading to repeat of Love Theme (part 1)

Second Subject Love Theme (part 1)
Bars 213 – 243   D♭ **Maj**

(compare and contrast with bars 184 – 192)

Bar 213   Nine-bar melody extended sequentially on flutes and oboes accompanied by wind, horns and strings.

- violin and viola broken chord figure
- swaying horn figure
- pizzicato cello and double bass
- four-bar motif in bar 221 repeated up a 3rd in bar 225 and again in bar 229 but altered
- no percussion
- dominant pedal (A♭) on the bassoon and low strings

Bar 235   Love Theme repeated.

- clarinets join flutes and oboes
- bass trombone joins harmonic support
- Perfect cadence at bars 142 – 143

©Higgins & Higgins

| Codetta | Bars 243 – 272 | D♭ Maj |

TRACK 44

Bar 243 Seventeen bars.

- descending block chords on harp
- D♭ tonic pedal for nine bars on cello and double bass
- dialogue between first bassoon and top strings (bars 245 – 248)
- dialogue between corno inglese and bassoon and cello from bar 250
- tonic pedal on first violin from bar 250

Bar 260 Thirteen bars.

- sustained wind over descending harp chords
- pizzicato cello and double bass notes
- soft dynamic – *pp*
- final F♮ on viola

EXERCISE

1. What is syncopation? Name THREE places in this overture where Tchaikovsky uses it.

2. Outline THREE ways Tchaikovsky achieves tension in this overture.

3. Explain the following terms:
   (a) con sordini
   (b) a.2
   (c) div
   (d) tremolo

DEVELOPMENT

The Development uses two themes – the Strife Theme and the Friar Lawrence Theme. These represent the feuding families and the mediator. As the section progresses, you will hear their 'discussions' becoming more and more heated as the tension builds up to a climactic Recapitulation. The FL Theme has moved from the lighter wind to the heavier brass – more serious – and each repeat is played up a semitone showing frustration creeping in.

Section	Key	Bar	Track
Intro and FL + Strife	B min – F♯ min	273	45
FL + Strife second time	G min	302	46
Fl + Strife third time	B min	335	47

| FL Theme and Strife | Bars 273 – 301 | B Min – F♯ Min |

TRACK 45

Bar 273 Seven-bar build-up.

- absence of a key signature
- dialogue between strings and wind
- three-note Strife rhythm (two semiquavers and a quaver)
- semiquaver scales based around C♯ major (dominant of F♯ minor)

©Higgins & Higgins

Bar 280 Five bars of FL Theme theme in F♯ minor on horn with Strife idea on second violin accompanied by remaining strings and bassoon.

- polyphonic texture
- pizzicato tonic on the cello and double bass and bassoon tonic pedal
- sequences
- staccato

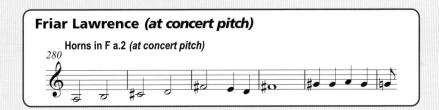

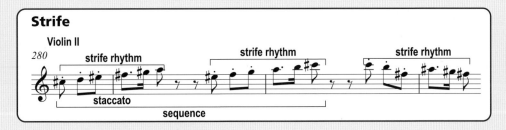

Bar 285 Eight bars of dialogue between brass and wind over a syncopated string.

- semitone motif idea on trumpet and trombones answered by flutes, oboes and clarinets
- regular repeated off-beat crotchet accompaniment of (B♭) played by the two violins

Bar 293 Nine bars.

- FL Theme first on horns and then on first flute and clarinet
- off-beat rhythm continued on strings
- three-note Strife rhythm
- scales based on D (dominant of G minor)

| FL Theme and Strife | Bars 302 – 334 | G Min |

(compare and contrast with bars 280 – 297)

Bar 302 Repeat of the FL Theme and Strife arrangement up a semitone to G minor.

Bar 320 Fifteen bars of dialogue and overlapping ideas.

- three-note semiquaver and quaver rhythm across the orchestra
- sequences in bars 326 – 330
- strong rhythmic two-bar idea in bars 331 – 332 and as a sequence in bars 333 – 334
- crescendo

©Higgins & Higgins

| FL Theme and Strife | Bars 335 – 352 | B Min | |

(compare and contrast with bars 280 – 297)

Bar 335 Eight bars of (4+4) FL Theme on trumpets with orchestra accompanying.

- three-note Strife rhythm; off-beat
- FL Theme on the beat
- cello, double bass, tuba and bassoon have a descending line
- repeats music of bars 335 – 338 with raised 3rd, 4th and 6th to give a major sound with a hint of F♯ minor (the dominant key)

Bar 343 Eight-bar scale and stabbing chords as in bars 143 – 150 in Exposition.

RECAPITULATION

The Recap omits the first few statements of the main themes. The story has moved on and there is a lot of tension. The Recap begins thirty nine bars into the Exposition – with the same eight-bar lead in (as heard above at the end of the Development). We expect to hear both subjects in the tonic key. However, Tchaikovsky chooses to use the relative major this time for the second subject material – it had not been used in the Exposition.

Section	Key	Bar	Track
Strife (1st subject)	B min	353	48
Love Theme (part 2) (2nd subject)	D maj	368	49
Love Theme (part 1) (2nd subject)	D maj	389	50
Altered Love Theme (2nd subject)	D maj	419	51
Strife theme and FL (1st subject)	B min – C min – C♯ min	441	52
Transition (final conflict)	C♯ min – B min	462	53

| First Subject Strife Theme | Bars 353 – 367 | B Min | |

(compare and contrast with bars 151 – 161)

Bar 353 A repeat of the Strife Theme from bar 151.

- extra bar of Strife rhythm in bars 361 – 363
- different transition to D major and the Love Theme (part 2)
- Perfect cadence at bars 366 – 367
- F♯ timpani must re-tune to A

| Second Subject Love Theme (part 2) | Bar 368 – 388 D Maj | |

(compare and contrast with bars 193 – 200)

Bar 368 Eight bars (2x2 + 2x2) with upbeat on first oboe, accompanied by second oboe, clarinet, horns and a new violin motif.

- restless motif repeated successively on second and then first violin
- D chord in the horns

©Higgins & Higgins

(compare and contrast with bars 201 – 212)

Bar 376 Eight bars (extended) with up-beat; remaining wind and cello added to accompaniment.

- tonic pedal on bassoons and cello from bar 380
- sequences
- scale of E♭ in triplets on the strings over a B♭ in double bass in bars 387 – 388

> **Second Subject Love Theme (part 1) Bar 389 – 419 D Maj**

(compare and contrast with bars 213 – 243)

Bar 389 Thirty bars, repeating the music from bar 213 with changed orchestration.

- dynamic – *f*
- theme in 8ves on violins, viola and cello with piccolo doubling the first violin
- repeated quaver triplet accompaniment on wind
- swaying horn idea
- bass line provided by double bass, tuba and bassoon
- dominant pedal A on bassoon, tuba and double bass (bar 396)
- timpani enter in bar 405
- full brass section join with accompaniment (bar 410)
- flute, clarinets and bassoons join playing theme and the bass drum enters (bar 411)
- 'A' timpani must re-tune to F♯

> **Altered Second Subject Love Theme (part 1) in imitation**
> **Bars 419 – 440   D Maj**

Bar 419 Ten bars (5+5) on cello and bassoon answered by flutes and oboe.

- cello and bassoon play four bars of Love Theme in 8ves
- flutes and oboe imitate a bar later with a wider leap and altered ending
- clarinet and cor inglese echo bar 422
- strings have a distinctive repeated note semiquaver accompaniment
- double bass play pizzicato
- violin has a rising triplet quaver scale in bar 423
- At bar 429, the flutes, oboes and clarinets answer the horns and the strings provide a strong triplet quaver accompaniment followed by two-bar broken scale

Bar 436 Five bars of Love Theme first on the strings and echoed by wind.

> **First Subject Strife and Friar Lawrence**
> **Bars 441 – 461   B Min – C Min – C♯ Min**

Bar 441 Five-bar link using Strife rhythm.

(compare and contrast with bars 151 – 154)

Bar 446 Four-bar Strife Theme played by piccolo; first flute, trumpet and violin accompanied by remaining instruments without cymbals.

©Higgins & Higgins

Bar 450   Four bars of FL Theme in C minor played by first oboe, horn and trumpet, accompanied by remaining brass, wind and string.

- busy semiquaver accompaniment

Bar 454   A repeat of bar 446 up a semitone in C minor.

Bar 458   A repeat of bar 450 up a semitone in C♯ minor.

Transition	Bars 462 – 484	C♯ Min – B Min

TRACK
53

Bar 462   Five bars (2+2+1) using Strife rhythm.

- three-note Strife rhythm; off-beat
- sequences

Bar 467   Six bars full orchestra.

- falling two-note idea on piccolo, flute, clarinets and tremolo strings
- orchestra play off-beat rhythm
- trombone, tuba, bassoon and double bass semibreve G♯ (bar 471)

Bar 473   Eight bars (4+4) on full orchestra.

- horns, trumpet and trombone punctuate the bars playing on the 3rd beat in bars 473 and 474 followed by tremolo strings.

Bar 477   Repeat of the idea from bar 473 at a lower pitch.

- minim played by clarinet, bassoon and trombones
- only low strings and bassoons play (bar 479)

Bar 481   Final four bars on bassoons, cello and double bass with timpani roll announcing the final tragedy. The Exposition comes to an end on an F♯ which is the dominant of B.

CODA

Theme	Key	Bar	Track
Funeral March	B maj	485	34
Link	B maj	494	35
Love Motif	B maj	510	36

Funeral March	Bars 485 – 494	B Maj

TRACK
34

Bar 485   Nine and a half bar (4+5½) march on timpani and double bass with emotive Love Motif on bassoon and string accompanied by tuba and remaining strings.

- Moderato assai (very moderate)
- pizzicato crotchets on double bass
- repeated triplet rhythm on the timpani
- tonic pedal on the tuba
- Love Motif in unison, heard first on bassoon, violin and cello and then on bassoon, viola and cello; extended

©Higgins & Higgins

| Link | Bars 494 – 509 | B Maj | TRACK 35 |

Bar 494 Fifteen bars on wind and horns.

- chorale arrangement in block movement
- melodic line echoing FL Theme
- mood of reconciliation and hope
- resting on the chord of F♯ (dominant of B) in bar 508
- rising arpeggio chords on the harp (reading enharmonically as F♯ major)

| Love Motif | Bars 510 – 522 | B Maj | TRACK 36 |

Bar 510 Eight bars (2+2+4) on full orchestra.

- two-bar Love Motif starting on 3rd beat on violins and viola
- two-bar ostinato (repeated figure) on double bass and bassoons; played three times
- arpeggio chords on harp
- syncopated accompaniment on wind

Bar 519 Final four bars of off-beats B major chords; full orchestra; refers back to Strife.

EXERCISE

1. **Fill in the missing notes from the following themes in the *Romeo and Juliet Overture*.**

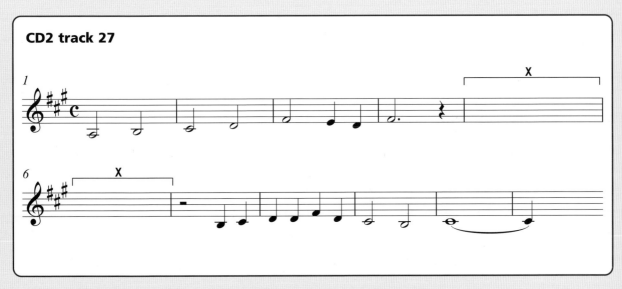

©Higgins & Higgins

CD2 track 41

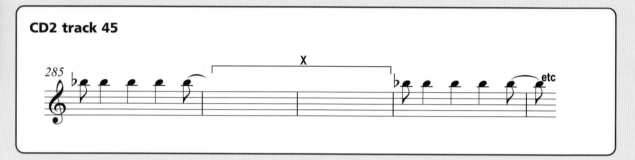

CD2 track 45

2. Give THREE ways the Friar Lawrence Theme is developed in this overture.

3. Which theme changes the most in this overture? Give reasons for your answer.

4. Explain sonata form and show how Tchaikovsky uses it in this overture.

5. Explain the following terms

   (a) muta in F♯
   (b) dolce ma sensible
   (c) stringendo accelerando
   (d) con sord

6. Give THREE features of Romantic music you hear in this work. Outline were these features occur.

7. Name and explain THREE instrumental techniques Tchaikovsky uses in this work. Outline where they are used.

8. List all the transposing instruments Tchaikovsky uses in this work. Remember to state the key of each.

©Higgins & Higgins

Course A – Barry

Contents

THE 20TH CENTURY AND IRELAND

The 20th Century has experienced two world wars, the formation of the United Nations and the European Union, the growth of the modern Olympics, advances in world and space travel and a booming film and recording industry. It has been a time of wide ranging invention and creation. However, we also find poverty and starvation co-existing alongside great economic wealth and power. There have also been awful moments of disaster like Chernobyl but some wonderful events like Live Aid.

Ireland too has had an eventful hundred years. It became a free state and survived thirty years of unrest to finally end the century at peace. The country has suffered depression and emigration but the Celtic Tiger of the nineties ensured a prosperous start to the 21st century.

Art music in the 20th century has seen so many different styles emerge that no one umbrella term can be used to describe the music of the time. Composers often merge a variety of styles.

20th Century Style

Texture: Many traditional melodic, harmonic, rhythmic and tonal rules are replaced and labelling the texture may not be as straightforward as in previous eras. The compositional and instrumental techniques used are important when analysing the texture of a modern piece.

Melody: Melodic lines of some compositions can now be built on a small motif which grows and develops through the piece. This motif may be a series of notes, a rhythm, an interval or any other sound. Many 20th century composers do not use conventional key structures, preferring to use tonal centres. Others write atonally (not in any key) or choose to use a number of keys together (polytonality). As a result, conventional harmonic progressions, including cadences, may be absent. Dissonant (clashing) harmonies can result from the combination of notes used.

Instruments: There is a wide range, variety and combination of instruments available. One of the most important developments during this time is in the experimental techniques used to produce the sound on these instruments. Also, the advances in technology enable many sounds to be synthesised (created). This means that it is possible to generate a music sample without using any conventional instruments.

Form: The structure of a work may not always be obvious. Some pieces simply evolve from an idea. The combination of ideas, rhythms and sounds is important and the order in which this is done – the form – may depend on the story of the composition.

Features: Time signatures and tempi can change frequently in a 20th century piece. The compositional and instrumental techniques used are important in its construction. Composers often include detailed comments on the score to help the performer understand what they want. There is a wide range of compositional styles which make it difficult to generalise, as some composers experiment greatly while others revert back to older periods for inspiration.

Contemporaries include: Arnold Schoenberg (1874 – 1951 Austria), Igor Stravinsky (1882 – 1971 Russia), Pierre Schaeffer (1910 – 1995 France), Witold Lutoslawski (1913 – 1994 Poland), Karlheinz Stockhausen (1928 – 2007 Germany), Steve Reich (1936 – USA), Raymond Deane (1953 – Ireland) and Christopher Norton (1953 – New Zealand).

©Higgins & Higgins

BARRY'S LIFE

Gerald Barry was born in Clare in 1952. He studied in UCD and later in Germany with Stockhausen. As a fulltime composer, Barry has received a number of important commissions from different quarters. These include *Chevaux-de-frise* for the BBC which was first performed at the Proms in 1988 and the *Triumph of Beauty and Deceit* which was written for Channel 4 television in 1995. Other works include the opera *The Intelligence Park* which was first performed in 1990.

Barry's music is widely performed in Europe and America and he travels extensively to attend these concerts. Contemporary music has this advantage over other periods: the composer's opinion can be sought and given before any performance. Barry has been a member of Aosdána, the state sponsored academy for creative artists, since 1985.

BARRY'S STYLE

Barry's music is complex and often difficult to perform. He likes widely contrasting sections and achieves this by using different textures, dynamics, tempi and registers. He likes to write multi-sectioned works.

Features:
(i)   Fusion – the use of existing material, such as traditional airs, with his own
(ii) Doubling at less common intervals, such as a 2nd
(iii) Canon at a less common distance, such as a crotchet or a quaver
(iv) Importance of rests in his music
(v)   His melodies can be played on all instruments. Like Bach, his interest is in the melodic line rather than the instrumental timbre.

20th CENTURY FORM

COMPOSITIONAL TECHNIQUES

Canon

This is the strictest form of contrapuntal imitation. The voices repeat a melody at a specific time and pitch interval. They overlap and imitate note for note. Occasionally, the imitating voice may alter an opening interval to suit the harmony.

Retrograde

A line of music played in reverse so that it is the same forward as backwards. There are a few ways this can happen. The following examples illustrate this technique.

Example 1

In this example, an instrument plays a four-bar melody. This melody uses the same notes and rhythm if read forward or backward (like a palindrome in language). The first note is a minim C, as is the last note. The second note is a crotchet E, as is the second last note and so on.

©Higgins & Higgins

Example 2

In this example, the retrograde is worked out over two instruments playing simultaneously. The first note of Voice I is the same as the last note of Voice II; the second note of Voice I is the same as the second last note of Voice II and so on. You can also read it the other way – the first note of Voice II is the same as the last note of Voice I and so on.

Example 3

This final example shows how a second phrase can be formed by rewinding the notes forward. Phrase 1 ends at 'X'. This note – C – is the last note of phrase 1 and the first note of phrase 2. The second last note of phrase 1 is the second note of phrase 2 and so on. It is different to example 1 where the one phrase is a retrograde of itself. Here there are two phrases, the second created from the first.

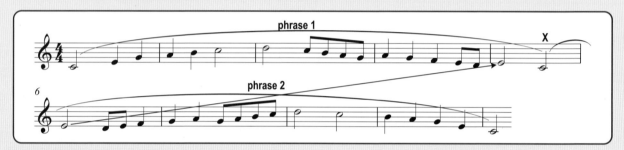

Inversion

This is when a chord, motif or melody is turned upside down.

INSTRUMENTAL TECHNIQUES

Harmonics

A harmonic is an overtone and there are two types – natural and artificial. On a string instrument, the performer lightly touches the string to achieve an interval above. A natural harmonic is on an open string. In this quartet, Barry chooses mainly artificial harmonics. This is achieved on a stopped string by lightly touching it with a second finger. It is indicated with a diamond above the stopped note **(See also: CD1, track 8)**. The sound is wispy and delicate.

C flat is not an open string on the cello and must be made by stopping a string in the correct place.	With the C flat already in place, a second finger then touches the string in the correct place to form the F flat harmonic.
C flat 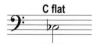	C flat with an F flat harmonic 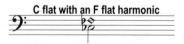

Vibrato

Vibrato is a slight altering of the pitch of a note by controlled vibration of a player's finger on a stopped string. It adds richness to the sound and is usually used, unless a composer indicates that the music is to be performed *senza vibrato* (no vibrato) **(See also: CD1, track 10)**

©Higgins & Higgins

Piano Quartet No. 1

This quartet was commissioned by the ICA (Institute of Contemporary Arts) and was performed for the first time in London in 1992. It uses the Classical combination of instruments for a piano quartet. It is not in a traditional form but there are points to notice about the make up of the eighteen sections. There is a certain symmetry in the layout of the sections. The first and last are created from Irish airs and are heard only once in the work. Some of the sections are heard a number of times – never the same and sometimes completely distorted.

Notice also, that the sections are longer in the first half of the piece with the shortest sections coming at the end. It is also unusual that there is a lot of new music at the end of the piece – it is more usual to have Recap material here. The final seven sections contrast greatly with each other in all aspects, showing Barry's love of extremes.

Section	Bar	Compositional Technique	Track
A	1	Inversion of Irish tune and Canon	54
B^1	53	Melody + accompaniment X three	55
C^1	108	Two melodies + accompaniment X two	56
C^2	140	Two melodies X two	57
B^2	170	Three-part Canon X five	58
C^3	256	Three melodies X four	59
D^1	318	Irish Air, Melody and accompaniment	60
D^2+B^3	335	Two melodies + accompaniment X two	61
E^1	357	Canon and Retrograde	62
C^4	373	Two melodies	63
C^5	403	Three-part Canon X two	64
E^2+D^3	426	Two melodies X two	65
C^6	458	Three-part Canon	66
C^7	469	Two melodies, Inversion and Canon	67
F+C^8	490	Retrograde, Augmentation and Polymetre	68
C^9	512	Three-part Canon	69
G	519	New material created from old	70
H	528-	Irish Air and three-part Canon	71

It is abstract music – it doesn't tell a story. There are only a few unusual instrumental techniques used, leaving the music uncluttered. Barry suggests that the string players play *senza vibrato* (without vibrato) for most of the piece and this allows for clarity of line. The time signatures change constantly along with the tempo. Accidentals apply only to the notes they precede.

Instruments   Violin, Viola, Cello and Piano

©Higgins & Higgins

Section A	Bars 1 – 52	C Maj

TRACK
54

This section is in two parts. The first part is repeated exactly (apart from bar 26). The second part also has a repeat; the music is the same each time.

Bar 1   Twenty six bars of four-part canon at the 8ve with upbeat. Polyphonic texture.

- inversion of *Sí Bheag, Sí Mhór*
- four-part canon at the 8ve and at a crotchet distance
- open string 'E'
- *senza vibrato*
- repeat bar with the indication to play the music softer the second time
- instruction to play light staccato
- tempo of a dotted minim equal to 108
- different dynamics – f (loud) first time and mp (mod soft) second time

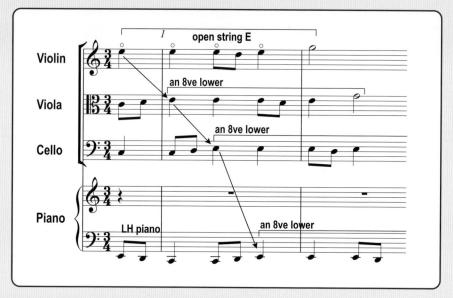

Bar 27   Twenty-six bars of five-part canon at the 8ve.

- piano splits into two voices (right hand and left hand) to give a five-part canon
- canon begins on the 1st beat on left hand; answered by right hand, cello, viola and violin
- range is wide to allow each voice enter an 8ve higher
- dynamic is loud

If you read the score backwards and upside down on the left-hand piano part, starting at bar 52, you will see the Irish air on which this tune is based – **(See also: page 82)**.

Section B¹	Bars 53 – 107	C Maj

TRACK
55

Bar 53   Seventeen-bar rhythmic melody with upbeat on violin accompanied by viola. Homophonic texture. A contrast to the previous section. In C major despite the presence of C♯.

- triadic character of the melody
- *senza vibrato*

©Higgins & Higgins

- slower tempo of a dotted minim equal to 72
- loud dynamic
- indication to play roughly
- open string G
- augmented 8ves and 4ths
- changing time signatures including 5/8 (five quaver beats in bar)
- repeated two-note staccato accompaniment

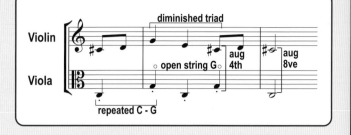

(compare and contrast with bars 53 – 71).

Bar 72 Seventeen bars repeated with added cello.

- cello plays an inverted version of the viola two-note accompaniment
- drone effect

(compare and contrast with bars 53 – 71)

Bar 89 Seventeen-bar melody repeated on all instruments.

- music is repeated without accompaniment
- string instruments play an 8ve apart
- violin is two 8ves higher than at bar 53
- piano is playing hand clusters using the same range as the violin and viola
- dynamic is very, very loud

Section C¹	Bars 108 – 139	A♭ centre

This section uses two melodies and is a contrast to the previous section. The gentle flow is interrupted often, however, by sharp and abrupt time signature changes.

Bar 108 Sixteen bars; strings. No piano. Two melodies and accompaniment. Polyphonic.

- repeated notes
- changing time signatures including 3/16 – three semiquavers in bar
- *senza vibrato*
- repeated sustained soft harmonics on the cello

Bar 124 Sixteen bars repeated with different instruments and a different arrangement. The piano part intertwines both melodies in both hands.

- right hand and left hand play an 8ve apart and double the string parts
- melodies move down an 8ve leaving gaps in violin part as notes not available
- very different to bar 108 in dynamic, speed and style

Section C²	Bars 140 – 169

In this section Barry varies the ideas by widening the distance between the intervals. The section is in two parts and the second part develops the intervals even further.

Bar 140 Fifteen bars of C melodies played on viola and cello only. Polyphonic texture.

- rhythmically and melodically similar to **C¹**
- constantly changing time signatures

©Higgins & Higgins

- intervals get wider, uncertain key centre as a result
- slower tempo
- softer dynamic and *senza vibrato*

Bar 155 Fifteen bars repeated with intervals shifting again.

Section B²	Bars 170 – 255

TRACK 58

This section has five parts to it, each in three-part canon.

Bar 170 Eighteen bars of three-part canon on the strings in the order of violin, viola and cello. Polyphonic texture.

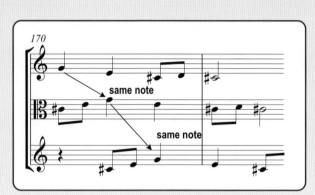

- canon at the unison and at a crotchet distance
- upbeat is missing on the violin
- very loud
- fast, with the instruction to play it searingly (with bite!)

Bar 188 Seventeen bars of three-part canon with upbeat on strings in the order violin, cello and viola. Right-hand piano doubles strings an 8ve lower. Polyphonic texture.

- right hand plays in bass clef
- appears to play block chords

Bar 205 Seventeen bars of three-part canon in the order cello, viola and violin with right-hand and left-hand piano doubling at the 8ve.

Bar 222 Seventeen bars of three-part canon in 5ths at the 8ve on strings and piano in the order violin and viola, cello and right hand with left hand playing in 5ths. Polyphonic texture.

- soft dynamic
- light articulation
- occasional double-stopping on violin

Bar 239 Seventeen-bar repeat from bar 222 onwards with double-stopping on all strings.

- very loud dynamic
- open string double-stops
- drone effec
- canon at the 8ve

©Higgins & Higgins

Section C³   Bars 256 – 317

TRACK 59

This section has four parts, each with a variation of the C material.

Bar 256 Sixteen bars on strings with no piano. Polyphonic texture.

- viola and cello play music from **C²**
- violin doubles the cello at dissonant intervals of the 2nd and 7th
- slow tempo of a crotchet equal to 76
- *senza vibrato*
- open strings
- changing time signatures

Bar 272 Sixteen bars on strings with single piano line. Polyphonic texture.

- faster tempo
- louder dynamic
- double-stops in places
- piano line occasionally doubling the string parts

Bar 288 Fifteen bar on strings and left hand piano. Polyphonic texture.

- tempo has increased
- dynamic is loud
- range is extended with violin playing up an 8ve and left hand playing both melodies doubling the strings at dissonant intervals

Bar 303 Fifteen bars on strings with right-hand and left-hand piano. Polyphonic texture.

- dynamic is very loud
- right hand is added, playing what the left hand played at bar 288
- violin part extended upwards
- left hand doubling this time at the 2nd

Section D¹   Bars 318 – 334   A Min

TRACK 60

This is new music which is based on the Irish tune – Beidh Aonach Amárach.

Bar 318 Seventeen bars on viola and cello. Homophonic texture.

- shortest time signature of the piece is used here, 1/8 – one quaver beat in bar
- first two notes are B – F (aug 4th)
- repeated notes
- similar accompaniment to **B¹**
- instability because of the constantly changing time signatures
- two-note repeated accompaniment (dominant chord E – B)
- fast tempo
- loud dynamic and wild sound

©Higgins & Higgins

EXERCISE

1. **Fill in the missing notes from sections of the Piano Quartet on the staves below.**

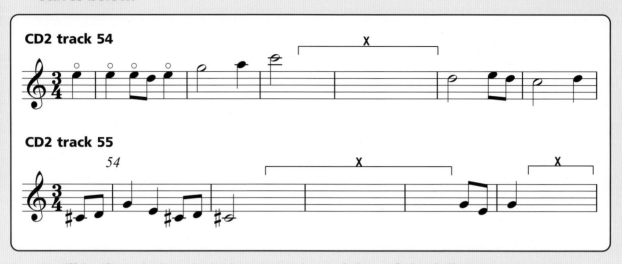

2. **2. Fill in the missing time signatures in each bar of the following excerpt:**

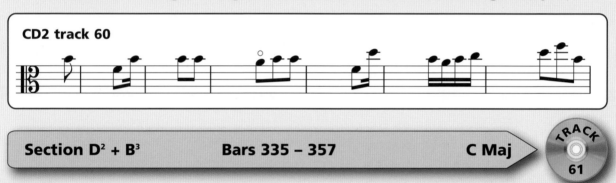

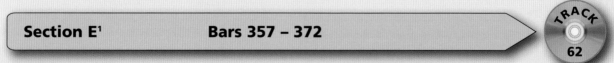

| **Section D² + B³** | **Bars 335 – 357** | **C Maj** | *TRACK 61* |

Bar 335 Nine bars with upbeat, rhythmically altered version of **B** and **D** combined with accompaniments. Polyphonic texture.

- loud dynamic
- viola and cello play the **B³** melody in unison
- violin and right-hand piano play the **D²** melody in unison
- B melody is in diminution (quavers and semiquavers in place of crotchets and quavers)
- left hand combines the two-note accompaniment from **B¹** (C and G) with the two-note accompaniment from **D¹**

Bar 344 Fourteen bars with upbeat.

- repeats music of bar 335 but with different time signatures
- some notes missing
- ends on the middle quaver F in bar 357

| **Section E¹** | **Bars 357 – 372** | *TRACK 62* |

Bar 357 Four-part canon at the 8ve and at a quaver's distance. **E¹** is a retrograde of **D²** Polyphonic texture

- **E¹** is **D²** played in reverse
- last note of **D²** is first note of **E¹**
- second note of **E¹** is second-last note of **D²** and so on

©Higgins & Higgins

- canon at a quaver distance in the order violin, viola, cello and left-hand piano
- loud dynamic and accents
- repeat sign and changing time signatures

Section C⁴   **Bars 373 – 402**

Bar 373 Fifteen bars of both **C** melodies on piano. This is the only section for a solo instrument. Polyphonic texture. Flamboyant, as a tribute to Horowitz.

- 8ves in both hands
- fast tempo
- loud dynamic

Bar 388 Repeated with changed intervals.

Section C⁵   **Bars 403 – 425**

Bar 403 Thirteen bars of one **C** melody on strings in three-part canon at the octave and at a crotchet distance. Polyphonic texture.

- shortened version of the violin melody from **C³** used
- slow tempo
- soft dynamic
- *senza vibrato*

Bar 416 Ten-bar repeat, with notes omitted.

Section E² + D³   **Bars 426 – 457**   **B♭ Min**

Bar 426 Sixteen bars of **E** and **D** combined up a semitone from original A minor to B♭ minor on strings and right-hand piano. Polyphonic texture.

- **E** was a retrograde of **D**
- **D³** is played in unison by cello and right-hand piano

©Higgins & Higgins

- **E²** in unison on violin and viola all rhythmically altered
- fast tempo
- loud and accented dynamic

Bar 442 Sixteen bars repeated with parts now doubling at the 8ve.
- louder dynamic
- violin an 8ve higher
- piano part is an 8ve lower and in the left hand

| Section C⁶ | Bars 458 – 468 | B♭ centre |

TRACK 66

Bar 458 Eleven bars of one **C** melody in three-part canon at the 8ve and at a quaver distance, on strings played only once. Polyphonic texture.
- music of **C⁵** up a semitone
- slower tempo
- soft dynamic
- instrumental technique of *flautando* (play on the fingerboard giving a wispy sound)

| Section C⁷ | Bars 469 – 490 |

TRACK 67

Bar 469 This section sounds like new material even though it uses both **C** melodies. It is a big contrast to the preceding and following sections. Polyphonic texture.
- violin plays an inverted version of **C⁶** melody with viola; canon in unison at a crotchet distance
- cello plays other **C** melody
- faster tempo
- piano doubles string parts with dissonant harmonies added
- very loud dynamic

Bar 483 The tempo gets faster and the added double-stops add intensity to the piece; high pitch and final accelerando.

| Section F + C⁸ | Bars 490 – 511 |

TRACK 68

Bar 490 This section uses the compositional techniques: **augmentation**, **polymetre** and **retrograde**. The **F** material is new and both **C** melodies are heard. Contrasting ideas in rhythm and speed played simultaneously. Polyphonic texture.
- one-bar rest to breathe
- fast tempo
- triplet characteristic of the **F** melody (jig-like)
- loud dynamic
- **F** melody heard on violin playing forward and on right-hand piano playing backwards (reading the violin forward from bar 491 and right-hand piano backwards from bar 511)
- **C** melodies are heard in augmentation (longer notes) on the viola and cello

©Higgins & Higgins

Section C⁹   Bars 512 – 518

This is the shortest section in bars. It is the slowest in tempo.

Bar 512   Seven bars of one **C** melody in three-part canon at the double 8ve and at a crotchet distance. Polyphonic texture.

- wide range to cater for the distance between parts
- little vibrato used
- slow tempo
- bar rest to breathe at the start

Section G   Bars 519 – 527

This sounds like new music but is made from all the previous sections. It is the shortest section in duration.

Bar 519   Nine bars made from notes taken from the beginning and ending of the previous sections. Homophonic texture.

- strong rhythmic punch of all instruments playing together
- loud dynamic
- sudden (*subito*) fast tempo
- accents and the constantly changing time signatures

Here is the violin part with some of the source bars indicated. Notes were taken from the start of each section to create the first half of this section. Similarly, notes were taken from the end of the sections to create the second half of this section.

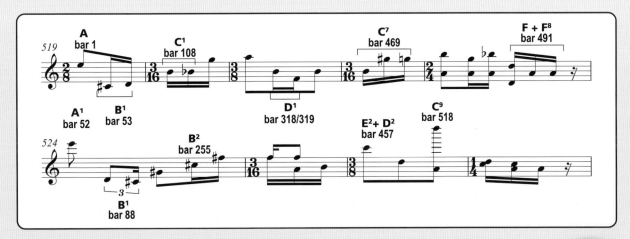

Section H   Bars 528 – 571

*This section is in three parts and is based on the Irish tune – Lord Mayo's Delight – **(See also: page 83)**.*

Bar 528   Fourteen-bar two-part canon at the unison at a crotchet distance on viola and cello. Polyphonic texture.

- instrumental technique *flautando* which gives a light texture
- low register
- comparison with the first part of the Irish tune

©Higgins & Higgins

Bar 542 Sixteen-bar three-part canon at the unison and at a crotchet distance in the order viola, cello and left-hand piano. Polyphonic texture.

- compare with the second part of the Irish tune
- constantly changing time signatures
- soft dynamic
- dotted rhythm
- occasional notes from the violin are played *flautando*

Bar 558 Fourteen-bar three-part canon at the unison at a crotchet distance on strings in the order violin, viola and cello. Polyphonic texture.

- return to the first part of the Irish tune; low register
- notes missing from violin part played by viola
- light texture (*flautando*)
- left-hand piano returns for the last beat; unfinished and open sound of the ending

---

EXERCISE

1. **Insert a time signature at each bar marked by an asterisk (*)**

2. **Write the retrograde of the following short melody:**

3. **Write the inversion of the following melody:**

4. **Identify and explain THREE modern features in this Piano Quartet.**
5. **Identify and explain THREE of Barry's features in this Piano Quartet.**
6. **Explain Retrograde.**
7. **Which of the following tempo marks is the slowest? Explain.**

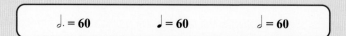

©Higgins & Higgins

Course A – Queen

Contents

1970 – 1980

The Seventies were a time of change and development. The decade saw great advances in electronic inventions such as the home computer and the microwave oven. While the Vietnam war came to an end, the Cold war between East and West still existed and the arms race continued. The hippy culture fell out of style and there was an ever-increasing importance attached to ones image. It was a time of excess, inflation, oil crisis, growth in women's rights and the jumbo jet.

In music, the early 1970s was the era of the group. It was a time of heavy publicity with posters promoting tours. Advertising, merchandising and album sales were of high importance. Concerts included light shows with live props while the fashion was for flashy clothes, platform shoes and long hair.

It was the heyday of the extended guitar solo which featured a lot of improvisation. There were also many diverse music genres to choose from. Disco was born and Rock music split into a number of different styles including Heavy Metal, Glam, Punk and Progressive Rock. After *Sgt Pepper's Lonely Hearts Club Band* by The Beatles, many albums were concept albums.

Seventies' Style

Instruments: Guitars, synthesiser, drums and electronic amplification. Guitar solos, riffs and licks are instrumental techniques used.

Features: Many high-tech studios were built to cater for the demand in albums being recorded using stereo panning, distortion, overdubbing and multitracking. There were many different Rock styles and each had different features. Progressive Rock was seen as an attempt to elevate Rock music on to a higher intellectual plane and to be taken seriously as an art form. It was album-based and featured large-scale compositions. Bands infused their music with Classical sounds. Glam Rock was simple, catchy, silly and fun but what mattered most was the image. There was also a cool arty side to Glam Rock where every aspect from clothes to album cover had to have an elegance and sophistication. Heavy Metal gave out a tougher personality with screaming vocals and high decibel guitar solos. Punk was a reaction to all of this. It was a movement based on anger, teenage angst and a rejection of the virtuoso musician. Its ethos was 'anyone can do it'!

Melody: Rock music tended to have a rebellious side and featured a strong rhythm and repetition. A lot of the music was built around high volume and distortion with the drums and guitars the driving force. The lyrics usually commented on society. The 'Power Ballad' as a Rock Pop form was important as it allowed musicians to use emotion and melancholy to draw the listener in.

Form: Rock songs usually took a strophic form which was made up of a number of verses and a repeated chorus. While each verse used different words, the music was the same, or almost the same. The chorus contrasts harmonically, rhythmically and melodically from the verse. There could be long improvised guitar solo sections between verses or choruses.

Contemporaries include: 1970s Pop musicians include Eric Clapton (1945 –), Elton John (1947.-), David Bowie (1947 –), Bruce Springteen (1949 –), The Rolling Stones (1962 –), Pink Floyd (1964 –), Genesis (1967 –), Fleetwood Mac (1967 –), Led Zeppelin (1968 –), Deep Purple (1968 –), ABBA (1971 – 1982), and The Eagles (1971 –).

QUEEN

Freddie Mercury alias Farok Bulsara (1946 – 1991), Brian May (1947) and Roger Taylor played in a number of different bands in the late 1960s while in college. They came together in 1970 and Queen was formed with the line-up completed in 1971 when John Deacon (1951) joined. They signed with Trident in 1972 (where they linked up with Roy Thomas Baker who was to produce their first nine albums) and EMI in 1973. Freddie received a diploma in Art and Design in 1972, Brian became a physics teacher (obtaining his PhD in Astro–Physics in 2008), Roger obtained his degree in biology in 1972 and John received a degree in electronics also in 1972. They all then concentrated on the band.

All four composed songs for the group and include Roger's *These are The Days of Our Lives* from *Innuendo*, John's *I Want to Break Free* from *The Works*, Brian's *Sweet Lady* from *A Night at the Opera* and Freddie's *Killer Queen* from *Sheer Heart Attack* which received a Novello award. They spent time experimenting with their image and much of their early releases received mixed reviews. However, they had established a strong fan base and their tours in 1974 and 1975 were sold out. John Reid became their manager in 1975, the year *A Night at the Opera* was released and when *Bohemian Rhapsody* was released from this album in November it marked a turning point for the band. It spent nine weeks at number one in the UK and was to become one of the most successful songs of all time. The short film which the band shot to accompany the song included the famous pose of the four heads gazing toward the light, and established a precedent for the Rock video.

The band continued to release hit after hit, touring throughout the world and were part of the *Live Aid* concert in 1985. Freddie recorded even after he became ill and when he died in 1991, the band were able to release an album of new songs called *Made in Heaven*. While Roger and Brian continue with solo careers, occasionally reuniting to perform Queen songs, John has pulled back from public life.

QUEEN'S STYLE

They were four educated, creative and talented people who provided rich harmonic accompaniments to the many songs they wrote. Freddie was the lead vocalist and dynamic front man. He had studied Classical music as a child and played piano. Brian's expertise was in guitar playing and his arrangements and layering of sound along with his individual guitar solos gave the band its distinctive edge. Roger was the drummer and supplied the high falsetto vocals and John was the non-singing bass guitarist. They played other instruments when required and in the 80s, after the invention of MIDI, Brian in particular was able to access all the instrumental sounds needed for their records. They did not use synthesisers during the 70s and recorded in 24-track record studios which enabled them to produce large, almost orchestral, sounds.

Features:

(i) Classical influence in vocals. Freddie's love of opera and all things theatrical are apparent in a lot of their songs.

(ii) Use of classical harmonies with added notes and circle of 5th progressions.

(iii) Experimentation with new recording techniques like panning and multitrack recording.

(iv) Brian's guitar tracks – multitracked to produce large orchestral style arrangements.

(v) Fusion of styles. Queen combined elements from a vast range of musical genres.

©Higgins & Higgins

In the 1970s, the recording practices had changed due to the continued advances in technology. Bands now expected to spend months in studios perfecting and experimenting with tracks. Queen were no different from other bands and were constantly looking for new and different sounds.

BOHEMIAN RHAPSODY

(The following analysis is based on the full score rather than on the piano version as it indicates the harmony in greater detail.)

Taken from their 1975 album *'A Night at the Opera'*, Bohemian Rhapsody was a six-minute song that many felt too long to be a single. However, with the support of Capitol Radio's DJ, Kenny Everett, there was massive demand for it in the UK even before it was released and it spent seventeen weeks in the charts, nine at number one.

The album, produced by Roy Thomas Baker, contains twelve songs all of which were written by band members – *Bohemian Rhapsody* was written by Freddie Mercury. Facts to know about the album are that:

(i)   The songs range in style from folk to opera.
(ii)   It took almost six months to produce.
(iii)   Only members of the band perform on the album – no session players or singers.
(iv)   No synthesiser was used.
(v)   *Bohemian Rhapsody* took three weeks to record and includes over 180 vocal overdubs.

Bohemian Rhapsody has Rock, Pop, Ballad and Classical features. It uses a number of different time signatures and goes through a number of different keys. Although the video shows all the band members singing, a lot of the vocals both solo and harmony – were recorded by Freddie and then bounced to one track. As for the lyrics, Freddie wanted people simply to listen to the song and make up their own mind as to what was meant. There are some unifying elements which help to link up the sections.

Theme	Bar	Key
Introduction	1	B♭ maj – G min
Verse 1	15	B♭ maj – E♭ maj
Verse 2	33	B♭ maj – E♭ maj
Guitar Interlude	47	E♭ maj
Operatic Section	55	A maj – A♭ maj –- E♭ maj
Rock Section	96	E♭ maj
Recap and Coda	123	E♭ maj –- F maj

Instruments   Guitar, Bass Guitar, Drum Kit, Piano and Vocals

©Higgins & Higgins

Introduction   Bars 1-15   Bb Maj / G Min

There is no instrumental introduction

Bar 1   Four bars of *a capella* (unaccompanied singing).

- close harmony which was multitracked
- repeated notes and syncopation
- change of time signature to 5/4 in bar 3 as music follows rhythm of words
- chord progressions which include 7ths
- Bb⁶ (or Gm⁷), C⁷ (major supertonic/ dominant of dominant), F⁷ and Bb.

On the staves below, write out the first four bars of melody in the introduction. Remember, to pick out the correct line. It begins on F.   EXERCISE

Bar 5   Eleven bars of vocal harmony accompanied by piano with cymbals in bars 12/13 and bass guitar in bar 15.

- melody contains repeated notes and syncopation
- piano enters with Gm chord
- 8ves in left hand from bar 5
- piano broken chords
- Eb major broken chord motif in bar 7 (which recurs later)
- countermelody in bar 8 – 12
- chromatic idea in bars 10 – 11 (which recurs later)
- panning in bar 11
- word painting in bar 12 – 13 with flanged cymbals resembling wind
- Perfect cadence in Bb major at bars 14 –15

Verse 1   Bars 15-32   Bb Maj – Eb Maj

While the chord is Bb, the presence of G gives it a minor feel as in the opening bar of the song.

Bar 15   A two-bar instrumental leads to a ballad-like verse 1.

- right hand plays broken chord idea
- left hand plays 1st beat 8ves in the bass and 3rd and 4th beats in the treble
- two-bar accompaniment used through the verse
- bass guitar enters in bar 15 and doubles the left hand

Bar 17   Eighteen bars (4+4+2+6+2), solo voice accompanied by piano and bass guitar. Percussion are added after eight bars.

- range of melody fits within an 8ve
- features many repeated notes
- homophonic texture
- syncopated rhythm
- bass guitar glissando at end of bars 20 and 30

©Higgins & Higgins

- descending chromatic bass line in bars 23, 24 and 27
- cymbal fill in bar 24
- E♭ major in bar 25
- standard drum beat with some added quaver hi-hat and cymbals from bars 25 – 30 with a fill in bar 28

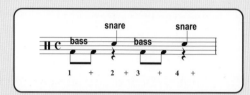

- repeated left hand rhythm of a quaver + two semiquavers in bar 28
- final bars hint at a plagal cadence A♭ minor (**iv**) – E♭ major (**I**) in Bar 30 – 31
- piano plays chromatically, bringing the key back to B♭ major at bars 31 and 32 (a developed version of bar 7)

On the staves below, write out the first eight bars of the melody of verse 1. EXERCISE

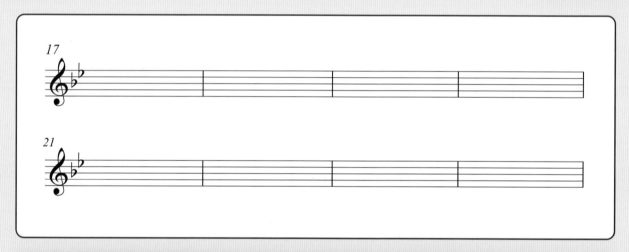

| Verse 2 | Bars 33 – 47 | B♭ Maj – E♭ Maj |

(compare and contrast with bar 15 – 16)
Bar 33   Two-bar piano interlude.

(compare and contrast with bar 17 – 29)
Bar 35   Thirteen bars (4+4+2+3), solo voice with backing vocals accompanied by piano, percussion and bass guitar with electric guitar joining in after eight bars.

- repeats the music of verse 1
- drums accompany from start of verse 2
- word painting in bar 37; bell tree suggesting shivers
- overdubbed guitar from bar 42 moving the music from Ballad to Rock
- extra layers of vocals from bar 43 with harmony and countermelodies added
- descending bass lines as before
- increased rhythm in bar 46 with the drum fill
- bass guitar doubling left hand rhythm (from bar 28)
- Perfect cadence at bars 46 – 47
- backing vocals continue under the guitar interlude for two bars as the two sections overlap

Guitar Interlude   Bar 47 – 55   E♭ Maj

Bar 47   Nine-bar solo guitar lick accompanied by piano, bass guitar, percussion and overdubbed guitars.

- rapid semiquaver scales and repeated three-note rhythm
- use of glissandos in bars 47, 48 and 54
- vibrato in bars 48, 50, 52 and 53
- descending chromatic line in the accompanying overdubbed guitars and in left hand and bass guitar in bar 49 and again in bars 53 and 54
- power chords (where the doubled root and fifth are played) in bar 50
- the left hand rhythm in bar 50 (compare and contrast with bar 28)
- abrupt and enharmonic move from E♭ major to A major using an added D♭ in bar 54 which becomes a C♯ in the next bar

Operatic Section   Bar 55 – 95
                      A Maj – A♭ Maj – E♭ – Maj 4/4 (at 4/8 speed)

There is an abrupt change of key, texture and tempo (where the crotchet now takes the quaver speed).

Bar 55   Two-bar solo piano introduction playing staccato chords on each beat.

Bar 57   Eleven bars (2+2+2+5) of alternating solo voice and vocal harmonies accompanied by piano with percussion in some bars.

- chromatic movement in bars 57 and 58 (see bars 10 and 11)
- *soh – doh* effect of vocal harmony (bar 59)
- word painting (bar 61) as percussion reflects the words
- falsetto vocals in bars 61- 66
- panning in bars 63-67
- unaccompanied antiphonal singing bars 63 and 64
- piano doubles the vocals
- rising harmony in maj 3rds (A♭ – C – E)
- parallel 5ths in bar 65
- 2/4 bar
- bell-like arrangement of the chord of Cm⁷ in bar 66 and 67 which is spread out over 5 voices each entering one after the other and held over into the next section

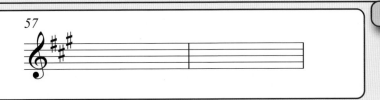

Cm⁷ chord spread out

min 3rd lower

maj 3rd lower

min 3rd lower

EXERCISE

On this stave, write out bars 57 and 58:

57

©Higgins & Higgins

Bar 68 Six bars repeated with added accompaniment and in A♭ major.

- melody of bars 68 and 69 now more closely resembles bars 10 and 11
- six-part chromatic vocals and piano
- percussion and bass guitar in bars 70 – 73
- Bar 74 is a one-bar piano link (see bars 7 and 32)

Queen

On this stave, write out bars 68 and 69:

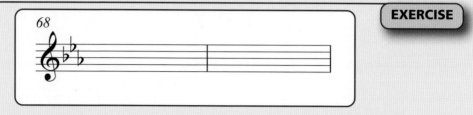

EXERCISE

Bar 75 Repeats bars 68 and 69.

Bar 77 Ten bars of alternating solo and vocal harmony with piano, bass guitar and percussion accompanying.

- *soh – doh* effect
- homophonic texture
- urgent repetition of the music
- F♯⁷ chord arranged similar to bar 66 and 67
- panning in bars 82 – 84

Bar 86 Two bars of rising stabbing block chords on vocals, piano, bass guitar and percussion as intensity continues to increase.

Bar 88 Eight bars of vocal harmony accompanied by piano, bass guitar, percussion and joined by overdubbed guitars as the section moves towards heavy rock in style.

- repeated chords and notes
- sequence in vocal part in bars 92 and 93
- repeated quavers on the left hand
- power chords from bar 92, all on a B♭⁷ chord (**V⁷**)

Bar 95 prepares the music for a change to compound time in the next section by introducing triplets in the accompaniment. These bars contain some distortion.

Rock Section	Bars 96 – 122	E♭ Maj	12/8 – 4/4

Bar 96 Four-bar guitar riff overdubbed with percussion. No piano.

- syncopation and key of E♭ major

Bar 100 Fourteen bars (3+1+3+4+3) of solo voice accompanied by overdubbed guitars, bass guitar and percussion. (Second Song)

- repeated notes, syncopation
- power chords in the accompaniment
- distortion
- repeated B♭ in the bass guitar (a dominant pedal)
- 6/8 bar interrupting the rhythm at bar 103
- six bars of **ii – V** (sometimes adding the 7th to both) between 107 – 112 resolving on to **I** in bar 113 (E♭ major)

©Higgins & Higgins

Bar 113 Ten bars of guitar overdubs with percussion. Piano re-enters in bar 121

- repeats four-bar riff
- four bars of panned rising guitar licks, first overdubbed and then solo
- piano re-enters playing in 8ves for two bars with power chords accompanying
- metre changes back to simple time with 4/4 in bar 122

Recap and Coda	Bars 123 – 138	E♭ Maj – F Maj

Bar 123 Five bars back at original speed.

- vocal harmony similar to bar 43 accompanied by percussion
- overdubbed panned guitars playing rising arpeggios
- falling harmony (**I -Vb – vi**) played by left hand
- music calms down and returns to gentler Ballad style of opening song

Bar 128 Solo voice with piano, bass guitar and percussion and some lead guitar.

- free rhythm (rubato)
- percussion drop out at end of bar 129
- melancholic melody for four bars ending with Perfect cadence in E♭ major in bar 131 – 132
- piano plays simple accompaniment similar to verse 1
- panned lead guitar in bars 134 and 136
- one-bar of solo voice accompanied by piano playing motif similar to bar 32
- ends on an F major chord on piano
- gong-hit

> **EXERCISE**

1. **Make a list of all the bars where there is a descending bass line.**
2. **Make a list of all the recurring ideas and chart the bars where they occur.**
3. **Give THREE Rock features found in this song. Explain each feature.**
4. **Give TWO Ballad features found in this song. Explain each feature.**
5. **Give TWO Classical features found in this song. Explain each feature.**
6. **There are a number of recording techniques in this song. Name at least one from each section.**

Queen

165

Course B – Mozart

Contents

1750 – 1810 CLASSICAL PERIOD

The Classical period dates, roughly, from 1750 to 1810. The word 'classical' is used to suggest a number of things. 'A classic' infers a superior object; referring to something as having classical proportions assumes a perfect and natural balance without extravagance. This period was a time when all composers sought to construct music which had a balance between keys, giving the listener a clear idea of where the music was going. Composers followed set structures and their task was to add interest and surprise without altering the outlines. The music should be straightforward and undemanding to the listener and maintain a certain elegance. We expect flowing melodies, regular phrasing, clear form and simple accompaniments.

By the end of the 18th century, art music was no longer the domain of the nobility but extended to a rising middle class. The demand for public concerts led to a demand for public concert halls. This in turn allowed composers the freedom to compose more from their own desire and less from the requests of a patron.

Classical Style

Texture: Light and clear, mainly homophonic with a melody above a chordal accompaniment

Melody: Elegant and expressive within a formal structure, with clear-cut phrases and well-defined cadences. Long trills were often used to emphasise important cadential points. Melody was mainly in treble instruments – usually the first violin, flute, oboe or clarinet.

Instruments: The orchestra increased in size and range during this time. Generally, it would consist of twelve violins, eight other string instruments, a flute, two oboes, two bassoons and a horn. The clarinet, as the youngest of the woodwind instruments, did not become a regular member of the orchestra until the 19th century. Occasionally, there would be trumpets and some timpani.

The piano, invented at the beginning of the 18th century, soon replaced other keyboard instruments such as the harpsichord. The continuo, which consisted of a keyboard instrument and cello, and which had been present in Baroque music, was no longer used and a conductor now directed the orchestra.

Form: Chamber music, along with the symphony, concerto and sonata gained importance as a result of the shift towards more standard instrumental groups. Sonata form was developed and became the basic structure for first movements of these large-scale works.

Features: One main compositional feature used by piano composers was the **Alberti bass**. This is a repeated figure in the left hand part which is made up of the notes of a chord played in a broken pattern. Other features include use of related keys, dominant and tonic pedals and clear dynamic contrasts.

Contemporaries include: Christoph Gluck (1714 – 1787 Germany), C.P.E Bach (1714 – 1788 Germany), Franz Josef Haydn (1732 – 1809 Austria), J.C. Bach (1735 – 1782 Germany) and Ludwig van Beethoven (1770 – 1827 Germany).

©Higgins & Higgins

MOZART'S LIFE

Wolfgang Amadeus Mozart was born in 1756 in Salzburg, Austria. His father, Leopold, was a composer and violinist while his older sister, Maria Anna, was also a talented musician. Wolfgang could play the harpsichord by the age of four, was composing at five and performing at six. He spent his childhood travelling the length and breadth of Europe performing and composing. He learnt his craft by listening to the music of other composers.

He settled in Vienna, 'the land of the piano', in 1781, where he composed, performed and taught. In 1782 he married Constanze Marie. He died of fever in 1791.

Mozart's works were catalogued by Köchel and appear with a K number to indicate their chronological order. The K488 piano concerto was written in 1786 along with a number of other important compositions including an opera, the *Marriage of Figaro* and the *Prague* symphony. Compositions include 41 symphonies, chamber music (string trios, quartets and quintets), religious music (17 masses and 1 requiem), solo music for the piano and violin (sonatas and fantasias), concertos (27 piano and various others), serenades and operas. Some of Mozart's earlier pieces are arrangements of other composers' music while some are not complete works.

MOZART'S STYLE

Mozart was a skilled composer and pianist and as one of the important composers of the Classical period, his style is intertwined with the Classical style. It was a time of clear form and structure and Mozart seemed to have had an innate sense of symmetry which, combined with his brilliance in a wide range of areas, allows his music to stand apart from most of the composers of the period in its excellence.

Features:

(i)   He uses many themes, linked by brilliant passage-work made up of scales and arpeggios.

(ii)   In the Classical period, music usually modulated to related keys. Mozart would sometimes surprise the listener by introducing an unexpected key change

(iii)   Mozart sought to develop the potential of the clarinet and included it in his orchestras, as well as writing solo pieces for it.

CLASSICAL FORM

Concerto
A concerto is a piece of music, usually in three movements, in which a solo instrument is contrasted or blended with the orchestra. The soloist will have the opportunity to show brilliance, especially in the cadenza.

Cadenza
A cadenza is a solo section usually inserted at the end of the 1st movement of a concerto. This is where the performer can show skill and virtuosity. The cadenza may be improvised and usually ends with a long trill which alerts the orchestra to re-enter.

Ternary Form
Ternary form (**A B A**) is a three-part form where the third part is identical or very similar to the first.

Mozart

©Higgins & Higgins

Sonata Form

A sonata form movement falls into three main sections – Exposition, Development and Recapitulation (Recap). The relationship between the keys is the basis of this form. There may be two Expositions in a sonata form movement of a concerto – one for the soloist and one for the orchestra.

Section ☞	EXPOSITION		DEVELOPMENT	RECAPITULATION	
Subject ☞	A (I)	B (II)	A/B (I/II)	A (I)	B (II)
Key ☞	TONIC	DOMINANT	VARIOUS	TONIC	TONIC

The **Exposition** is where we hear the themes played for the first time. They are divided into two groups called subjects (**A** and **B**). There can be any number of themes within these two subject groups. All the themes in subject **A** are in the tonic or home key. All the themes in subject **B** are in the dominant key in a major-key work, or the relative major in a minor-key work. If there are two Expositions, only one will change key.

The **Development** uses material from the Exposition. Motives, rhythms or fragments of ideas from either subject group can be developed by changing the texture, the key or the arrangement or by using compositional techniques such as dialogue and sequence. Modulations are to related keys such as the dominant, subdominant, and the related majors or minors.

The **Recapitulation** restates the music of the Exposition. However, the second subject themes, **B**, will now be in the tonic key, thus resolving the 'tension'.

The movement may begin with an Introduction which uses unrelated material, and end with a Coda which will refer back to the melodies heard. There may be a Codetta – a little Coda – to end the Exposition.

Sonata-Rondo Form

Sonata-rondo form uses the recurring idea of rondo form within a sonata form plan. Take **ABACADA** as a sample of rondo form. The recurring section is represented by **A**. Combining this with the sonata form chart above, sonata-rondo form could be shown as follows *(note the extra **A** section at the end of both the Exposition and Recapitulation)*

Section ☞	EXPOSITION			DEVELOPMENT	RECAPITULATION		
Subject ☞	A (I)	B (II)	A (I)	C (III)	A (I)	B (II)	A (I)
Key ☞	TONIC	DOMINANT	TONIC	VARIOUS	TONIC	TONIC	TONIC

The **C** section in the Development takes the place of the **A/B** material in sonata form and may be totally new music. The **A** sections should be in the home key. The other sections or Episodes, are normally in related keys.

In the Recapitulation, the **B** section in the tonic key replaces section **D** in the sample rondo form. This then fulfils the tonic/dominant requirement of sonata form.

©Higgins & Higgins

Piano Concerto no 23 – A Major K488

There are THREE movements in this concerto:

MOVEMENT	FORM	TEMPO	KEY	TIME
1st Movement	Sonata Form	Allegro (lively)	A maj	¢
2nd Movement	Ternary Form (**ABA¹**)	Adagio (slowly)	F♯ min	6/8
3rd Movement	Sonata-Rondo Form	Allegro assai (very lively)	A maj	¢

Instruments

Piano and the following orchestra:

Violins I and II (Vl)	1 Flute (Fl)
Violas (Vla)	2 Clarinets in A (Cl)
V'Cellos (Vlc)	2 Bassoons (Fag)
Double Basses (Cb)	2 Horns in A (Cor)

This orchestra is typical of that used during the Classical period. The clarinets are used instead of the oboe while the horns are valveless and have a limited range

FIRST MOVEMENT A MAJ. ALLEGRO (LIVELY)

The 1st movement is in **sonata form** and has two Expositions. Four themes (**A¹**, **A²**, **B¹**, **B²**) are introduced in the Orchestral Exposition, all in the tonic key. The Piano Exposition repeats these but modulates to the dominant key for the second subject themes **B¹** and **B²** and adds a 5th theme, **C**, which is then used for the Development. There is one Recapitulation which includes a cadenza. The movement ends with a Coda.

Section	Bar	Key	Track
Orchestral Exposition	1	A maj	1
Piano Exposition	67	A maj – E maj	2
Development	156	Various	3
Recapitulation	198	A maj	4
Cadenza and Coda	297	A maj	5

ORCHESTRAL EXPOSITION

Theme	Key	Bar	Track
A¹ (I^a)	A maj	1	6
A² (I^b)	A maj	19	7
B¹ (II^a)	A maj	31	8
B² (II^b)	A maj	47	9

©Higgins & Higgins

First Subject   A¹   Bar 1 – 8 and 9 – 18   A Maj   TRACK 6

Bar 1   Eight-bar melody (4 + 4) on first violin. Accompanied by the remaining strings.
- repeated tonic on low strings
- violins play a rising sequence in parallel 3rds
- Imperfect cadence in bar 8.

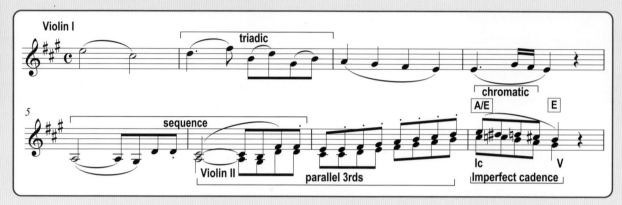

Bar 9   Eight-bar melody repeated but extended by two bars. First four bars on flute (and some clarinet) an 8ve higher with woodwind and horns accompanying.
- horns in A plays a tonic pedal
- Perfect cadence at bars 17 – 18

First Subject (Linking theme)   A²   Bar 19 – 30   A Maj   TRACK 7

Here, A² is a linking theme and not a transition theme – it does not change key. A² links A¹ and B¹. In sonata form, we expect the second subject to be in a new key in the Exposition. However, there is no change of key in the Orchestral Exposition of a concerto as this is kept for the soloist's Exposition.

Bar 19   Twelve-bar melody on violins with upbeat of three repeated quavers.
- repeated notes on low strings and bassoons (zu 2 both play same line)
- rising sequence in bars 19 – 21 and falling sequence in bars 23 – 24
- syncopation (dotted crotchet on 2nd beat) and repeated notes
- Imperfect cadence at bars 29 – 30

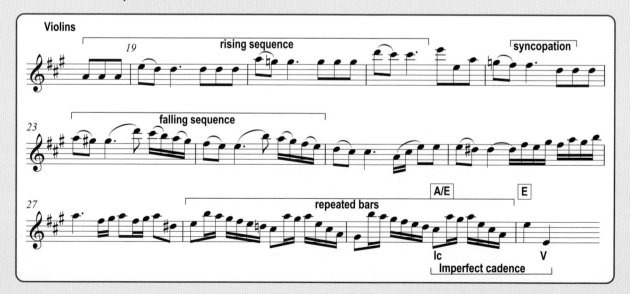

©Higgins & Higgins

Second Subject   B¹   Bars 31 – 38 and 39 – 46   A Maj

Bar 31   Eight-bar melody with upbeat, on first violin accompanied by remaining strings.
- dotted rhythm, repeated notes and chromatic movement
- falling sequence in bars 31 – 34 and bars 35 – 36
- Imperfect cadence at bar 38

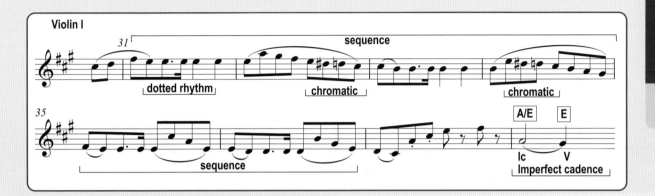

Bar 39   Eight-bar melody repeated on first violin with first bassoon playing an 8ve lower and flute joining in an 8ve higher.
- Perfect cadence at bars 45 – 46

Second Subject   B²   Bars 47 – 62   A Maj

This theme can be split into three parts.

Bar 47   First, a five-bar melody with upbeat, on first violin with second violin joining in.
- syncopation and repeated notes and arpeggio figure in melody
- syncopation and repeated notes in accompaniment

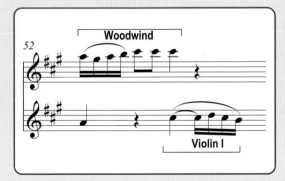

Second, a one-bar dialogue on woodwind and first violin played three times (bars 52 – 54).

- rising chromatic scale at bar 55

Third, the opening syncopated and arpeggio figure returns (bars 56 – 62).

- Perfect cadence in A major at bars 61 – 62

The remaining four bars bring the Orchestral Exposition to an end

©Higgins & Higgins

Mozart

PIANO EXPOSITION

Theme	Key	Bar	Track
A¹ (Iª)	A maj	67	10
A² (Iᵇ)	A maj	83	11
B¹ (IIª)	E maj	99	12
B² (IIᵇ)	E maj	115	13
C (III)	E maj	143	14

174

> **First Subject   A¹   Bars 67 – 74 and 75 – 82   A Maj**

(compare and contrast with bars 1 – 8)

Bar 67   Eight-bar melody (4+4) on piano with string accompaniment.
- left hand broken chord accompaniment in bars 67 and 68
- sequence in bars 71 – 72 is a decorated version of original
- Imperfect cadence in A major in bar 74

(compare and contrast with bars 9 – 16)

Bar 75   Eight bar decorated version of melody on piano with string accompaniment.
- triadic and semiquaver movement of bar 76
- Perfect cadence in A major at bars 81 – 82

> **First Subject (Transition theme) A²   Bars 83 – 98**
> **A Maj to E Maj**

A² is a transition theme here – it changes key.

(compare and contrast with bars 19 – 30)

Bar 83   Sixteen bars. Bars 83 – 86 the same as bars 19 – 22. From bar 87, the piano plays remaining twelve bars with orchestra.
- scale and broken chord passages in sequence on right-hand piano
- broken chord accompaniment on left hand
- descending accompaniment and dominant pedal from bars 93 – 96
- descending B major scale and chord of B (**V** in E major)
- Imperfect cadence

> **Second Subject B¹   Bars 99 – 106 and 107 – 114   E Maj**

(compare and contrast with bars 31 – 38)

Bar 99   Eight-bar melody on piano.
- left hand plays accompanying block harmony
- Imperfect cadence in E major in bar 106

(compare and contrast with bars 39 – 46)

Bar 107   Eight-bar melody repeated on flute, first bassoon and first violin
- right hand plays descending semiquavers scales in broken 8ves
- Perfect cadence in E major in bar 114

©Higgins & Higgins

Second Subject B²	Bars 115 – 136	E Maj

TRACK 13

(compare and contrast it with bars 47 – 62)

Bar 115 The melody is now on the piano with orchestral accompaniment. Extended
- Alberti bass on left hand
- horns in A plays tonic pedal (transposing instrument see G, hear E)
- dialogue between violins and piano in bar 120
- triplet chromatic scale (bar 123), then rapid scales and broken chords
- trill in bar 136 and Perfect cadence at bars 136 – 137

Bar 137 Soloist stops and the orchestra continues with short Codetta using **A²** material. Exposition appears to come to a close.
- violins (bars 141 – 142) play a rising sequence of a descending scale
- music ends abruptly on dominant chord B major

Third Subject C	Bars 143 – 156	E Maj

TRACK 14

Bar 143 A six-bar melody on the strings.
- first violin and viola play in 6ths after a two-beat rest
- strong contrapuntal feel; ♩. ♪ rhythm (**X** in excerpt below)

Bar 149 The piano plays a series of scales flowing between both hands.
- contrapuntal effect between right hand and left hand
- Perfect cadence at bars 155 – 156

DEVELOPMENT

Section	Theme	Key	Bar	Track
Part one	**C** (III)	E min, C maj, A min, D min	156	15
Part two	**C** (III)	C maj, A min, A maj	170	16

Part One	C Material Bars 156 – 70
	E Min – C Maj – A Min – D Min

TRACK 15

We expect the Development to use the related keys of A major – dominant (E major), subdominant (D major), and the three related minors (F♯ minor, C♯ minor, B minor). However, Mozart elects not to do this. There are subtle connections – using A minor instead of A major and E minor in place of E major. The key-sequence makes use of falling 3rds (E to C and C to A).

©Higgins & Higgins

Bar 156 A four-bar phrase (2+2) in E minor. Dialogue between clarinets, bassoons and horns answered by piano and strings.
- two-bar contrapuntal idea (**C** material) on wind and horns
- answered by homophonic piano and strings (repeated semitone motif)
- strings play staccato
- harmonic emphasis is dominant – tonic

Bar 160 Repeats above idea in C major. Flute joins other wind; horns are omitted.

Bar 164 Repeats idea but this time extended in two-bar groups. Key now A minor.
- piano continues with the contrapuntal wind music ending in F major
- strings then take this idea and end in D minor

Part Two C Material Bars 170 – 198	C Maj – A Maj

TRACK 16

Bar 170 The **C** material is again developed.
- first clarinet and flute play a motif from **C** theme in free canon at the 4th
- clarinet leaps a 10th, flute imitates but extends interval to a 12th
- clarinet has four entries (Bars 170, 172, 174 and altered in 176)
- right hand plays scales and broken scales in semiquavers
- left hand plays double 8ves in **V – Vb – I** (or **i**) progressions

Bar 177 After an F major chord, the piece begins a long dominant preparation on E which brings the music back to home key of A major for Recapitulation.
- repeated 'E's on low strings and horns in bars 178 – 181 and 182 – 185
- held 'E's in bars 180 – 181 and 184 – 185 on left hand
- right hand plays scales and broken chords (turns and triplets)
- rising chromatic scale (bar 197)

RECAPITULATION

Theme	Key	Bar	Track
A¹ (Iª) and **A²** (Iᵇ)	A maj	198	17
B¹ (IIª) and **B²** (IIᵇ)	A maj	229	18
C (III)	A maj	261	19

Although there are two Expositions, there is only one Recapitulation. You will notice that Mozart merges the Expositions for this, using elements from both. The second subjects are in the tonic key.

©Higgins & Higgins

First Subjects   A¹ and A² Bars 198 – 205 and 206 – 213

A Maj

TRACK
17

(compare and contrast with bars 1 – 8 and 9 – 16)

Bar 198   Eight-bars (4+4) on first violin with flutes and clarinets joining in
- full orchestra; string section the same as bars 1 – 8
- woodwind double in places merging first two statements of **A¹**

(compare and contrast with bars 75 – 82)

Bar 206   The piano repeats **A¹**. Highly decorated.
- grace notes in bar 206
- scales in parallel 10ths in bars 210 – 211

(compare and contrast with bars 83 – 98)

Bar 214   The **A²** music of bar 83.
- no modulation this time so it has a different ending
- piano plays an ascending scale ending on chord of E major (**V**)

Second Subjects B¹ and B² Bars 229 – 236 and 237 – 244

A Maj

TRACK
18

(compare and contrast with bars 99 – 106)

Bar 229   The **B¹** music of bar 99 is played in A major.

(compare and contrast with bars 107 – 114)

Bar 237   The **B¹** music of bar 107 played in A major
- full complement of woodwind from the start

(compare and contrast with bars 115 – 129

Bar 245   This repeats the **B²** music of bar 115 -129 in A major. It is mostly the same with the accompaniment slightly altered.
- abrupt ending from bars 141 – 142 used at bars 259 – 260

Third Subject C Bars 261 – 284   A Maj

TRACK
19

(this statement of the third subject was not in either Expositions)

Bar 261   Six bars on piano first and then wind. Similar to bar 143 but in A major.
- contrapuntal section
- clarinets and bassoons take melody and piano plays semiquavers

Bar 272   A strong dominant preparation again with a pedal on low strings and horns.
- Alberti bass left hand (E major) under rapid right hand scales
- ends similar to bar 136

Bar 284   Similar to Codetta music at bar 137.

(compare and contrast with bars 143 – 149.)

Bar 290   **C** played on the orchestra. No piano.
- extended a bar
- stops on chord of A major in 2nd inversion, A/E (**Ic**) at bar 297

©Higgins & Higgins

CADENZA AND CODA

This cadenza was written by Mozart. Its purpose is to showcase the soloist's skill. There is a connection to the music heard in the 1st movement.

Cadenza   Bar 297

- rapid scale passages, triplets and chromatic movement
- cadenza comes to an end with a long trill on a chord of E^7 (**V^7**)
- harmony of A/E (**Ic**) from bar 297 resolves to A (**I**) in bar 299

CODA   Bars 299 – 314   A Maj

Bar 299   No piano. This uses the **B^2** material and is similar to the music from bar 55.

Bar 310   Dialogue between flute and first violin and between low strings and horns.
- second violin plays a broken chord pattern

Bar 313   The last five chords are A – E^7 – A – E^7 – A (**I – V^7 – I – V^7 – I**) giving a strong final cadence to this movement.

---

1.   Fill in the missing notes from the following main themes in the 1st 【EXERCISE】
movement.

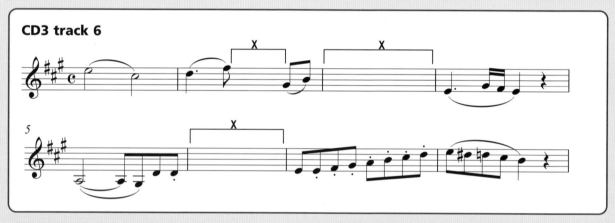

CD3 track 6

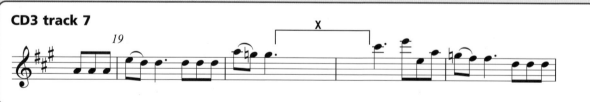

CD3 track 7

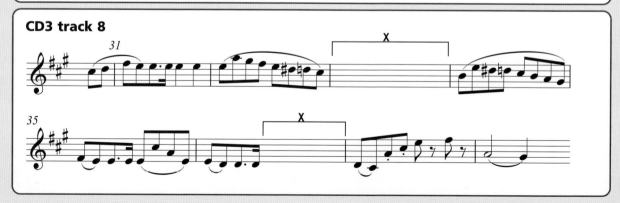

CD3 track 8

©Higgins & Higgins

2. **Compare AND contrast all six statements of the A¹ theme. Make sure you mention instruments playing the melody, instruments playing the accompaniment, type of accompaniment, cadence, key, pitch, dynamic and length in your answer.**

3. **Compare AND contrast all six statements of the B¹ theme using the same pointers as above.**

4. **What is the important difference between each statement of the A² theme?**

5. **Name and describe the compositional techniques Mozart uses in this movement.**

6. **Name and explain the instrumental techniques Mozart uses in this movement**

SECOND MOVEMENT F♯ Min   ADAGIO (SLOW)

The 2nd movement is in **ternary form** with three clear sections and a final coda. Three themes are introduced in Section **A** which begins in F♯ minor (not a key Mozart used very often) and ends in its relative major, A major. Section **B** uses one new idea. Section **A¹** reprises two of the **A** themes but alters the third. All are in F♯ minor.

It is a **siciliana**, a common form in the 18th century, which features compound duple or quadruple time, a swaying rhythm and usually a minor key. In this movement Mozart shows the developing expressive qualities of the piano which was still a relatively new instrument.

Section	Key	Bar	Track
A	F♯ min – A maj	1	20 – 22
B	A maj	35	23
A¹	F♯ min	53	24 – 25
Coda	F♯ min	92	26

SECTION A

Theme	Key	Bar	Track
Theme 1	F♯ min	1	20
Theme 2	F♯ min	12	21
Theme 3	F♯ min – A maj	20	22

©Higgins & Higgins

Theme 1   Bars 1 – 12   F♯ Min

Bar 1   Eleven-and-a-half bar (4+7½) piano solo.

- homophonic texture, chromatic movement, dotted rhythm
- wide leaps, wide range, grace notes and syncopation in melody
- chromatic harmony in bar 9 with chord of G major
- block chord accompaniment on left hand (crotchet/quaver rhythm)
- Imperfect cadence in bar 4 and Perfect cadence at bars 11 – 12

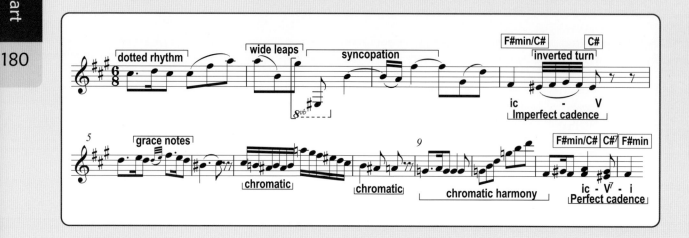

Theme 2   Bars 12 – 20   F♯ Min

Bar 12   Eight-bar melody (2+2+4) on first violin doubled at 8ve by first clarinet (bars 12 and 16) and flute (bar 14). The bassoon imitates (bars 13 and 15) at a bars distance and at the interval of a 7th. It is contrapuntal in texture.

- no piano in this theme
- two-bar idea treated canonically, played as a rising sequence three times
- syncopation in bars 18 and 19
- repeated broken chord accompaniment on second violin
- Perfect cadence at bars 19 – 20

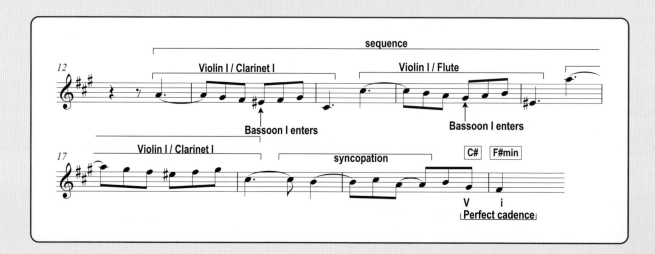

©Higgins & Higgins

| Theme 3 | Bars 20 – 28 | F# Min – A Maj | TRACK 22 |

Bar 20 Eight-bar homophonic melody (2+2+4) on piano.

- a turn, dotted rhythm, staccatos and chromatic movement
- variation with repeated notes in bar 23
- block chord crotchet/quaver accompaniment
- modulation to A major at bar 25 as strings enter
- Imperfect cadence in A major in bar 28

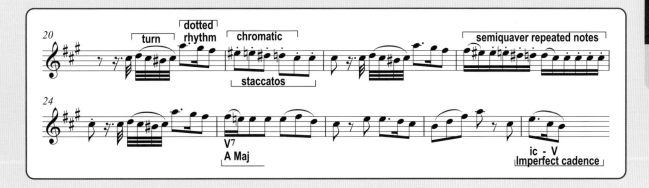

Bar 28 Section **A** comes to an end as A major is established.

- wide leaps, arpeggios and repeated motives
- dominant pedal on horns and then low strings

SECTION B

| Theme 4 | Bars 35 – 52 | A Maj – F# Min | TRACK 23 |

Bar 35 Four-bar melody (2+2) on woodwind.

- flute plays a two-bar melody doubled a 3rd lower on first clarinet
- distinctive accompaniment of triplet arpeggios on second clarinet
- two bars of rising scales on woodwind

Bar 39 Melody repeated on piano, flute and first clarinet.

- right hand plays melody with first clarinet; flute doubles at 8ve
- second clarinet plays in 3rds below and left hand plays arpeggios
- horns plays a dominant pedal
- Perfect cadence in bar 42

©Higgins & Higgins

Bar 43 Eight bars (3+2+3) of dialogue and sequences on orchestra and piano.

- clarinets and bassoons start and piano answers (bars 43 and 44)
- strings and piano start and flute and bassoons answer (bars 46 and 47)
- demisemiquaver scales and triplet descending scales
- ornament (turn) and wide leap on piano
- broken chords on strings (bar 48)
- trill on chord of E major resolving to A major in bar 51 (Perfect cadence)

Bar 51 Two-bar transition from A major to F♯ minor.

SECTION A¹

Theme	Key	Bar	Track
Themes 1 and 2	F♯ min	53	24
Theme 2* and link	F♯ min	68	25

Theme 1	**Bars 53 – 68**	**F♯ Min**

(compare and contrast with bars 1 – 12)

Bar 53 The music of bar 1 is repeated and extended.

- Interrupted cadence (**V – VI**) stopping on D major for a bar
- theme is extended for four bars using familiar material
- Perfect cadence at bars 67 – 68

Theme 2	**Bars 68 – 76**	**F♯ Min**

(compare and contrast with bars 12 – 20)

Bar 68 Repeats the music of bar 12.

Theme 2*	**Bars 76 – 84**	**F♯ Min**

(replaces Theme 3 with a variation of Theme 2)

Bar 76 Four-bar melody on piano and strings.

- right hand plays a semiquaver version of Theme 2
- first violin answers with Theme 2 in quavers a bar later, a 7th lower
- grace note and turn on right hand
- Alberti bass on left hand

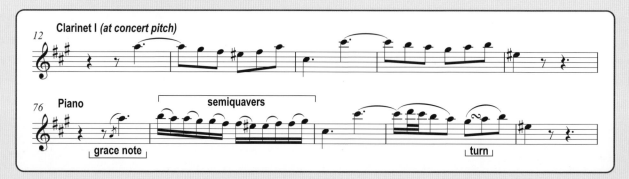

©Higgins & Higgins

Bar 80   Four bars of left hand and first bassoon in dialogue.

- arpeggios and 8ve leaps on piano and first bassoon
- dominant pedal on horns and low strings

Bar 84   Eight-bar link passage (4+4) with wide leaps on piano.

- four-bar harmony of **i – VI – ii°b – ic V** on pizzicato strings
- lower strings play on the beat and violins play on off-beat

Bar 88   Four bars repeated with wind accompaniment.

CODA   Bars 92 – 99   F♯ Min

Bar 92   Eight bars (2+2+2+2). Theme 2 melody on flute with violin broken chord.

- repeated dominant (C♯) semiquavers on right hand
- first clarinet doubles flute an 8ve lower at bar 94
- first bassoon joins an 8ve lower than clarinet at bar 96
- Perfect cadence at bars 97 – 98 and two bars of very soft tonic chords

---

EXERCISE

1. **Fill in the missing notes from the following themes in the 2nd movement.**

1. **Outline the differences between Theme 1 in section A and Theme 1 in section A¹.**
2. **Name and describe the compositional techniques Mozart uses in Theme 2.**

©Higgins & Higgins

4. **Name and explain THREE ornaments used by Mozart in this movement.**
5. **The rhythm in bar 3 of Theme 1 is syncopated. Explain.**
6. **Explain the following accompaniments:**
   (i) Alberti bass
   (ii) Dominant pedal
   (iii) Block chord
   (iv) Broken chord

THIRD MOVEMENT   A MAJ   ALLEGRO ASSAI (VERY LIVELY)

The 3rd movement is in **sonata-rondo** form, combining, sonata form, which has an Exposition, a Development and a Recapitulation, with rondo form which has a main recurring group **A** between a number of other different groups usually referred to as episodes. Subject group **A** has three main themes as well as one important link theme and one transition theme. The second subject group **B** has two themes and one important link theme. There is a third subject group **C** which has three new themes, one of which is extended and developed. The recurring subject group **A** appears only once in its entirety at the beginning. After that, the themes are split up. It is in A major and has two minim beats in the bar.

Mozart uses related keys for each subject – E major (dominant) for the second subject group, with F♯ minor (relative minor of the tonic) and D major (subdominant) used in the Development section. However, he uses the minor version of both the tonic (A minor) and the dominant (E minor) also.

Section	Subject/Episode	Key	Bar	Track
Exposition	A	A maj	1	27
	B	E min – E maj	106	
	A	A maj	202	
Development	C	F♯ min – D maj	230	28
Recapitulation	A	A maj – A min	312	29
	B	A maj – A min	330	
	A	A maj	441	
Coda		D maj – A maj	481	30

EXPOSITION

Theme	Key	Bar	Track
A¹ (Iª)	A maj	1	31
A² (Iᵇ)	A maj	16	32
Link	A maj	32	33
A³ (Iᶜ)	A maj	62	34
Transition	A maj – E maj	77	35
B¹ (IIª)	E min	106	36
Link	E maj	129	37
B² (IIᵇ)	E maj	176	38
A¹ (Iª)	A maj	202	39

©Higgins & Higgins

| First Subject | A¹ | Bar 1 – 8 and 9 – 16 | A Maj |

TRACK 31

Bar 1 Eight-bar melody (4+4) on piano with scales, grace notes and rests.

- 5th and 8ve leaps, Alberti bass accompaniment, homophonic texture
- Perfect cadence at bars 7 – 8.

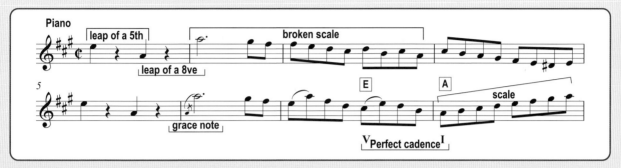

Bar 9 Eight-bar melody repeated and varied on first violin, orchestra accompanies.

- repeated tonic crotchets in accompaniment
- wind and horn play sustained harmony; strings play a broken chord
- Perfect cadence at bars 15 – 16

| First Subject | A² | Bar 16 – 24 and 24 – 32 | A Maj |

TRACK 32

Eight bars split into two clear four-bar sections for strings, wind and horns.

Bar 16 Four-bar phrase on strings.

- begins on 2nd minim beat, violins playing in parallel 3rds
- three-note motif, rising sequence
- remaining strings imitate rhythmically; polyphonic texture
- Imperfect cadence in bar 20

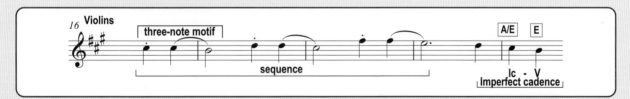

Bar 20 Four-bar answering phrase on clarinets, bassoons and horns.

- polyphonic texture, one-bar four-note falling sequence on second bassoon
- Perfect cadence at bars 23 – 24

Bar 24 Eight-bar melody repeated.

- variation in bassoon part, sequence in bars 29 and 30 (bassoon)
- Perfect cadence at bars 31 – 32

©Higgins & Higgins

| First Subject | Link Passage | Bars 32 – 61 | A Maj |

Bar 32 Eight bars on the orchestra.

- rapid scale passages and repeated notes on strings and bassoons
- syncopation and wide leaps on violins from bar 35

Bar 40 Six-bar idea (2+2+2) on orchestra.

- dialogue between first violins and flute answered by horns
- repeated notes in middle strings

Bar 46 Six bars repeated.

- flute plays melody, dialogue between clarinets and bassoons
- rising scales in parallel 3rds; dominant pedal on horns
- three-note idea on violins which echoes the flute part

Bar 52 Ten bars (3+3+4) on the orchestra.

- three-bar melody with triplets played twice by flutes and first violins
- repeated notes, block accompaniment and **V – I** chords at bars 58 – 61

| First Subject | A³ | Bars 62 – 69 | A Maj |

Bar 62 Eight bars (4+4) on piano.

- parallel 10ths and tonic pedal on left hand (bars 64 – 65)
- higher range and grace notes (bar 66)
- Imperfect cadence in bar 69

Bar 70 Eight-bar melody varied on clarinets and horns; piano takes over at bar 74.

- Perfect cadence at bars 76 – 77

| First Subject | Transition Theme | Bars 77 – 105 | |
| | | | A Maj – E Maj |

Bar 77 Six bars (2+2+2) on piano and strings.

- Alberti bass accompaniment; turns on right hand
- tonic pedal and sustained harmony

Bar 84 Six bars repeated in the dominant key.

Bar 90 Sixteen bars.

- dominant pedal, chromatic movement, sequences and trill
- Perfect cadence at bars 104 – 105

©Higgins & Higgins

TRACK
36

Second Subject   B¹   Bars 106 – 113   E Min

Bar 106   Eight-bar melody (4+4) on flute and first bassoon with orchestra.

- flute and first bassoon play two 8ves apart
- first note G natural places theme in E minor instead of E major
- broken chord accompaniment on second violins
- Imperfect cadence in bar 109 and Perfect cadence at bars 112 – 113

Bar 114   Eight bars repeated and extended on piano with orchestral accompaniment.

- Alberti bass, chromatic decoration and key change to C major (bar 121)
- wide leaps, descending arpeggios, dominant 7th (bars 121 – 124)
- syncopation and Perfect cadence (bars 124 – 125)
- two-bar rising chromatic scale on strings and piano (bars 125 – 126)
- Perfect cadence in E major at bars 128 – 129

TRACK
37

Second Subject   Link Theme   Bars 129 – 151 and 151 –175

This section can be divided into two halves, the second a variation of the first. Both piano and orchestra are in constant motion throughout. There is a strong rhythmic pulse and a number of repeated motives. It begins and ends in E major but travels through a number of keys on the way.

Bar 129   Six bars on piano with simple string accompaniment.

- left hand plays one-bar, rising arpeggio motives in sequence
- right hand plays a strong two-note quaver – minim rhythm

Bar 135   Six bars (2+2+2). Piano accompanied by clarinet, first bassoon and flute.

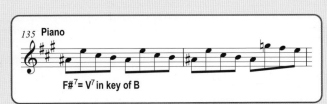

- right hand plays quaver motif
- bar 137 is **V⁷** in E Major (B⁷)
- bar 139 is **V⁷** in A Major (E⁷)

Bar 141   Eleven bars on piano and strings.

- strings and left hand play parallel scales, dotted crotchet – quaver rhythm
- right hand plays a four quaver motif in sequence
- scale passages lead to a trill and Perfect cadence at bars 150 – 151

Bar 151   The music of bars 129 – 151 is repeated with some variations.

- piano parts switch hands, string and wind play on alternate minims
- bars 157 – 162 use same harmony as bars 135 – 140, different motif
- grace notes, triplets and trills
- scales at bars 166 – 175 use even rhythm and broken 8ves on piano
- dominant pedal (horns bar 171), Perfect cadence at bars 174 – 175

©Higgins & Higgins

Second Subject   B²   Bars 176 – 181 and 182 –187   E Maj

Bar 176   Six-bar melody on piano with string and horns accompanying.

- rising idea with repeated notes and Alberti bass accompaniment
- tonic pedal on horns and string pizzicato chords on first beats

Bar 182   Six-bar melody repeated on flute, clarinet and bassoon with piano (Alberti bass), horns and pizzicato strings accompanying.

- polyphonic texture with countermelody on right hand
- tonic pedal on horns, double bass and cello

Bar 187   Transition from E major to A major.

- repeated **V – I** harmony, rising three-note motif on piano
- dominant pedal on flute (Bar 198)

First Subject A¹ and Transition   Bar 202 – 229
A Maj – F♯Min

(compare and contrast with bars 1 – 8)

Bar 202   Eight-bar melody on piano.
- syncopation in bar 207

(compare and contrast with bars 9 – 16)

Bar 210   Eight-bar melody altered and extended using familiar motives.
- dominant pedal (C♯) on horns from bar 222
- Imperfect cadence in F♯ Minor at bar 229

DEVELOPMENT

Theme	Key	Bar	Track
C¹ (IIIᵃ) and **C²** (IIIᵇ)	F♯ min	230	40
C³ (IIIᶜ)	D maj	262	41

Third Subject C¹ and C²   Bars 230 – 246 and 246 – 262
F♯ Min

C¹ and C² are two distinct eight-bar themes. C² is an orchestral reply to the piano C¹ theme and for that reason they are analysed together.

Bar 230   **C¹** – Eight-bar melody on piano with string accompaniment.

- fast flowing melody of falling scales and rising triadic motives
- sustained block chord support and Perfect cadence at bars 237 – 238

©Higgins & Higgins

Bar 238 **C²** – Eight-bar (2+2+4) reply on orchestra. Polyphonic texture.

- two-bar melody on flute and first clarinet answered by second clarinet
- bassoons play harmony; horns have dominant pedal
- Imperfect cadence at bar 244 – 245

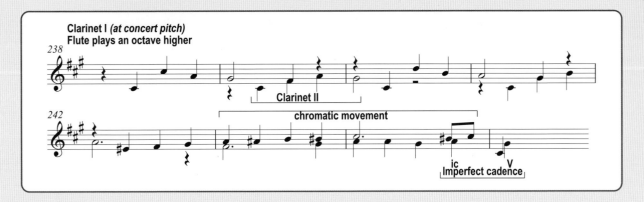

Bar 246 **C¹** melody repeated on piano.

- F♯ major chord in bar 254 as music hints at B minor

Bar 254 **C²** melody repeated on orchestra

- bassoon and clarinet answered by bassoon and flute
- modulation through B minor to D major, dominant pedal (A) on horns

---

Third Subject C³ and Transition
Bars 262 –269 and 270 – 312   D Maj – A Maj

TRACK 41

Bar 262 Eight-bar melody with four bars on clarinets and four bars on flute accompanied by piano and remaining wind.

- elaborate broken chord accompaniment on right hand
- Imperfect cadence in bar 269

©Higgins & Higgins

Bar 270 Melody repeated on piano with string accompaniment.
  • Perfect cadence in D major at bars 276 – 277

Bar 278 Sixteen bars using **C³** material.
  • eight bars on wind with piano accompaniment, dominant pedal on horns
  • eight bars on piano with string accompaniment,
  • Alberti bass, syncopation (bar 282), Perfect cadence at bars 292 – 293

Bar 294 Transition to A Major.
  • sequences on piano, dominant pedal (E) on horns (bars 300 – 303)
  • falling four note sequence from bar 308
  • Perfect cadence in A major at bars 311 – 312

RECAPITULATION

Theme	Key	Bar	Track
A³ (I^c)	A maj and A min	312	42
B¹ (II^a)	A maj and A min	330	43
Link	A maj	363	44
B² (II^b)	A maj	412	45
A¹ (I^a) and **A²** (I^b)	A maj	441	46

First Subject A³ Bars 312 – 319 and 320 – 329
A Maj and A Min

(compare to bars 62 – 69)

Bar 312 Eight-bar melody on piano with added ornament.
Bar 320 A variation of **A³** melody in A minor on flute and first bassoon.
  • four-note descending idea (piano bar 325, strings bar 326, wind bar 327)

Second Subject B¹ Bars 330 – 337 and 338 – 363
A Maj and A Min

(compare to bars 62 – 69)

Bar 330 Eight-bar melody in A major on flute, clarinet with bassoon playing in 8ves; accompanied by strings with a dominant pedal on the horns.

(compare to bars 114 – 129)

Bar 338 Eight-bar melody extended on piano accompanied by strings and wind.
  • Perfect cadence at bars 362 – 363

Second Subject Linking Theme
Bars 363 – 385 and 385 – 411 A Maj

(compare and contrast with bars 129 – 151 and bars 151 – 175)
Bar 363 Similar music but in A major.

©Higgins & Higgins

Second Subject B² Bars 412 – 417 and 418 – 423 A Maj

(compare and contrast with bars 176 – 181)
Bar 412 Same as bar 176 but in A major.

(compare and contrast with bars 182 – 187)
Bar 418 Similar to 182 but in A major and without flute at first.

Bar 423 Linking passage.
- some similarities to music from bar 187 with no modulation

First Subject A¹ and A² Bars 441 – 471 A Maj

(compare and contrast with bars 1 – 16)
Bar 441 A¹ – Similar bar 1 – 16.
- syncopation in bar 446 and a chromatic scale in bar 448

(compare and contrast with bars 16 – 32)
Bar 456 Similar to bar 16 – 32.
- piano joins in bar 464 with a variation

Bar 472 Link passage similar to bar 32 with some variations.

CODA

Second Subject B² Bars 481 – 488 and 489 – 496 D Maj

(compare and contrast with bars 176 – 181)
Bar 481 Theme extended to eight bars on piano with pizzicato string accompaniment and dominant pedal (A) on horns as before.

(compare and contrast with bars 181 – 186)
Bar 489 Theme extended on wind with countermelody on piano, string accompaniment as before.

(compare and contrast with bars 40)
Bar 496 Uses the music from the first subject at bar 40 to end this movement.
- scales in parallel 10ths on piano
- strong dominant – tonic (**V** – **I**) progressions (bar 514)
- final three tonic chords

---

1. **Fill in the missing notes from the following themes in the 3rd movement:**   EXERCISE

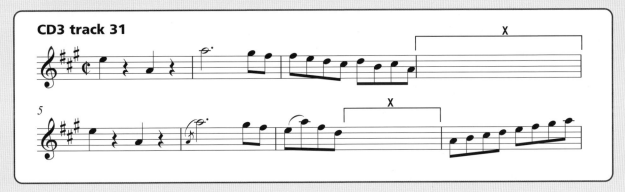

©Higgins & Higgins

CD3 track 38

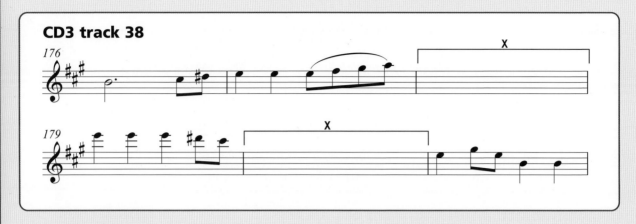

CD3 track 41

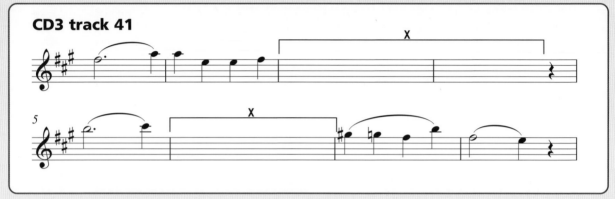

2. Explain the differences between sonata form and sonata-rondo form.

3. Explain the following compositional techniques as Mozart uses them in this movement. Name one place each occurs.
    (i)   Alberti bass
    (ii) Polyphonic texture
    (iii) Variation

4. Compare and contrast each statement of the following themes:
    A¹ (six times), B¹ (four times) and B² (six times).

5. What is the difference between a 'link theme' and a 'transition theme'?

6. Explain 'zu2' and 'pizz'.

©Higgins & Higgins

Course B – Berlioz

Contents

19th CENTURY FRANCE AND THE ROMANTIC PERIOD

For all Germany's importance as the homeland of early Romantic music, Paris, as the largest and culturally richest city in Europe, became the capital of Romanticism. The word 'romantic' can be used to imply many things from love and passion to imagination. In the arts, it usually means that fantasy and expression are more important than the Classical features of balance and symmetry.

The Romantic period was a time when composers sought to create a drama, describe an emotion and paint a scene. The mysteries of nature and the supernatural became the inspiration for many musical works. Composers expanded on traditional Classical patterns and used large concert rooms to accommodate the less intimate performances. Since the French revolution of 1789 had seen the near extinction of the aristocracy, 19th century audiences came from a wide range of social groups.

Romantic Style

Texture: This refers to how melodies and harmonies are arranged. With the emphasis in Romantic music on dramatic expression, textures often changed quite quickly from section to section. Usually homophonic with melody and accompaniment, there could also be polyphonic sections where main themes combined to illustrate a point in the story. As the range and power of the instruments increased, so did the variety in tonal colour.

Melody: Long expansive melodies, which sometimes included unusual modulations, a wide range, dramatic leaps and chromatic moments could be heard on any instrument in the orchestra. Harmonies now used chords with added notes as well as 'new' types of chords and progressions.

Instruments: The 19th century orchestra was big and included a many more instruemnts, especially, brass and percussion, than in the 18th century. Interesting combinations of instruments which created different timbres and tonal colours helped the composer to set the required mood. The piano, which had only been invented at the beginning of the 18th century, had developed into the ideal vehicle of Romantic expression.

Form: Composers continued to use the symphony, concerto and sonata of the Classical period. However, the number of movements was no longer restricted to three, the forms were extended and the rules relaxed to allow for increased expression. The importance of the story being told led to the development of programme music and the symphonic poem. Piano music moved away from abstract pieces to ones portraying particular emotions and the solo song with piano, which became known as the **art song** or **lied**, was developed.

Features: The main features of Romantic music include a wide dynamic range and modulation to non-related keys. The use of a *leitmotiv* – a recurring theme said to represent a particular idea, mood or character – also became common. Large-scale doubling of parts added to the texture of the compositions where necessary.

Contemporaries include: Ludwig van Beethoven (1770 – 1827 Germany), Franz Schubert (1797 – 1828 Austria), Fryderyk Chopin (1810 – 1849 Poland), Franz Liszt (1811 – 1886 Hungary), Richard Wagner (1813 – 1883), César Franck (1822 – 1890 France), Camille Saint Saëns (1835 – 1921 France) and Edvard Hagerup Grieg (1843 – 1907 Norway).

©Higgins & Higgins

BERLIOZ'S LIFE

Hector Berlioz was born near Lyon, France on the 11 December 1803. His father was a doctor and Hector initially studied medicine in Paris before moving, against his fathers wishes, to the Conservatoire to study music. He had learnt flute and guitar as a child but his interest was in composing rather than performing. Having grown up in a literary family, some of his compositions were influenced by the works of William Shakespeare. While in Paris, he met and befriended many of the artistic luminaries of the time including Liszt and Chopin.

He fell deeply in love with Irish actress Harriet Smithson in 1827 when he saw her on stage in productions of *Hamlet* and *Romeo and Juliet*. Heartbroken when she did not respond to his many letters, he composed *Symphonie Fantastique*, which reflected his feelings at the rejection. The five-movement work was completed in 1830 and established Berlioz as a composer and orchestrator of great talent.

After spending some time in Italy, having won the Prix de Rome in 1830, he returned to Paris, met Harriet and they married in 1833. They had one son and were divorced in 1844. He toured extensively outside France and died in Paris in 1869.

Compositions include symphonies and overtures for orchestra, secular and sacred choral music – his requiem is scored for sixteen timpani and four brass bands – and a number of operas.

BERLIOZ'S STYLE

Berlioz was a romantic through and through. His music is filled with images of nature, the macabre, the supernatural, death, redemption and love. Many of his compositions were inspired by his own life experiences. He had a love of poetry and was a lifelong devotee of the works of Shakespeare. He was influenced by both the Classical structures of Beethoven and the spectacular *grand opera* tradition that was centred in Paris. He was also a man of humour and many comic elements can be found in his compositions.

Features:

(i) He was a master of orchestration, writing a book on the subject in 1844. While using large orchestras, Berlioz showed his genius with instrumental timbre by combining and contrasting instruments to achieve effective tonal colours. He wrote poetic melodies, rousing marches and vivid choruses always creating the correct atmosphere.

(ii) He would often combine main themes together.

(iii) He was particular about how his music should be performed and provided clear and precise musical markings.

(iv) His melodies are expressive. Phrase-lengths vary and rhythms are inventive. His arrangements include both unison and contrapuntal textures.

ROMANTIC FORM

Ternary Form
Ternary form (A B A) is a three-part form where the third part is identical or very similar to the first.

Symphony
A symphony is a piece of music for orchestra in three movements – fast, slow, fast. If a 4th movement is added, it is usually placed after the slow movement and it takes the form of a minuet and trio.

©Higgins & Higgins

The 1st movement is in sonata form and the last in sonata or sonata-rondo form. The 2nd movement could be in sonata or variation form. By the end of the Classical period, the symphony had become longer. The courtly minuet was replaced by a livelier scherzo. The composers of the Romantic period continued to expand on the form – Beethoven's symphonies are large-scale works, with his 9th including a choir.

Symphonie Fantastique

Symphonie Fantastique is a symphony in five movements unified by a recurring theme – the *idée fixe*. It is **programme music** with each movement portraying a different stage in the composer's reaction to her rejection of his advances. Berlioz provides clear instructions to the orchestra and conductor as to how he wanted everything to be played. He also distributed the following programme notes to the audience to help their understanding of the work.

Programme Notes *(designed by Berlioz)*

For the first performances of the *Symphonie Fantastique*, Berlioz provided the following programme, indicating that it was indispensable for a complete understanding of the dramatic outline of the work.

Part One: Dreams—Passions

The author imagines that a young musician, afflicted with that moral disease that a well-known writer calls the *vague des passions*, sees for the first time a woman who embodies all the charms of the ideal being he has imagined in his dreams, and he falls desperately in love with her. Through an odd whim, whenever the beloved image appears before the mind's eye of the artist, it is linked with a musical thought whose character, passionate but at the same time noble and shy, he finds similar to the one he attributes to his beloved.

This melodic image and the model it reflects pursue him incessantly like a double *idée fixe*. That is the reason for the constant appearance, in every movement of the symphony, of the melody that begins the first Allegro. The passage from this state of melancholy reverie, interrupted by a few fits of groundless joy, to one of frenzied passion, with its gestures of fury, of jealousy, its return of tenderness, its tears, its religious consolations—this is the subject of the first movement.

Part Two: A Ball

The artist finds himself in the most varied situations – in the midst of *the tumult of a party*, in the peaceful contemplation of the beauties of nature; but everywhere, in town, in the country, the beloved image appears before him and disturbs his peace of mind.

Part Three: A Scene in the Country

Finding himself one evening in the country, he hears in the distance two shepherds piping a *ranz des vaches* in dialogue. This pastoral duet, the scenery, the quiet rustling of the trees gently brushed by the wind, the hopes he has recently found some reason to entertain—all concur in affording his heart an unaccustomed calm, and in giving a more cheerful color to his ideas. He reflects upon his isolation; he hopes that his loneliness will soon be over. But what if she were deceiving him! This mingling of hope and fear, these ideas of happiness disturbed by black presentiments, form the subject of the Adagio. At the end, one of the shepherds again

©Higgins & Higgins

takes up the *ranz des vaches*; the other no longer replies. Distant sound of thunder – loneliness – silence.

Part Four: March to the Scaffold

Convinced that his love is unappreciated, the artist poisons himself with opium. The dose of the narcotic, too weak to kill him, plunges him into a sleep accompanied by the most horrible visions. He dreams that he has killed his beloved, that he is condemned and led to the scaffold, and that he is witnessing *his own execution*. The procession moves forward to the sounds of a march that is now sombre and fierce, now brilliant and solemn, in which the muffled noise of heavy steps gives way without transition to the noisiest clamour. At the end of the march the first four measures of the *idée fixe* reappear, like a last thought of love interrupted by the fatal blow.

Part Five: Dream of a Witches' Sabbath

He sees himself at the Sabbath, in the midst of a frightful troop of ghosts, sorcerers, monsters of every kind, come together for his funeral. Strange noises, groans, bursts of laughter, distant cries which other cries seem to answer. The beloved melody appears again, but it has lost its character of nobility and shyness; it is no more than a dance tune, mean, trivial, and grotesque: it is she, coming to join the Sabbath. A roar of joy at her arrival. She takes part in the devilish orgy. Funeral knell, burlesque parody of the *Dies Irae* [a hymn sung in the funeral rites of the Catholic Church], *Sabbath round-dance*. The sabbath round and the *Dies Irae* are combined.

The movements to be studied from the symphony are:

Movement	Title	Key	Time
Second	Un Bal	A maj	3/8
Fourth	Marche au Supplice	G min	¢

SECOND MOVEMENT –
Valse. Allegro non troppo (lively but not too much)

Instruments

Violins I and II (Vl)
Violas (Vla)
Cellos (Vlc)
Double Basses (Cb)
2 Harps (Arpa)

2 Flutes (Fl) & Piccolo (Picc)
2 Oboes (Ob)
2 Clarinets in A (Cl)
2 Horns in E (Cor)
2 Horns in C (Cor)

The 2nd movement is in **ternary form (ABA[1])** with an Introduction and Coda. It is in A major and has three quaver beats in the bar. The important features of this movement are the waltz theme, the accompaniments and the changing orchestration each time a theme recurs. It is important to note the combination of instruments Berlioz uses throughout the symphony. They are different to what would have been used in Mozart's time with the emphasis moving away from treble instruments.

©Higgins & Higgins

The *idée fixe* is heard in the **B** section where Berlioz uses the key of F major – a key far removed from the home key of A major – to reflect the distance between him and his beloved. This theme was heard initially in the 1st movement (bars 72 – 111) played on the first violin and flute. The time signature there is 2/2 and is adapted to fit the much shorter 3/8 time of the 2nd movement. One feature of the theme which is used throughout the symphony is the sigh motif (eg. bar 87) – a two-note descending idea which gives a sighing effect.

Idée fixe	**First Movement**	**Bars 72 – 111**	**C Maj**

TRACK
47

idée fixe 1st movement

The mood of the 2nd movement is set from the Introduction which opens with tremolo strings that give a sense of anticipation and excitement. The uncertain moments before a dance begins is also conveyed by the shifting tonality of the opening 30 bars which move from A minor to A major through many unrelated keys. His use of dynamics also help the mood. This leads to the definite 1,2,3 of the waltz accompaniment for the main theme.

When the artist sees his beloved at the ball, we hear the *idée fixe* played over the waltz theme. As she disappears, his heart beats erratically; he returns to the ball which is in full flow. Towards the end, he catches a quick glimpse of her again.

Section	Bar	Key	Track
Introduction	1	A min – A maj	48
A	36	A maj – F maj	49
B	121	F maj	50
A¹	176	A maj	51
Link	257	A maj	52
Coda	302	A maj	53

INTRODUCTION

Bar 1   Two-bar tremolo on violins and viola. A minor.

Bar 3   Thirty-four bars, rising arpeggios on double bass answered by harp accompanied by tremolo violins, viola and cello.
- double bass quavers; solo harp answers in triplet semiquavers

©Higgins & Higgins

- changing chords every two bars
- dynamics in melody and accompaniment from bar 12
- flutes and oboe join from bar 27; harp triplets in bars 30 – 31
- chord of A major in second inversion (Ic) in bar 30 on full orchestra
- descending scales (bars 32 – 36); Perfect cadence at bars 35 – 36

Bar	Key	Bar	Key
5	F maj	19	G♯ dim
7	F♯ dim	20	A♭ maj
9	F♯ min	22	B♭ min
11	F♯ maj	24	B dim
13	B min	26	B⁷ maj
15	G maj	30	A maj

SECTION A

There are three themes in section A. Each theme has a two-bar lead in.

Theme	Key	Bar	Track
1	A maj	36	54
2	A maj	54	55
3	A maj	66	56
1	A maj	94	57

Theme 1	Bars 36 – 54	A Maj

TRACK 54

Bar 36 Two-bar waltz rhythm; double bass and cello on 1st beat; viola and second violin on 2nd and 3rd beats.

Bar 39 Sixteen-bar melody(4+4+4+4) on first violin accompanied by strings.

- upbeat start, step movement, chromatic movement
- sigh motif, glissandos, repetition and variation
- slow down (**rall**) and **a tempo** (back in time) in bars 49 and 51
- Perfect cadence at bars 53 – 54

©Higgins & Higgins

| Theme 2 | Bar 54 – 66 | A Maj |

TRACK 55

Bar 54   Two-bar lead in to Theme 2. Semiquaver broken chords on harp; pizzicato quaver arpeggios on double bass and cello; tremolo middle strings.

Bar 56   Eleven-bar theme (5+1+5) on first violin accompanied by strings and harp.
- triplet link (bar 61), sigh motif (bars 59, 60 and 65)
- second five bars are a variation of first five
- step movement, pizzicato and tremolo accompaniment
- second harp joins (bar 61); flutes, clarinets and horns join (bar 62)
- Perfect cadence at bars 65 – 66

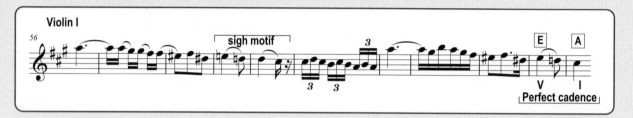

| Theme 3 | Bar 66 – 93 | A Maj |

TRACK 56

Bar 66   Two-bar lead to Theme 3. A rising scale on first flute and clarinets in 3rds. Theme 3 has two phrases.

Phrase 1

Bar 68   Ten-bar melody on violins (in 3rds) accompanied by viola and cello.
- chord of A major (bar 68), one-bar idea played five times as a sequence
- homophonic texture, semiquaver movement, repeated notes, accents
- range of melody is a maj 7th from C♯ (bar 68) to D♮ (bar 76)
- wind, horn, double bass and harp join in bars 75 and 76
- Imperfect cadence at bars 76 – 77

Phrase 2

Bar 78   Eight bars on first violin and cello accompanied by second violin, viola, horns, first flute and clarinets.
- eight-note turning motif on first violin; cello imitates at an 8ve and at two quavers distance
- repeated notes; contrapuntal texture; pizzicato second violin and viola
- Imperfect cadence (with trill) on first violin and cello at bars 84 – 85

©Higgins & Higgins

- three-note idea on flute and clarinet in dialogue with horns

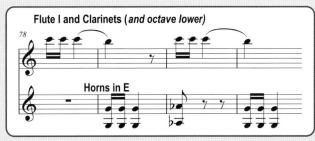

Bar 85   Nine-bar link.
- rising harps; chromatic movement on the wind (bar 89)

Theme 1	Bars 94 – 120	A Maj – F Maj

(compare and contrast with bars 39-54)

Bar 94   Sixteen-bar theme extended on first violin with orchestral accompaniment.
- no upbeat, no slow down in bar 104
- waltz rhythm; 1st beat strings, 2nd beat harps, 3rd beat wind and horns
- theme extended sequentially by 11 bars using a two-bar motif
- modulation to F major; tremolo strings from bar 117
- sudden drop in dynamics to **pppp** (*presque rien* – almost nothing)

SECTION B

(compare and contrast with idée fixe in first movement bar 72)

Bar 121   Eight bars of the *idée fixe* on first flute and oboe accompanied by strings.
- upbeat; tremolo violins and viola
- double bass and cello play broken arpeggio figures (staccato)

Bar 129   Thirty-two bars on flute and clarinet playing in unison for three bars and then in 8ves; accompanied by strings.
- contrapuntal texture, wide leaps and chromatic movement
- repeated dominant pedal (C♮) on double bass for fourteen bars
- Theme 1 used in imitation and dialogue on strings in accompaniment

©Higgins & Higgins

- strong waltz beat on low strings
- Perfect cadence in F major at bars 159 – 160

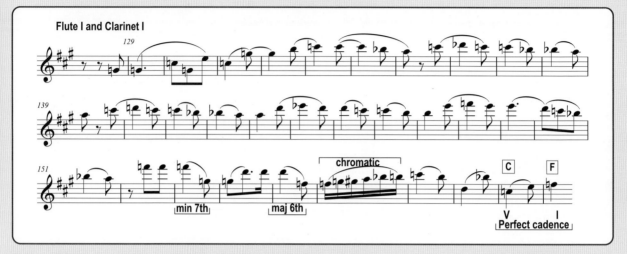

Bar 160 Sixteen-bar transition from F major – A major.

- wide leaps, off-beat semiquavers on strings and wind (faltering heartbeat)
- pedal E on horns from bar 163 (dominant of A)
- final chord of E (**V**) on full orchestra at bar 175

SECTION A¹

Theme	Key	Bar	Track
1 and 2	A maj	176	58
3	A maj	203	59
1	A maj	232	60

Themes 1 and 2   Bars 176 – 203   A Maj

TRACK 58

(compare and contrast with bars 36 – 66)

Bar 176 Theme 1. Sixteen-bar melody on second violin, viola and first cello accompanied by orchestra.

- no lead-in and no tempo change; three semiquaver upbeat
- three instruments play theme; new demisemiquaver motif on first violin
- distinctive three-note rhythm on wind and horn; harp joins in bar 183
- pizzicato tonic on second cello and double bass (tonic pedal)
- Perfect cadence at bars 190 – 191

©Higgins & Higgins

Bar 191 Theme 2. Two-bar lead-in on harps, low strings and wind followed by eleven-bar theme on violins and viola accompanied by remaining instruments.

- two harps this time, three instruments play theme
- repeated notes on wind
- Perfect cadence at bars 202 – 203

Theme 3	Bars 203 – 232	A Maj

Phrase 1
(compare and contrast with bars 66 – 77)

Bar 203 Two-bar lead in; rising scale on first flute and clarinets; falling scale on cello.

Bar 205 Ten-bar melody on first flute and oboe accompanied by wind and strings with harp in bar 205.

- rising harp triplets in bar 205
- pizzicato broken chord accompaniment on strings

Phrase 2
(compare and contrast with bars 78 – 85)

Bar 215 Eight-bar melody on first violin with cello, first flute and first clarinet imitating.

- dialogue is between second violin and viola
- Imperfect cadence at bars 221 – 222

(compare and contrast with bars 85 – 93)

Bar 222 Eleven-bar link

- no harps, chord of D major (**IV**) in bar 227 on all instruments
- descending broken scale on wind; second flute changes to piccolo
- one-bar rest in bar 232

Theme 1	Bars 233 – 256	A Maj

(compare and contrast with bars 36 – 54 and 94 – 120 and 176 – 191

Bar 233 Sixteen-bar melody extended on piccolo, flute, oboe and clarinets with harps joining in bar 240; accompanied by horns and strings.

- waltz accompaniment on double bass, cello, viola and second violin
- first violin repeated notes; syncopated horn accompaniment
- rall and 1° tempo (bars 243 – 245)
- final eight bars repeated including a second rall and 1° tempo
- first violin joins melody (bar 253); Perfect cadence (bars 255 – 256)

LINK	

Bar 257 Eight bars on wind and two horns; harp arpeggios; descending motif on violins; tremolo on lower strings.

- polyphonic texture, repeated notes, triplets and dynamics

©Higgins & Higgins

Bar 265 Eight-bar answer on first violin; melody on wind.
- off-beat crotchets in accompaniment
- Perfect cadence at bars 271 – 272

Bar 273 Sixteen bars repeated from bar 257.
- first violins move up an 8ve, harp more active
- waltz rhythm returns, wind join the strings in final bars

Bar 288 Fifteen bars.
- motif used on wind and first violin similar to bar 45
- waltz rhythm accompaniment; Perfect cadence at bars 301 – 302

CODA

Bar 302 Eighteen bars on first clarinet accompanied by first horn, flute and harps.
- *Idée fixe* with tonic pedal on flute and horn

Bar 320 Full orchestra.
- heartbeat effect (bars 320 and 361); off-beats from bar 327
- similarity to Theme 1 of music on strings from bar 338 (double bass)
- repeated note accompaniment on wind (bars 346); waltz rhythm (bars 353)
- Perfect cadence at bars 367 – 368

1. **Fill in the missing notes from the following themes of the 2nd movement on the stave below:**   EXERCISE

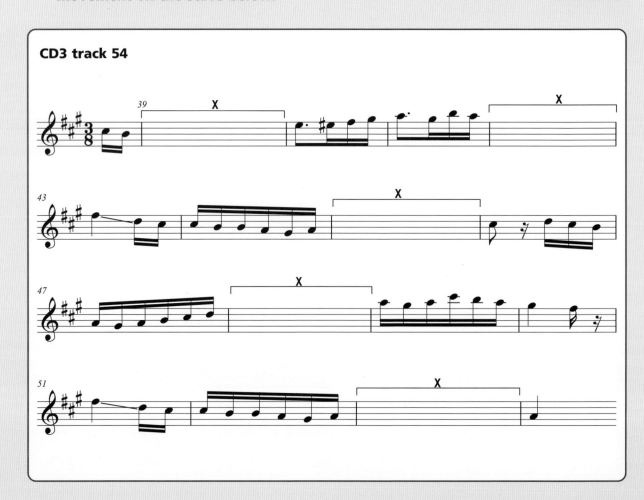

©Higgins & Higgins

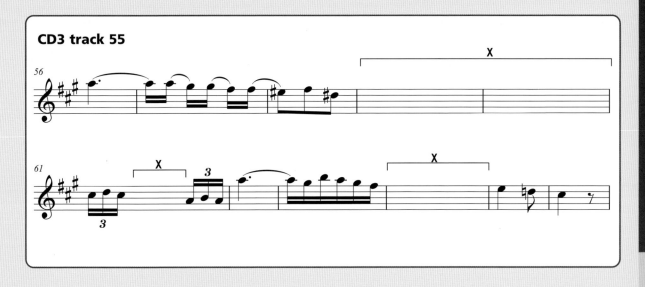

CD3 track 55

CD3 track 56

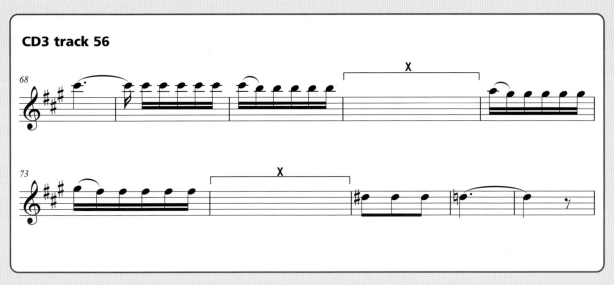

CD3 track 50

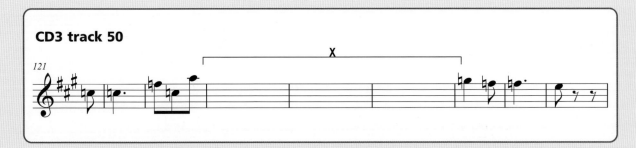

2. **Compare and contrast all FOUR statements of Theme 1. Remember to mention instruments, accompaniment, length and tempo.**

3. **Compare and contrast BOTH statements of Theme 3. Remember to mention instruments, accompaniment and texture.**

4. **Describe the events as they occur in the B section. Remember the story and explain how Berlioz tells it through music.**

5. **Give TWO similarities and THREE differences between Section A and Section A¹.**

©Higgins & Higgins

FOURTH MOVEMENT – *Marche au Supplice*
Allegretto non troppo (a little lively but not too much)

Instruments

Violins I and II (Vl)	2 Flutes (Fl)	2 Horms in B♭ (Cor)
Violas (Vla)	2 Oboes (Ob)	2 Horms in E♭ (Cor)
Cellos (Vc)	2 Clarinets in C (Cl)	2 Trumpets in B♭ (Tr)
Double Basses (Cb)	2 Bassoons (Fg)	2 Cornet à piston in B♭ (C à p)
		1 alto Trombone (Tbn)
Drum (Tamb)		2 tenor Trombone (Tbn)
4 Timpani in G, B♭, D, F (Timp)		2 Ophicléide (Oph)
Cymbals (Ptti)		
Bass Drum (G C)		

The 4th movement does not fall into a clear recognised form but is built around two strong themes. It begins with an Introduction followed by an Exposition with two main subjects in related keys. There are two Developments. The movement ends with a Coda, is in G minor and has two minim beats in a bar. Watch out for possible changes in instrumentation and accompaniments each time a theme is heard. Note also the precise instructions Berlioz includes in the score.

In this movement, Berlioz dreams that he has killed his beloved and is sentenced to death. While this seems sombre, it is only a dream and there are some light-hearted moments that show the composer's comic side.

Theme	Key	Bar	Track
Introduction	G min	1	61
Exposition	G min – B♭ maj	17	62
Development 1	G min – B♭ maj – G min	78	63
Development 2	G min – D♭ maj	114	64
Coda	G min – G maj	140	65

INTRODUCTION

TRACK
61

Bar 1   Seventeen bars on timpani and horns accompanied by double basses.
   • timpanists play 1st quaver with two sticks; play others with right stick only
   • horn players mute the sound with their hand; syncopated rhythm
   • divided double basses pluck tonic chord of Gm
   • very soft (*pp*) dynamic building to very loud (*ff*)
   • repeated chords aid the gradual build of tension
   • harmony change to **V'd** (D⁷/C♯) in bar 13
   • resolves in bar 17 to the chord of i (Gm)

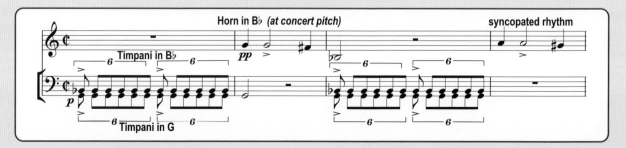

©Higgins & Higgins

EXPOSITION

Section	Key	Bar	Track
Descending Theme	G min – E♭ maj – G min	17	66
March	B♭ maj	62	67

First Subject – Descending Theme (five times)
Bars 17 – 60   G Min – E♭ Maj- G Min

Bar 17   Eight bars on cello and double bass in G minor.

- monophonic texture, G melodic minor scale descending, dynamic *ff* to *p*
- range of two 8ves using a two-bar rhythm three times
- bassoon and viola join for the Imperfect cadence at bars 23 – 24

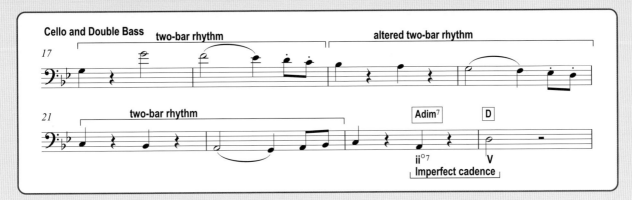

Bar 25   Eight bars on cello and double bass with viola in 3rds; G minor – E♭ major.

- countersubject on bassoons; two-bar motif, three times, rising sequence
- polyphonic texture; crescendo on bassoon
- Perfect cadence in E♭ major at bars 31 – 32

Bar 33   Eight bars on first and second violins in 8ves in E♭ major.

- timpani sextuplet rhythm from Introduction; countersubject on low strings
- polyphonic texture
- viola takes theme in bar 38 (too low for violins)
- full orchestra returns for Imperfect cadence in bar 40

Bar 41   Eight bars repeated in E♭ major.

- ending altered so music can return to G minor

©Higgins & Higgins

Bar 49   Eight-bar Descending Theme extended on cello and double bass; violins and viola play Descending Theme as an ascending theme; strings pizzicato.

- polyphonic texture; quaver countersubject on bassoons
- use of raised 6th and 7th of melodic minor scale (ascending version)
- final two bars repeated twice to extend the theme by four bars
- Perfect cadence at bars 59 – 60

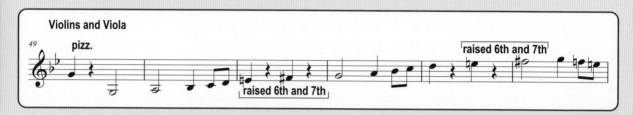

Second Subject – March Theme Bars 62 – 77   **B♭ Maj**

TRACK
67

There is a two-bar lead-in to this theme. A strong B♭ tonic is repeated on the ophicléide (in 8ves) and timpani accompanied by strings and bassoons. A B♭ major scale leads to the March Theme.

Bar 62   Sixteen bars (8+8) on first flute, clarinet, horn and cornet in B♭ major accompanied by remaining wind, brass and timpani, homophonic texture.

- dotted rhythm; syncopated rhythm from the Introduction
- 8ves on the ophicléide and bassoon providing a tonic pedal of B♭
- first eight bars end on F major (**V**) (bars 68 – 69)
- added string scale in bar 73
- second eight bars end on B♭ major (**I**) (bars 76 – 77)

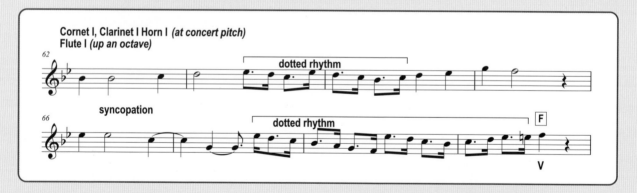

Note the repeat barlines in bar 77. Some recordings observe this while others don't. This recording does not.

©Higgins & Higgins

DEVELOPMENT 1

Bar 78   Eleven-bar link (4+7) on full orchestra in G minor.

- four bars of dialogue between brass and wind
- sextuplet motif on strings
- Descending Theme split up across the orchestra (bars 82 – 88)
- timpani rhythm returns in bar 87

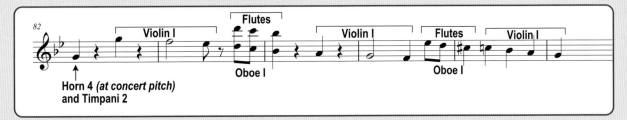

(compare and contrast with bars 62 – 77)
Bar 89   Sixteen-bar March Theme on full orchestra in B♭ major.

- added strings; arpeggio and broken chords in triplets on middle strings
- busy motif on first violin; double bass has a tonic pedal effect

(compare and contrast with bars 78 – 88)
Bar 105   Nine-bar link in G minor.

- triplet crotchets and descending chromatic scale in bar 113

DEVELOPMENT 2

Bar 114   Ten bars (2+2+2+4) on trombones, ophicléide and bassoons with orchestra.

- two-bar motif (Descending Theme) played three times as a rising sequence
- repeated sextuplet motif on the wind
- repeated crotchets and grace notes on strings
- bars 120 – 122 descending motif in diminution (shorter rhythm)
- timpani and the rising chromatic scale from bar 121

Bar 123   Seventeen bars of Descending Theme on full orchestra.

- Descending Theme played in G minor (bar 123); wind, brass and low strings
- ascending in D♭ major (bar 131); timpani rolls; cymbals and bass drum
- tremolo on violins and violas
- enharmonic change of C♯ to D♭ in bars 130 – 131
- Perfect cadence in G minor at bars 139 – 140

©Higgins & Higgins

CODA

Bar 140 Fifteen bars.
- dotted rhythm used on strings
- repeated three-note dotted motif on wind, horn and cornet
- **V – i** block chord all instruments (except string) bars 143 – 144 / 147 – 148
- descending scale on strings to end section

Bar 154 Eleven bars of dialogue; wind and brass answered by strings and timpani.
- dotted rhythm block chords; Db major answered in G minor (a tritone apart – the sign of evil in music)
- *ff* dominant chord (D major) in bar 160; descending scale in triplets in bar 161

Bar 164 Five-bar solo of *idée fixe* on first clarinet, the guillotine chop at bar 169.

Bar 170 Final bars feature full G major chords on orchestra with timpani rolls.

EXERCISE

1. **Fill in the missing notes from the following themes of the 4th movement.**

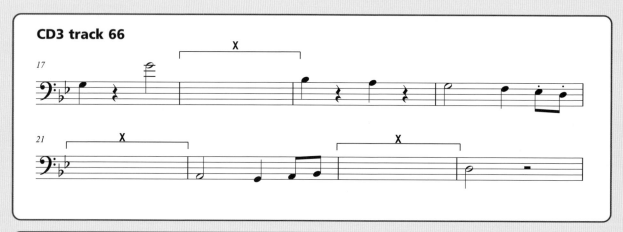

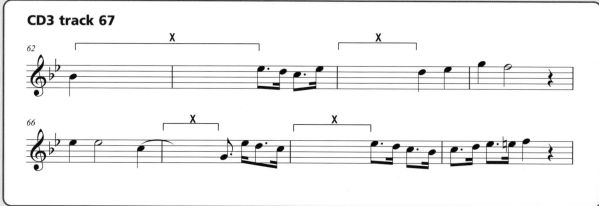

2. **Compare and contrast each of the five Descending Theme statements in the Exposition. Mention instruments, key, accompaniment and texture.**

3. **Name TWO features of Berlioz style found in this movement. Explain.**

4. **Identify and explain the compositional techniques used in this movement.**

5. **Describe TWO ways Berlioz captures the mood of a march.**

Berlioz

210

Course B – Deane

Contents

THE 20TH CENTURY AND IRELAND

The 20th Century has experienced two world wars, the creation of the United Nations and the European Union, the growth of the modern Olympics, advances in world and space travel and a booming film and recording industry. It has been a time of wide ranging invention and creation. However, we also find poverty and starvation co-existing alongside great economic wealth and power. There have also been awful moments of disaster like Chernobyl but some wonderful events like Live Aid.

Ireland too has had an eventful hundred years. It became a free state and survived thirty years of unrest to finally end the century at peace. The country has suffered depression and emigration, but the Celtic Tiger of the nineties has ensured a prosperous start to the 21st century.

Art music in the 20th century has seen so many different styles emerge that no one umbrella term can be used to describe the music of the time. Composers often merge a variety of styles.

20th Century Style

Texture: As many traditional melodic, harmonic, rhythmic and tonal rules are replaced, labelling the texture may not be as straightforward as in previous eras. The compositional and instrumental techniques used are important when analysing the texture of a modern piece.

Melody: Melodic lines of some compositions can now be built on a small motif which grows and develops through the piece. This motif may be a series of notes, a rhythm, an interval or any other sound. Many 20th century composers do not use conventional key structures, preferring to use tonal centres. Others write atonally (not in any key) or choose to use a number of keys together (polytonality). As a result, conventional classic harmonic progressions, including cadences, may be absent. Dissonant (clashing) harmonies can result from the combination of notes used.

Instruments: There is a wide range, variety and combination of instruments available. One of the most important developments during this time is in the experimental techniques used to produce the sound on these instruments. Also, the advances in technology enable many sounds to be synthesised (created). This means that it is possible to generate a music sample without using any conventional instruments.

Form: The structure of a work may not always be obvious. Some pieces simply evolve from an idea. The combination of ideas, rhythms and sounds is important and the order in which this is done – the form – may depend on the story of the composition.

Features: Time signatures and tempi can change frequently in a 20th century piece. The compositional and instrumental techniques used are important in its construction. Composers often include detailed comments on the score to help the performer understand what they want. There is a wide range of compositional styles which make it difficult to generalise, as some composers experiment greatly while others revert back to older periods for inspiration.

Contemporaries include: Arnold Schoenberg (1874 – 1951 Austria), Igor Stravinsky (1882 – 1971 Russia), Pierre Schaeffer (1910 – 1995 France), Witold Lutoslawski (1913 – 1994 Poland), Karlheinz Stockhausen (1928 – 2007 Germany), Steve Reich (1936 – USA), Gerald Barry (1952 – Ireland) and Christopher Norton (1953 – New Zealand).

©Higgins & Higgins

DEANE'S LIFE

Raymond Deane was born in 1953 in the West of Ireland. He took music classes there and when, at the age of ten the family moved to Dublin, he continued with these at the College of Music and then at UCD, graduating in 1974. He studied abroad for some time but is now based in Dublin where he works as a freelance composer and pianist.

Deane has received many commissions from Ireland and abroad and his works have been widely performed. He writes for a wide variety of genres – choral, chamber, orchestral and electroacoustic. They include *Enchainment* (1981 – 1982) for large orchestra, the *Macabre Trilogy* (1993 – 1996) for chamber ensemble and the opera *The Poet and his Double* (1991). His electroacoustic composition *Passage Work* for tape with voice and chamber ensemble was performed by the Crash Ensemble in 2001. He has been a member of Aosdána, the state sponsored academy for creative artists, since 1986.

DEANE'S STYLE

Deane studied with Stockhausen in Germany where he was influenced by 'serialism' – a structural 'series' of notes which governs the development of a composition. However, he has developed it to suit the time and moment in which he composes and is not rigid in his choices.

Features:

(i)   Incorporating existing music ideas into his compositions.
(ii) Starting a piece with a small idea and allowing it to grow.
(iii) Using diatonic and chromatic music simultaneously in a piece – one group playing tonally while a second plays atonally.
(iv) Exploring instrumental techniques to produce different timbres. For example, a violin can be made to sound like a guitar.
(v)   Breaking down the norm, resulting in a different norm. The idea of order and disorder.

20TH CENTURY FORM

COMPOSITIONAL TECHNIQUES

Subtraction and Addition Principles

In the subtraction principle, a motif is repeated a number of times, each time with one note removed until only one note remains. The addition principle works in reverse, starting with one note of the motif and each repetition adding a note until the original motif is restored.

Inversion

This is when a chord, motif or melody is turned upside down.

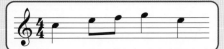 

Retrograde

A line of music played in reverse so that it is the same forward as backwards. In this example, the same instrument plays a four-bar melody. This melody uses the same notes and rhythm if read forward or backwards (like a palindrome in language). The first note is a minim C as is the last note, the second note is a crotchet E as is the second last.

©Higgins & Higgins

INSTRUMENTAL TECHNIQUES

arco is an instruction to play with a bow. Normally associated with string instruments. In this piece, Deane asks that some of the percussion instruments, such as the cymbals, be played with a bow. The result is a wispy, harmonic like sound.

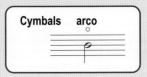

Bartok pizzicato
If written over a string instrument, it means a 'snap pizzicato'. The string is pulled up and allowed to snap back to the fingerboard **(CD1, track 5)** However, if written over a wind instrument, it can mean a finger slap or a 'spat' articulation to make a short percussive sound.

col legno battuto (c.l.) is an instruction to a string player to strike the string with the wood of the bow. **(CD1 track 16)**

harmonics (flag)
A harmonic is an overtone and there are two types – natural and artificial. On a string instrument, the performer lightly touches the string to achieve an interval above. The sound is wispy and delicate. A natural harmonic is on an open string and is indicated by a circle over the note. An artificial harmonic is achieved on a stopped string by lightly touching it with a second finger. It is indicated with a diamond above the stopped note. **(CD1 track 8)**

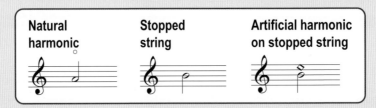

There are places where the composer suggests which violin or cello string the player should use for the harmonic. For example *flag (I)* on the cello in bar 9 means the harmonic is to be played on the first or 'A' string

glissando means to slide. On a string instrument, the performer draws his finger either up or down between two adjacent notes on a string. **(CD1 track 15)**

l.v. stands for laisser vibrer and usually refers to percussion instruments. It means that a sound is allowed to vibrate until it dies away.

sul ponticello is an instruction to a string player to play near the bridge so as to produce a metallic tone quality.

sul tasto is an instruction to a string player to play on the fingerboard.

pizz is a left-hand pizzicato. **(CD1 track 4)**
+

across the bridge  Play above the bridge to produce a shrill sound.

martellato means 'hammered'.

©Higgins & Higgins

Seachanges with Danse Macabre

Seachanges (with *Danse Macabre*) is a chamber piece commissioned by Concorde in 1993. It is one of the Macabre Trilogy (with *Catacombs* and *Marche Oubliée*) all three having death as their subject. *Seachanges* has a number of Mexican influences – Deane had visited there that year – such as the preoccupation with death and the Folk music and instruments of the Mariachi.

There are references in this work to two existing pieces of music associated with death.

The *Dies Irae*   (Day of Judgment)

The *Dies Irae* is an ancient Gregorian Chant sung at a Roman Catholic Requiem Mass. It moves in small intervals – 2nds and 3rds – and follows the rhythm of the words.

The *Danse Macabre* is a medieval dance of death with pulsating rhythm and sinister imagery.

The other important musical reference in this piece is to a melody that had come to the composer while strolling on a beach in Sligo. He used it in his suite *The Seagull Dreams of its Shadow*. While on a beach in Mexico the following year, the melody returned to him and he was taken by the contrast in his surroundings on both occasions.

The work is based around a three-note cell – G, A, C. These notes, and the intervals they make, are varied and distorted as the work progresses.

There are seven 'sections' to this one-movement work:

Section	Bar	Compositional Material	Tonal Centre	Track
Introduction	1	three-note cell (G, A, C)	G	69
A¹	17	Inversion of Main Melody	G	70
	27	Main Melody and Inversion	G	71
B	46	Danse Macabre (Totentanz)	Atonal	72
A²	74	Main Melody	D	73
C	92	Dies Irae	Atonal	74
A³	128	Main Melody	E♭	75
Coda	141	Danse Macabre and Dies Irae	C – A	76

This is descriptive music which has a number of different moods. The time signatures and tempi change often. Deane uses many instrumental and compositional techniques in the piece, a very wide range and a lot of extreme dynamics.

©Higgins & Higgins

Deane

215

Deane

216

Instruments

Piccolo and Flute in G	Piano
Cello	Violin
Percussion (pitched and unpitched)	

Pitched Percussion

- Crotales (tiny, antique cymbals)
- Marimba (a keyboard-like instrument with wooden bars. Mellow sound)

Unpitched Percussion

- Cymbals
- Bass Drum
- Guiro (wooden instrument played by scraping a stick over notches on the surface)
- Gong
- Maracas
- Tambourine
- Rainstick (a hollow stick with beads inside that you shake)

A number of times in this piece, the players (other than the percussionist) are asked to leave their instruments down and play the maracas.

Introduction	**Bars 1 – 16**	**Tonal Centre G**

The rhythm of this section is semibreves or longer. However, not all the instruments can sustain the note once it is played. The sound fades on the piano and crotales as the note is struck once only, irrespective of its value, unlike the string and wind instruments where the playing action is continuous for the value of the note.

This section conjures up images of desert heat and the piercing sun.

Bar 1   Sixteen bars of the three-note cell. The tempo is a crotchet equal to around 80.
- high pitch
- harmonics
- rests
- extreme dynamics
- sudden A♭
- tremolo cello
- *15ma* (up a double 8ve)
- left-hand pizzicato
- changing time signatures
- sparse texture
- accents

A¹

Inversion	**Bars 17 – 27**	**Tonal Centre G**

This section can be divided into two parts, each playing a version of the theme which is based on the three-note cell.

Bar 17   Four bars using an inversion of the three-note cell on the piano with percussion (gong, maracas, bass drum, violin, tambourine, and cymbals) interrupting, all over a sustained G on cello.

©Higgins & Higgins

- descending broken chords on piano
- harmonics on the strings
- extreme dynamics
- accents
- *8 ba...*(an 8ve lower)
- tonic pedal (G)
- tremolo violin
- semiquavers and demisemiquavers
- arco cymbal (playing with a bow)
- grace note on the piccolo
- col legno battuto on violin (back of bow)
- pizzicato and left-hand pizzicato on violin

Bar 21   Six bars of the Inversion of the Main Melody on the cello accompanied by remaining instruments including percussion (cymbals, marimba and maracas).

The first note of the Inversion (G) can be heard on the violin for the 2nd and following subtraction principle statements.

The flute and marimba part is made up of variations of the intervals formed by the notes in three-note cell (inverted and transposed).

- harmonics on cello and harmonics and glissando on violin
- accents and trills on flute
- sextuplets on the violin
- subtraction principle (6,5,4,3,2,1)
- Bartok pizzicato on the flute
- arco cymbal
- tremolo
- pizzicato cello

Main Melody and Inversion Bars 27 – 45   Tonal Centre G

Bar 27   Ten bars on violin (Main Melody) and cello (Inversion) accompanied by flute, piano and percussion (marimba and maracas).

- subtraction principle
- four-note rhythm on percussion
- descending broken chord on piano (bar 34)
- *15ma* on piano
- sustaining pedal on piano
- pizzicato and left-hand pizzicato on strings

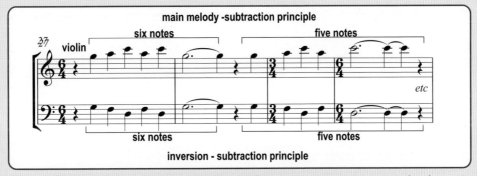

Seachanges by Raymond Deane ©Contemporary Music Centre, Ireland.
Reproduced by kind permission.

©Higgins & Higgins

(compare and contrast with bars 27 – 36)

Bar 37   Nine bars repeating the previous music with a different arrangement – marimba (Main Melody), piccolo (Inversion) and percussion (crotales and maracas). The piano shadows the piccolo.

The crotales play a shortened version of the Main Melody (diminution) in bars 37 and 44. Its semiquaver rhythm in the following bars also uses the notes of the three-note cell.

- subtraction principle
- four-note rhythm on crotales and strings
- percussive semiquaver strings
- left-hand pizzicato on strings
- double-stopping
- sustaining pedal on piano
- maracas rhythms
- soft pedal on the piano (UC)

Danse Macabre *(Totentanz)*   Bars 46 – 73   Atonal

TRACK
72

This is a rhythmic section where all the instruments used play the Totentanz rhythm. The grouping of the pairs of quavers may vary from statement to statement.

Bar 46   Nineteen bars of *Totentanz* rhythm. Percussion used are maracas, guiro, marimba and cymbal. The tempo is now a crotchet equal to 120.

The violin is told what strings to play (II is the A string, III the D string). This helps to play in a harsh way as indicated.

- use of parallel 5ths
- single bow per note on violin
- chromatic and glissando strings
- strumming like a guitar on strings
- piercing 'across the bridge' on strings
- piano chords (from three-note cell)
- piercing B on piccolo
- tremolo 5ths on the marimba
- tremolo aug 4ths (tritone) on the piano
- rest bars relieving of tension

Totentanz rhythm

tritone (aug 4ths)

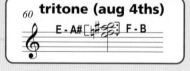

(compare and contrast with bars 27 – 36)

Bar 65   Main Melody (right hand) and Inversion (left hand) on piano with tremolo accompaniment.

- 8ves on piano
- sustaining pedal (a little) on piano
- tritone on marimba
- loud dynamic ending soft
- temolo 5ths on the strings (sul pont)
- high register from bar 60

©Higgins & Higgins

- descending glissando 5ths on strings
- block accented piano chords from bar 68
- maracas from bar 69
- cymbal from bar 71
- strumming strings from bar 71
- sul tasto bar 73
- subtraction principle

| A² | Bars 74 – 91 | Tonal Centre G |

Bar 74 Fourteen bars of gentle Main Melody (violin) and Inversion (cello) with flute countermelody and piano chords (based on chromatic, inverted and distorted versions of the three-note cell) and percussion (crotales, gong, cymbal and rainstick). Tempo is a crotchet equal to 80.

The composer has indicated that the 3/2 time signature was meant for the strings, with the remaining instruments playing in the freer 6/4 time. However, he suggests that this is not strict and the different signatures will be omitted in revised scores.

- minim and semibreve rhythm
- D drone/pedal on strings
- subtraction principle
- cymbal to refer to flute rhythm in bar 77
- tremolo 5ths on strings from bar 84
- rising piano broken chords (bar 85); subtraction principle (9,8,7,6,5,4)
- rainstick from bar 85
- tremolo flute

(compare and contrast with bars 65 – 67)

Bar 88 Main Melody (left hand) and Inversion (right hand) on piano with glissando and tremolo accompaniment over a G pedal on strings.

- strings are playing a distorted version of the three-note cell and its inversion.
- subtraction principle

| Dies Irae | Bars 92 – 127 | Atonal |

This section is based on an inversion of the Dies Irae plainchant. The intervals of a 2nd, 3rd and their inversions dominate throughout. The composer also uses canon at a bar distance at the unison between the marimba and violin.

Bar 92 Twenty bars (after one-bar link) of canon with percussion accompaniment (guiro). Tempo is a crotchet equal to 120.

Bar 94 is an inversion (ascending versus descending) and a retrograde of the Dies Irae *(page 215), which is also based on the three-note cell.*

- violin plays one note per bow
- guiro plays 7,11 or 5 notes
- guiro played by the pianist
- 2nds, 3rds, 6ths, 7ths in melodic line

©Higgins & Higgins

- *Dies Irae* in 5ths on cello at bar 99
- piercing piccolo *Dies Irae* from bar 106

Bar 113 Sixteen bars. Marimba, maracas and bass drum used.

- tremolo piccolo parallel with cello
- marimba in 5ths parallel with violin
- glissandos
- piano accented descending block chords
- hint at *Totentanz* rhythm (bar 118)
- constant reference to the plainchant
- constant permutations of the three-note cell
- homophonic texture from bar 125
- pizzicato and left-hand pizzicato

A³	**Bars 128 – 140**	**Tonal Centre E♭**

Bar 128 A thirteen-bar duet for flute (Main Melody) and piano (inversion) with rhythmic accompaniment. Percussion instruments used are marimba, cymbal and gong. Tempo is a crotchet equal to 80.

Gradually, throught the section, the Totentanz rhythm becomes more and more important. The quavers are played as triplets instead of duplets.

- addition principle on piano (1,2,3,4,5,6)
- subtraction principle on flute
- six-quaver rhythm on marimba
- three-note cell (chord) on marimba
- rhythm on violin and across bridge on cello
- sustaining pedal on piano
- added *Totentanz* rhythm from bar 134

Coda	**Bars 141 – 174**	**Tonal Centre C – A**

This final section combines both the Totentanz and the Dies Irae. It ends with all performers playing maracas

Bar 141 Strong rhythm and loud dynamic re-introduces familiar material. The percussion instruments used are crotales, marimba, cymbal, bass drum, guiro, gong and maracas.

- 8ves (cello) and 6ths (violin)
- C major chord formed by strings.
- piano chord notes derived from three-note cell

©Higgins & Higgins

- flute derived from *Dies Irae*
- C major disappears from strings at bar 150
- chromatic movement.
- guiro has *Totentanz* rhythm in bar 157
- strumming violin at bar 157
- glissando strings in bar 158
- parallel 5ths
- repeated 'A's from bar 163
- tremolo aug 4ths on piano from bar 164

The piece ends with everyone playing the Totentanz rhythm on the maracas. All pitch is abandoned.

1. **Fill in the missing notes or rhythm at 'X' in the following excerpts from Seachanges (with Danse Macabre) on the staves below:** **EXERCISE**

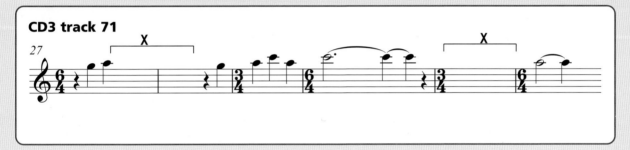

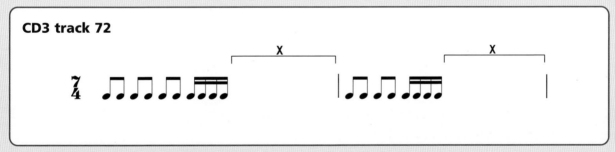

2. **Identify and explain TWO features of 20th century music found in this work.**

3. **Compare and contrast A¹, A² and A³. Mention instruments, accompaniment, tempo, dynamics and tonal centres. You must mention all three sections in your answer.**

4. **Compare and contrast bars 65 – 67 with bars 88 – 90. Mention instruments, accompaniment, dynamics and tonal centres.**

5. **Explain the following instrumental techniques:**

   (a) **col legno battuto.**
   (b) **pizz.**
   (c) **arco.**
   (d) **l.v.**
   (e) **fz.**

6. **Identify and explain TWO Mexican influences in this work.**

©Higgins & Higgins

©Higgins & Higgins

Course B – Beatles

Contents

1960 – 1970

The Sixties were an exciting and turbulent time of social, political and technological change which were marked by race riots, assassinations, student demonstrations, anti-war protests and peace marches. These marches, along with the rise of feminism and gay rights and the easy availability of hallucinogenic drugs, helped to give the decade its lasting label – 'the swinging sixties' and the 'flower power generation'. It was also a decade of space exploration and fashion icons, and a time of great technological advances. These advances were important in the development of television, film and music.

While the 1950s had seen the emergence of a teenage market for both Pop music and Rock and Roll, the 1960s saw a move from Pop singer to Pop group. Pop music can be hard to define – it absorbs musical sounds from everywhere. While it is possible to separate it from Classical and Folk music, it may include elements of other styles. Produced commercially for profit, it was a singles-based industry. Rock music falls under the Pop music umbrella but was regarded as an album-based industry with the emphasis generally on live performances.

Sixties Style

Instruments: Guitars, drums and electronic amplification. Instrumental techniques included guitar solos, riffs and licks.

Features: The advances in technology in the sixties led to new recording possibilities. Track capacity grew from 2-track to 8- and 16-track. This gave more control and allowed sound to be layered, with multitracking and overdubbing. Other recording features included panning, delay, flanging and distortion.

Melody: Pop melodies were generally catchy, using lyrics dealing with teen problems. Rock music tended to have a more rebellious side. The drums and guitars were the driving force. The lyrics usually commented on society. The 'Power Ballad', as a Rock or Pop form, was important as it allowed musicians to use emotion and melancholy to draw the listener in.

Form: Pop/Rock songs usually took a strophic form which was made up of a number of verses and a repeated chorus. While each verse used different words, the music was the same, or almost the same. The chorus contrasted harmonically, rhythmically and melodically from the verse.

Contemporaries include: Elvis Presley (1935 – 1977), Tom Jones (1940 –), Cliff Richard (1940 -), Bob Dylan (1941 –), Jimi Hendrix (1941 – 1970), The Beach Boys (1961 –), The Rolling Stones (1962 –).

THE BEATLES

John Lennon (1940 – 1981), Paul McCartney (1942) and George Harrison (1943 – 2001) played in a number of bands during the late 1950s. By 1958 all three were together in the same group and in 1960 The Beatles were formed. Brian Epstein joined as their manager in 1961 and eventually secured a record deal with EMI producer George Martin in 1962. When Ringo Starr (1940) became their drummer, also in 1962, the line-up was complete.

©Higgins & Higgins

Initially, they were a cover band and secured residencies in the Indra Club in Germany and then the Cavern Club in Liverpool. Their fringed hair cuts and matching suits gave the band a distinctive image. As the Lennon/McCartney partnership became established, so did one of the qualities that set them apart – they wrote their own songs. With a string of number ones to their name in the UK and Ireland, they set about conquering the world and toured regularly between 1963 and 1966.

In August 1966, they gave their last live concert. Their interest in the advances in recording techniques saw them spend their time now in the studio rather than touring. An interest in eastern philosophy, yoga, meditation and world peace was also an influence in their lives. Their image became more relaxed and they embraced all the trappings of the hippy culture which included colourful dress, long hair, beards and drugs.

1967 was a creative year with the release of *Sgt Pepper's Lonely Heart's Club Band* and *Magical Mystery Tour* and showed the band's experimentation with texture, colour and sound-producing. However, following the death of Epstein the same year, and with the band members growing further apart, The Beatles officially disbanded in 1970 after their final album Let It Be was released.

THE BEATLES' STYLE

While their original sound was rooted in 1950s Rock and Roll, The Beatles did not have any difficulty moving between varying genres when writing songs. They were influenced by Ballad, Jazz, Country and Classical music and used ethnic instruments in recordings. George Martin's influence cannot be overlooked. He had a background in Classical music and was able to put all their ideas into coherent arrangements. In the mid sixties, they became more socially aware and their lyrics reflected this. 1967 was a time for Psychedelic Rock, a mellow style that attempted to replicate the mind-altering experiences of hallucinogenic drugs by describing dreams and using elaborate recording effects. It was in their experimental and progressive recording techniques that The Beatles excelled. As well as using the new tricks of the trade that came with multitrack recording, The Beatles invented their own sound-altering techniques.

Features:

(i) Production and recording techniques such as unusual placement of microphones and manipulation of tapes.

(ii) Use of added notes in chords, sometimes up to the 13th

(iii) Use of the major supertonic (which also reads as the dominant of the dominant)

(iv) Repeated notes in the melodic line

(v) Fusion of styles

In the early 1960s, a band would not usually enter the recording studio without having a selection of material ready to be recorded. By the 1970s, as a result of the advances in technology, it was quite normal to spend weeks and months in the studio experimenting and composing.

©Higgins & Higgins

Songs from the Sgt. Pepper's Lonely Hearts Club Band Album

(The following analysis of each song is based on the full score rather than on the piano version, as it indicates the harmony in greater detail.)

Of the thirteen songs on the album, twelve were written by John and Paul either on their own or together. *Within You Without You* was written by George. The album (LP) was very different to anything that had been recorded before for the following reasons:

(i)   It took an unprecedented 129 days to record between 1966 and 1967.
(ii)   The album sleeve was the first to feature printed lyrics.
(iii) There were two sides of continuous music on the LP, with no banding.
(iv) Choice of instruments used was unusual for the time.
(v)   Innovative use of sound effects and recorded tape to establish atmosphere and add quirky effects.

The three songs to be studied from the album are:

Song	Style	Key	Time
Sgt. Pepper's Lonely Hearts Club Band	Rock/Classical	G maj	4/4
She's Leaving Home	Pop/Ballad/Classical	E maj	3/4
When I'm 64	Pop/Jazz/Ragtime	C maj*	2/2

* The song was recorded in C major but altered to D♭ major in the studio

SGT. PEPPER'S LONELY HEARTS CLUB BAND

Note the use of F naturals (flattened 7th) in the melodic line which are not indicated in the piano version. While the key centre is G major, there are many modal moments with the flattened 3rd (B♭) and 7th. The song is in common time and the song has Rock and Classical features.

Section	Bar	Key
Introduction	10 seconds + Bars 1-4	G maj
Verse 1	5	G maj
Interlude	13	F maj – G maj
Chorus	18	G maj – F maj – G maj
Verse 2	35	G maj

Instruments

Lead Guitar, Rhythm Guitar, Bass Guitar, Drum Kit, 4 Horns and Vocals.

©Higgins & Higgins

Introduction 10 seconds and Bars 1 – 4 G Maj

The opening 10 seconds of the track are used to set the mood. The idea had been to invent a fictitious band and send a 'show' on the road. The album tracks were meant to run directly into one another as in a live performance. Sgt Pepper is the first track on the album and the Introduction gives the effect of instruments tuning up and the audience waiting for the show to begin. The sounds used for this were taken from previously recorded material. The tapes were then cut and spliced together in the studio to give the 10-second opening for this song. We hear strings tuning up even though there are no strings in the song.

Bar 1 Four bars on guitars and drums.
- variation of standard drum beat
- opening chords of A^7 (major supertonic or dominant of the dominant)
- C^7 (with an added B♭) and G^7 (with an F natural)
- rising motif on lead guitar and drum fill in bar 4

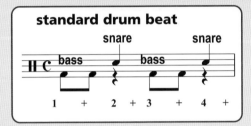

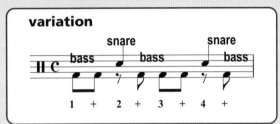

Verse 1 Bars 5 – 12 G Maj

Bar 5 Eight bars (2 x 4) for solo voice (Paul announcing band), drums and guitars.
- homophonic texture, upbeat start and panned vocals in bar 5
- repetition of notes, phrases and harmony on bass G^7, A^7 | C^7 , G^7
- syncopation, high register and drum fills in bars 8 and 12
- strong repeated plagal sound of **IV – I** (C^7 – G^7) in bars 10 – 12

EXERCISE

On the staves below, write out the first eight bars of the melody. Remember to include the upbeat of two semiquavers before bar 5.

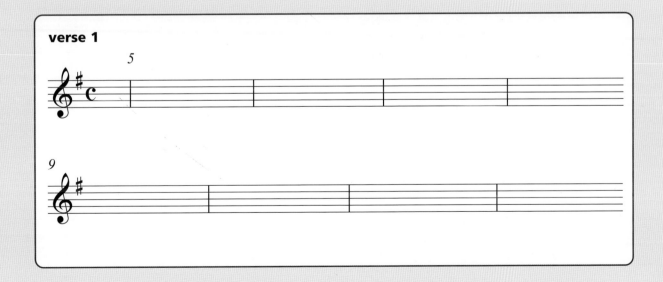

©Higgins & Higgins

Interlude   Bars 13 – 17   F Maj

Bar 13   Five-bar instrumental on four horns accompanied by drums and bass guitar.
- panning and reverb, audience sounds and Classical counterpoint on horns
- descending bass in bar 13 and chord progression C^7, F^7, C^7, D^7
- F major back to G major resting on dominant chord of D^7 at bars 16 – 17

Chorus   Bars 18 – 34   G Maj

Bar 18   Seventeen bars (4+4+4+5) of harmonised vocals accompanied by strong guitars and drums with horns joining at the end.

- upbeat start and syncopation
- hi-hat plays repeated quaver rhythm
- vocal rhythm changes to quavers
- strong repeated quavers on 1st and 3rd beats on bass and lead guitars
- chord progression of G – B♭ |C^7- G in bars 18 – 19 and 22 – 23
- C^7 – G^7 in bars 20 and 21 and descending bass in bar 20
- descending arpeggio chord of D^7 on horns and panned in bar 25
- sustained horn chords in bars 30 – 32 over a descending bass
- quaver movement in all instruments in bars 33 and 34
- dominant chord of D^7 over two bars to end section

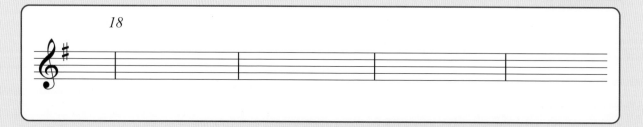

standard drum beat with hi hat

1 + 2 + 3 + 4 +

On the stave below, write out the first four bars of the chorus.   [EXERCISE]

18

Verse 2   Bars 35 – 42   G Maj

Bar 35   Eight bars using same music and accompaniment as bars 5 – 12 with different lyrics.

Bars 43 – 44 provide a two-bar link on the chord of C to the next song. The tracks run straight into each other, with the second track continuing the link by playing four bars using the chords of C, D and E.

[EXERCISE]

1. List the recording features found in this song.
2. Give THREE Rock features found in this song. Explain each feature.
3. Give THREE Classical features found in this song. Explain each feature.
4. List all the bars that have a descending bass line.

©Higgins & Higgins

SHE'S LEAVING HOME

Note that some piano scores are arranged in the key of E♭ major. However, this analysis is in E major, the key used by The Beatles. The song is in 3/4 time and has Pop and Classical features. It tells the story of a runaway teenager.

Section	Bar Verse 1	Bar Verse 2	Bar Verse 3
Introduction	1		
A	5	56	
B	13	64	
A	21	72	107
B	29	80	115
Chorus	37	88	123
Coda			143

Instruments

(string nonet and harp) 4 Violins – 2 Violas – 2 Cellos – 1 Double Bass – Harp

INTRODUCTION

Bar 1 Four bars (2+2) on panned harp.
- two-bar repeated melody with broken chord accompaniment based on tonic

VERSE 1

Bar 5 **Phrase A:** Eight bars (six-bar solo vocal + harp, interrupted in bar 10 by three bars of a panned cello answer); repeated block crotchet chords on each beat.
- Bm chord in bar 6 (flattened leading note D natural)
- F#⁷ chord in bar 11 (major supertonic or dominant of dominant)

On the staves below, write out the first six bars of the melody and the **EXERCISE** cello answer.

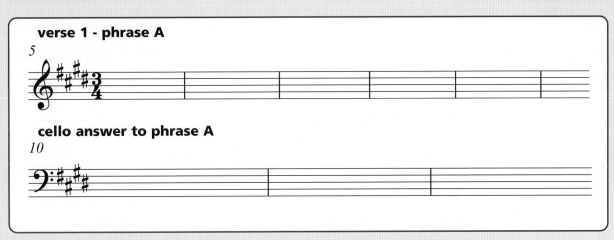

Bar 13 **Phrase B:** Eight-bar (4+4) solo vocal with harp chords and sustained upper strings
- only the dominant chord, B, with added notes used
- syncopated rhythm of quaver to crotchet on strings at bars 16 and 20

©Higgins & Higgins

On the staves below, write out the first four bars of the melody and the **EXERCISE**
syncopated accompaniment at bar 16.

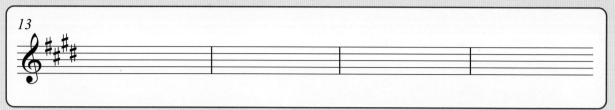

Bar 21   **Repeat of phrase A –** (with some rhythm changes in vocal line to fit the new words).
  - double bass joins with a descending line to portray going downstairs
  - descending violin (panned) in contrary motion to cello (bar 26)

Bar 29   **Repeat of phrase B –** (some rhythm changes in vocal line to fit new words).
  - richer string sound with low strings added this time

Chorus 1

Bar 37   Eight-bar (4+4) two-part vocal counterpoint (overdubbing) with string accompaniment.
  - sustained high-pitch narration (Paul), lower commentary of parents (John)
  - only the tonic chord used to harmonise; no harp
  - repeated 'on-beat rhythm' (upper strings), tonic pedal (low strings)

On the staves below, write out the first four bars of both melodies.   **EXERCISE**

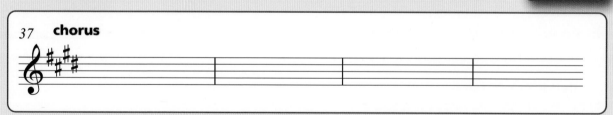

Bar 45   Repeat of four-bar phrase with top vocal up a 3rd.
  - harp re-enters in bar 47 and chord changes to the dominant

Bar 49   Seven bars of two-part vocals with harp accompaniment and sustained strings.
  - top vocal (Paul) is more active; final three block F# major chords

Verse 2

Similar to verse 1 but with a more involved accompaniment.

Bar 56   **Phrase A –** with sustained strings from the start.
  - four bars of rising cello arpeggio-type figures

©Higgins & Higgins

Bar 64   **Phrase B –** with sustained accompaniment and harp chords.

Bar 72   **Phrase A**
* syncopated rhythm; G♯ (sobbing) on violin in bar 76
* five beats repeated

sample rhythm pattern

Bar 80   **Phrase B**
* no syncopated accompaniment this time (see bar 16)

Chorus 2

Similar to chorus 1 with the following changes.

Bar 88   Twelve bars as before, more active broken chord pattern on inner strings.

Verse 3

*Sixteen bars shorter than verse 1 and 2 by omitting first **A** and **B** phrases.*

Bar 107   **Phrase A** *(compare and contrast with bar 21)*, richer counterpoint in bar 112.

Bar 115   **Phrase B** *(compare and contrast with bar 29)*
* tremolo strings used to portray anticipation of 'the appointment'

Chorus 3

Bar 123   *Similar to chorus 1 with the following changes:*
* upper strings play tonic chord notes using a repeated two-bar rhythm

sample rhythm pattern

Bar 135   Eight bars of two-part counterpoint over sustained chordal accompaniment.

Coda

Bar 143   Seven bars with the final bars similar to the introduction on harp.
* strong 2nd and 3rd beats; final Plagal cadence

EXERCISE

1   **Name THREE Classical features of this song. Explain each feature.**

2   **Name TWO Pop features of this song. Explain each feature.**

3   **Name a Ballad feature of this song. Explain.**

4   **Name the recording features used in this song. Explain each one.**

5   **Compare and contrast each verse. Mention instruments, accompaniment and length.**

6   **Give ONE example of word painting from each verse. Explain**

©Higgins & Higgins

WHEN I'M 64

This song was written by Paul for his fathers 64th birthday. He was an amateur Jazz musician and this song has Jazz and Pop features. It is written in a Ragtime style. This style was used specifically on the piano where a regular accompaniment in the left hand is played against a lively and syncopated melody in the right hand. Note the simple harmonic structure used here – primarily the chords of **I**, **IV** and **V**.

This analysis is in C, the key it was recorded in. However, the pitch was raised in the studio and we hear it in the key of D♭. The time signature is 2/2 time.

Section	Key	Bar
Introduction	C maj	1
Verse 1	C maj	5
Bridge 1	A min – C maj	2
Verse 2	C maj	40
Bridge 2	A min – C maj	56
Verse 3	C maj	73
Coda	C maj	89

Instruments

Vocals with Rhythm, Bass Guitar and Snare (with brushes), Piano, 2 Clarinets, 1 Bass Clarinet, a Drum Kit and Chimes.

Introduction

Bar 1 Six bars (4 + 2) on clarinets, bass guitar and drums, played with a swing.
- bass guitar and clarinet play harmonic support (1st and 3rd beats)
- first clarinet plays syncopated melody with second clarinet a bar later
- triplet rhythm in melody, sustained chord on clarinets (bars 5 and 6)
- bass and snare play standard rhythm with triplet variation

Both quaver and dotted quaver rhythm used in the sheet music are played in a triplet fashion.

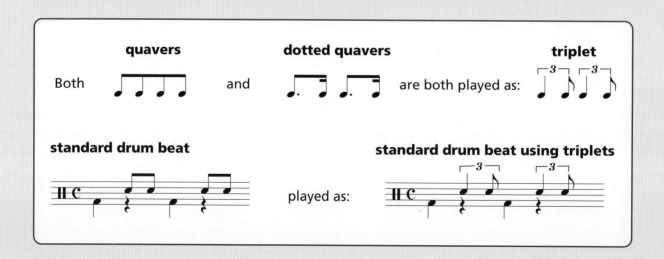

Verse 1

Bar 7   Eight-bar (4+4) solo vocal with clarinets, bass guitar and drums accompanying; piano joining at the end.
- panned vocals and clarinets; syncopated melody similar to introduction
- sustained clarinet chords (bars 7 – 9); clarinet melody (bar 10)
- chromatic movement (bars 11 – 14); rising chromatic scale on bass guitar
- piano block crotchet chords (bars 11 – 12); no drum beat (bars 13 -14)
- simple bass guitar harmonic support

On the staves below, write out the first 8 bars of the melody.   **EXERCISE**

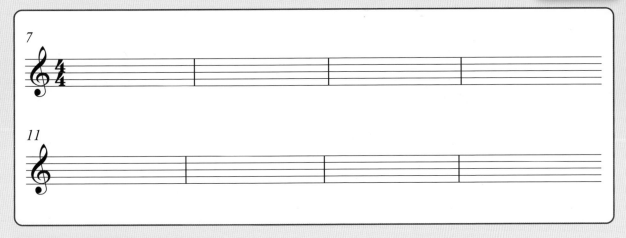

Bar 15   Eight-bar (4 + 4) solo vocal with clarinets, bass guitar and drum.
- compare bars 15 – 18 and bars 7 – 10 (chord of F instead of chord of G)
- clarinets play repeated crotchet chords in bars 19 – 22
- harmony moves in falling 5ths (A – D – G – C)
- Perfect cadence; triplet link on clarinets with added cymbals

Bridge 1

Bar 23   Eight bars in A minor, solo with backing vocals accompanied by piano, clarinets, drums and bass guitar.
- repeated crotchet chords on piano, snare drops out
- descending 3rds on clarinets and backing vocals ('oh')
- repeated left-hand piano 'two-note quaver figure', right-hand crotchet chords
- backing vocals repeat minim melody a bar later in crotchets (bar 28)
- repeated quaver rhythm on piano in bars 29 and 30
- panned vocals and reverb

Bar 31   Nine bars in A minor going to C major; solo with backing vocals accompanied by piano, clarinets, drums, bass guitar and chimes.
- chimes on 3rd and 4th beats in bar 34 and on 1st beat in other bars
- hi-hat fill in bars 35 and 36, clarinet motif in bar 37
- chord of G (**V**) in bars 38 and 39 giving an Imperfect finish

Verse 2

Similar to verse 1 with the following changes:

Bar 40   • snare-fill in bar 43 and 55 and panned clarinet motif in bar 47

©Higgins & Higgins

Bridge 2

Similar to bridge 1 with the following changes:

Bar 56
- repeated 'two-note quaver' idea in vocal line (bar 56), no backing vocals
- more complicated rhythm on cymbals from bar 65
- chimes rhythm changes to 4th beat (bar 68), 2nd beat (bar 69), 2nd and 3rd beats (bar 70) and 2nd beat (bars 71 and 72)

Verse 3

Same as verse 1 and 2 with following changes:

Bar 73
- half a verse only
- clarinet moves parallel with voice (mainly in 3rds and 6ths)
- rhythm guitar more involved from bar 77
- Paul's final note on 4th beat in bar 88
- Perfect cadence on vocals at bars 87- 88; no bridge

Coda

Four bars mirroring the Introduction with clarinets, bass guitar and drums; piano joining for final two chords.

Bar 89
- hi-hat rhythm
- Perfect cadence

EXERCISE

1. Name THREE Jazz features of this song. Explain each.

2. Name TWO Pop features of this song. Explain each.

3. Name the recording techniques used in this song. Explain.

4. Compare and contrast the three verses. Mention instruments, accompaniments and textures.

5. Compare and contrast the two bridges. Mention instruments, accompaniments and textures